Sustainable Development

Mobilisation and Globalisation

D.K. Bhatnagar

2008

CYBER TECH PUBLICATIONS
4264/3, Ansari Road, Daryaganj, New Delhi-110002 (India)
Ph.: 011-23244078. Fax: 011-23280028
E-Mail: cyberpublicationsdelhi@yahoo.com

Sustainable Development: Mobilisation and Globalisation

First Edition 2008

Published by G.S. Rawat

For Cyber Tech Publications

4264/3, Ansari Road, Daryaganj, New Delhi - 110 002

E-mail : cyberpublicationsdelhi@yahoo.com

Phone : 011-23244078,

Fax : 011-23280028

Preface

Social development and human well being have advanced only because people have taken risk. Time and again, we see the terrible toll that natural disasters inflict on vulnerable communities around the world.

The attempt to understand the mechanisms of development is a field of active research, both because of its own intrinsic interest and importance and because of its relevance to the problem of abnormal growth. For instance, agricultural mechanization is actively pursued, although it remains in the early stages of development and is considered impractical in many places because of the relatively small size of the cultivated areas. Flood control and irrigation projects, which include the construction of dams, canals, and reservoirs, have been accomplished on a large-scale. In the same period important changes have also occurred in cropping patterns.

We need more agricultural productivity to feed millions of population and for that we used to put more chemicals and fertilizers on the one hand but on the other we have to take care of soil fertility also. Soil should not lose its fertility otherwise it will not be treated as sustainable development. It extends cost benefit analysis and bio-economics and combines it with ideas of economic welfare. Economic tools are available for the public to evaluate alternative outcomes; for instance,

Last but not the least my publishers who appreciated this book and brought this work out in a record time.

—Editor

Contents

CHAPTER 1

An Introduction to the Sustainable Development

Sustainable development implies using renewable natural resources in a manner which does not eliminate or degrade them, or otherwise diminish their usefulness for future generations. It further implies using non-renewable (exhaustible) mineral resources in a manner which does not unnecessarily preclude easy access to them by future generations. Sustainable development also requires depleting non-renewable energy resources at a slow enough rate so as to ensure the high probability of an orderly society transition to renewable energy sources.

The current debate on globalization and the environment has revolved around four major themes, all informed by the multitude and complexity of a set of environmental concerns dubbed, even by the most conservative commentators, as symptoms of a global environmental crisis. From climate change to bio-diversity loss and from air pollution to fresh water contamination, the symptoms of a global environmental crisis have often been treated from an essentialist position. This theme acknowledges the significance of the natural interdependence of the environmental life support system (air, water, and soil) on a global scale. To that extent, the most common theme in the debate on globalization and the environment is that, if it is environmental then it must imply global consequences on the human and non-human world. This assumption implies that the impact of any large-scale development interventions (industrialization, raw material extraction and processing, mega-irrigation projects, timber logging, mining, fossil energy exploration, production and processing, and consumption, etc.) in the environment would influence the quality of the environmental life support system. Such large-scale environmental interventions are part of an ecological modernization process that has contributed to an unprecedented modification of the global environment. In essence ecological modernization carries the insignia of globalization and its capacity to produce momentous transformation in the way human lives are ordered and reordered, which in turn results in further modifications of the global environment. Ecological modernization can therefore defined as a manifestation of a complex and far-reaching development or process or modernization in one of its most common interactions with the natural environment. Sustainable development is defined as a pattern of social and structured economic transformations (i.e., development) which optimises the economic and societal benefits available in the present, without jeopardising the likely potential for similar benefits in the future.

A primary goal of sustainable development is to achieve a reasonable and equitably distributed level of economic well-being that can be perpetuated continually for many human generations. If the use and abuse of technology is an inseparable part of development and environmental modification then it is only logical that technology has also been conceived as the savior from global environmental destruction. In the process, the quest for ecological modernization becomes a global imperative resulting in ecological damage as well as ecological repair. Second, ecological modernization is associated with high per capita energy consumption and, also as a result of industrialization, the penetration of technology into almost every aspect of life, from household appliances to transport and the manufacturing of goods and services or development redefined as ecological modernization.

Paradoxically, under the ecological modernization project, a major reduction in energy consumption (the main contributor to air pollution, climate change, ozone layer depletion, and greenhouse effect, etc.) may not be possible without major alterations to today's lifestyles. The view that technological advancement and raw material fabrication are our potential saviors from an impending global environmental crisis is not supported by the current expansion of new environmentally harmful products. The implications of such developments for ecological modernization are immense, particularly in the event of further compression of the environmental space and the increase of ecological debt incurrent by the industrially advanced world.

The second theme in the debate is more concerned with the environmental consequences of the production of the goods and services required for the satisfaction of an increasing world population. The views expressed by social scientists attached to the Club of Rome are commonly known. For instance, Meadows *et al.* (1972) argue that if the current trends of industrialization, population growth, and depletion of non-renewable natural resources continue unchecked, the earth would reach *The Limits to Growth* within a hundred years. What is needed to reverse these trends; not only to curb population growth, but also to work towards a sustainability revolution (Meadows *et al.,* 1995)? Global economic growth would then set the limits to the capacity of the environment to provide the raw materials and energy resources needed to maintain economic growth. Generally, this theme is common in multilateral environmental initiatives and the manner in which they have responded to what has been dubbed the global environmental crisis. These initiatives are exemplified by a long sequence of global environmental conferences considered by the development lobby as an anticlimax to civilizational progression. Only by linking the multitude of socio-economic networks at various territorial levels around visible targets and common objectives can one realistically hope to achieve social justice, economic efficiency, environmental sustainability, and political democracy, as well as avoid the many possible sources (economic, political, ethnic) of global implosion.

The most doomsday-like scenario treats exponential development as a threat to long-term human survival in a healthy environment and transforms the daily struggles for survival to struggles over progress. This possible scenario would result in a global implosion summed up by Beck's (1995) risk society, characterized by uncertainty and lack of control over its future destiny. In the risk society: (1) Environmental hazards are global and cannot be delimited spatially, temporally, or socially; they encompass nation-states, military alliances, and all social classes, and, by their very nature, present wholly new kinds of challenge to the institutions designed for their control and the legitimatization of their anonymity. (2) The established rules of attribution and liability—casualty and guilt— break down. (3) The hazards can only be minimized by technological means, never entirely eliminated. The technocracy of hazard squirms in the thumbscrews of the safety guarantees which it is forced to impose on itself. (4) The lack of provision for catastrophe prevention or prediction plainly exposes the paradigm error; the bewitchment of reason caused by the false belief that the 20th century was only a continuation of the 19th. The security system, which anticipates social provisions for the worst conceivable case, broke down with the advent of large-scale (nuclear, chemical, ecological, genetic) hazards. Although Beck has moderated his position *vis-à-vis* the risk society thesis, it still poses some serious questions concerning what type of development developing countries should pursue.

The third theme is advocated by a large number of multilateral institutions and social scientists, mostly pro-South in their views on the relationship between the developing countries and the dominant global economic forces.[6] If that is the case, what is needed then is a differentiated rather than uniform approach to whether curbing economic growth should be adopted equality by poor and richer countries. Pro-

South social scientists also place a larger proportion of the blame for the global environmental crisis on the countries of the North.

On the other hand, social scientists of various radical environmental persuasions argue that, the global sustainable development movement usurps a neo-colonial ideology aim to frustrate the development of the South. This view, however, is not new; it originated in historical materialism and Engels' (1940) thesis on the *Dialectics of Nature* and Marx's contribution to the relationship between the expansion of capitalism and the destruction of the natural environment.

The fourth theme found expression in Agenda 21, as well as a variety of United Nations conventions, treaties, and declarations espouse, and a number of 'establishment' scholars who work within this dominant paradigm. The common view here is that global environmental protection could be realized by adopting sustainable development as a global ideal. As a global imperative, sustainable development is built around six axes;

(i) reviving growth;

(ii) changing the quality of growth;

(iii) meeting essential needs for jobs, energy, water, and sanitation;

(iv) conserving and enhancing the resource base;

(v) reorienting technology and managing risk and

(vi) merging environment and economics in decision-making.

The main thrust of sustainable development, therefore, is that global environmental protection and economic growth should proceed hand in hand. More importantly, sustainable development things on the premise that global environmental institutions and governance should manage global environmental problems.

Although some social scientists and activists were quick

to dub sustainable development's emphasis on reviving growth as a contradiction in terms, others began the search for methods and theories that could reconcile economic growth and global environmental protection. Some of the most stimulating research in this area is what Eckersley (1995:15) refers to as free market environmentalism, which conceives of sustainable development within the dominant free market paradigm. In this paradigm, nature itself is, to some extent, treated as a commodity subject to market principles linked to its ability to supply environmental goods and services.

(i) The market attaches a commonly recognized economic value to environmental resources. This value is dependent on the importance of the resource in question to environmental managers.

(ii) The market provides the means by which environmental resources can be exchanged.

(iii) As a direct response to valuation and exchange, the market has a direct bearing on the operation of multi-layered environmental management.

(iv) The market serves as an important means by which resource scarcity is regulated.

(v) Externalities highlight what can be termed market failure; that is, that the market does not capture the full environmental implications of human-environmental interactions. Free market environmentalism has to deal with this not at a resource, sector or national level, but all of these levels as well as integrating them at global level.

Ironically, while the debate on the global nature of the environmental crisis continues, the constellation of the world political and economic order began to shift away from global hegemony of two superpowers to unipolarity. In Axford's (1995) words, "global hegemony has slipped beyond the capacity of any single state, thus ushering in the emergence of a truly global managerial entrepreneurial class whose transnational economic transaction are efficiently enhanced by global private banks, financial markets and corporations." The advocacy of a rather muted free market principles and trade in production, services, and finance, has also worked its way to replace the primes of exchange relations informed by the sovereignty of national economies controlled by the state.

New trends in globalization, including robotization, the dematerialization of production (media and communication), and post-Fordism (franchising the great corporate conglomerations) are not environmentally neutral. The political economy of these new trends is exemplified by the structural power of mobile capital and private investment, which has contributed to the decline of the state and its ability to control economic activities and the factors of production, including environment and natural resources. Two observations merit some attention here: first, while the protection of the global environment requires a globally concerted action the prevailing economic globalization and its manifestation in trade, the information revolution and the accompanying technological advancements are growth driven. Second, globalization is born in the womb of a neo-liberal ideology hostile to attempts aiming at market regulation or control over the new entrepreneurial class's capacity to expand production, extract materials and exploit the riches of nature wherever they prove profitable. The question that begs a serious answer is whether it is possible to reconcile the ethos of neo-liberal globalization and the imperative of global environmental protection.

While the introductory section of this chapter has been devoted to the environment-development nexus seen as a process of ecological modernization, the following section takes issue with the debate on globalization and the environment, with specific reference to the debate on free market environmentalism and its potential contribution to global environmental protection. The section argues that development research has, to some extent, not been able to cope with the enormity of the configuration of the intricate relationship between globalization, sustainable development, and the quest for economic growth.

Globalization and the Environment

One of the questions we face is whether global resource competition for high and sustained growth would foster or hinder the realization of global projects such as free trade and global environmental protection. Is it practically possible to reconcile globalization, free trade, and global environmental protection? Even if it is possible to reconcile free trade and the environment protection on a global scale, what institutional mechanisms are needed to address these issues? In this respect, globalization and the environment can be explored by examining one of the most influential trends, which (if a perfect market ever existed) should ideally transform global trade and conversely the relationship between trade and environment in a globally open trade regime.

In essence, I argue that free market environmentalism is an extension of the ethos of neo-liberal globalization and therefore both treat global environmental protection as subservient to global capital flows and the expansion of trade and economic growth. However, paradoxically, the globalization of the environmental, issues and the quest for free trade constitutes the foundation stone of open globalization, which, if properly implemented, would allow for greater solidarity of a disenfranchised and diverse environmental movement (Martinez and Guha, 1997). This explains why all regional trading blocs have signed protocols and conventions, which have committed them to regional and global environmental protection laws.

However, there is no agreement as to the exact impact of the liberalization of trade and free market globalization on the environment. The anti free market lobby, including environmentalists, argue that trade liberalization is harmful to the environment because it puts more emphasis on growth and development at the expense of global environmental protection. They also argue for greater decentralization of economic and political activities to empower people and enable them to care for their local environments. Trade liberalization without proper environmental protection policies, legal instruments and economic incentives (or liabilities) often results in land degradation and environmental disasters in the marginal and fragile global commons. This will hold globalization responsible for the dangers that threaten our global future.

In a globally free trade regime, one of the institutions that will have a direct effect on the environment is the World Trade Organization (WTO), which represents the triumph of the trade liberalization lobby in conceiving the General Agreement on Tariff and Trade (GATT). The WTO is hailed as the epitome of how trade liberalization should lead to growth and therefore generates financial resources, which could be utilized to protect the environment. The WTO aims to liberalize four areas of economic activity previously considered to be the exclusive domain of the national legislation. These are: (a) trade in services, (b) intellectual property rights, (c) international investment flows, and (d) agriculture.

The WTO presumes that, by concentrating resources within each country into the most productive and competitive sectors, (i) free trade will enable countries to maximize their competitive advantage; (ii) a globally increased trade is essentially good for development, and the more people trade, the better off they will be.

Other aspects of global trade and the environment are articulated by Junior and Welford (1997:138), who argue that trade and economic globalization have greatly expanded the opportunities for the rich to pass on their environmental burdens to the poor by exporting both waste and polluting factories. Trade has a secondary impact on issues of equity as it results in impacts (positive or negative) on poverty, health, employment, human rights, democracy, labor laws, and self-determination. I add to these two points, one aspect of globalization that may have some positive result on the environment.

The pro-free trade lobby's assumptions have been contested by environmentalists who argue defiantly that the nature of comparative advantage in a globalized world has more to do with absolute price advantage then differences in comparative advantage. For instance, although many developing countries have comparative advantage in the production of tropical crops such as bananas, tea, and coffee, they continue to decrease in the international market due to their weak bargaining position in the world economy.

The meagre attention given to the environment in the GATT process would suggest that no or little value would be attached to the potential environmental destruction caused by excessive use of natural resources in response to such policies. This is particularly true for developing countries, which depend on primary commodity production which, in 1992, insisted on the inclusion of the environmental issues in the GATT process and negotiations.

However, it is difficult to analyze the development of world trade and its consequences on the environment in isolation from its differential effects on local communities, states, and regional entities. Wilson and Bryan (1996) explored the interdependence of local, national, regional, and global trade transactions and illustrated that multi-layered trade operations would result in the shrinking of environmental space. Earlier Opschoor *et al.* (1994) concluded that the expansion of global trade operations has resulted in an increased ecological debt and the shrinking of the environmental space available for the maintenance of the global environmental life support system. This process contributes, according to Opschoor *et al.* (1994), to the shrinking of the environmental space and the increase of the ecological debt, *i.e.*, an increased 'environmental reach' through far-reaching 'environmental foot steps.' A global condition in which the environmental space is shrinking at an accelerating rate is detrimental to the well-being of the industrial world as well as the developing world, where polluting industries have often been relocated in places of lax legal systems. The inter-dependence of the environmental life support system and its response to large- scale environmental damage or degradation, emanating from an increasing trade in primary products and goods and services, cannot be more revealing.

Is there a way out?

The picture that I have painted so far is a gloomy one in which global environmental actors as well as the development lobby seem to have been locked into a losing battle against the powerful tides of globalization and an impending environmental crisis. The question that follows is whether the social sciences live managed, somehow, to leave their imprints on the debate by explaining the 'social' and its relationship to 'nature' and how they influences each other on a global-scale and what policy issues have likewise preoccupied them. Social sciences have contributed to the debate in the field of environmental policies and respective institutional mechanisms responsible for the mitigation of global environmental problems. What can environmental policies and institutions deliver in such a situation that requires more than a balancing act, and what are their limitations? These are difficult questions to answer and are certainly beyond the scope of this chapter. However, I will attempt to delineate some of the main factors that influence global environmental policies and institutions and their response to the processes that simultaneously influence globalization and sustainable development.

In the field of international environmental policy, Vig defines them as ranging from broad policy declarations and informal agreements to highly articulated conventions and treaties. According to Vig (1999:*Ibid*),

> The range of international environmental policies currently in forces vast, covering protection of endangered plants and animals; protection against transboundary pollution of air, water, and soil; protection of the atmosphere against acidification, ozone depletion, and climate change; protection of the oceans

against oils spills and the dumping of radioactive and other hazardous chemicals, pesticides, and hazardous wastes, measures to combat desertification; and protection of Antarctica.

There is no gainsaying that international environmental policies represent a direct response to the consequences of ecological modernization. On a global scale this can be seen in the expansion of Western consumption patterns and life-styles that have subsequently strained the functioning of the fragile environmental life support system on which the production of globally consumed goods and services depend. However, international environmental policies require global environmental institutions with translational mandates to safeguard the protection of the global commons.

The major institutions entrusted with the implementation of international environmental polices are the United National General Assembly (UNGA), the United Nations Environmental Programme (UNEP), the Commission on Sustainable Development (CSD), the Global Environmental Facility (GEF). The three Bretton Wood Institutions (the International Bank for Reconstruction and Development, the IMF, and the World Trade Organization) have adopted reforms in the face of strong criticism for pursuing economic missions in ways that have further aggravated environmental problems.

Based on similar arguments, sustainable development has been alternatively defined in various manners also, some of them are as follows:

"Development that meets the needs of the present without compromising the ability of future generations to meet their own needs."

"Sustainable development ensures that the maximum rate of resource consumption and waste discharge for a selected development portfolio would be sustained indefinitely, in a defined planning region, without progressively impairing its bio-productivity and ecological integrity. Environmental conservation, therefore, contrary to general belief, accelerates rather than hinders economic development.

Therefore, the Development plans have to ensure:

- Sustainable and equitable use of resources for meeting the needs of the present and future generations without causing damage to environment.
- To prevent further damage to our life-support systems.
- To conserve and nurture the biological diversity, gene pool and other resources for long term food security."

"The primary objective of the Sustainable Development is to reduce the absolute poverty of the world's poor through providing lasting and secure livelihoods that minimise resource depletion, environmental degradation, cultural disruption and social instability."

The last several decades have seen unprecedented increases in economic output in many parts of Asia. The green revolution, the East Asian "miracle," explosive growth of the Asian middle class, and industrial expansion far outstripping that of other Third World regions have been lauded as successes. The material well-being of hundreds of millions of people has increased, along with tangible improvements in such quality-of-life indicators as literacy, life expectancy, and infant mortality.

Something, however, was amiss. One-dimensional measures of progress were missing the bigger picture, and the bigger picture included ubiquitous and accelerating environmental deterioration, social anomie, substitution of traditions of creative and spiritual vigour by materialism, and steadily worsening maldistribution of wealth and resources. By the 1990s, global rhetoric about combating poverty and protecting the environment sounded like empty slogans. It was only in the recent past that financial institutions such as ADB initiated a serious effort to combat poverty, the results of which would not be visible until some years later.

This chapter assesses the situation in the millennial year 2000. It uses the rubric "sustainable development", under which a wide-ranging exploration of dilemmas and possibilities may take place. "Sustainable" is a conservative term that suggests not taking from nature, society, or others without giving in return, "Development" is a cultural term that refers to creative energies of human beings and their expansion to bring into being higher quality of life for all individuals and societies. "Sustainable" does not mean that which preserves existing economic or social structures, and "development" is not synonymous with, but necessary condition for economic growth.

Sustainable development is Asia's greatest challenge. The alternative is a continuing descent into environmental destruction, social disruption, and cultural deterioration. Given the vast sums to be made and power to be accumulated through the creation of poverty and the destruction of nature, the prognosis could be grim.

Development as it has been experienced in Asia and the Pacific since the 1950s has left poverty, environmental deterioration, and social disintegration (especially social exclusion) in its wake. The ever-expanding market demands money to play. The ever-growing State demands power to play. The result has been creation of new hierarchies, new measures of deprivation, and new loci of polarisation. The process is not sustainable.

The fundamental question is whether or not ethics and social values will prevail over greed. The issues are, at root, about power in society and whether it is used for short-term, individualistic aggrandisement, or for intergeneration, social, and ecological betterment. Economics and technology matter, but only insofar as politics and culture demand sustainable development.

Environmental destruction, social deterioration, and poverty have the same root causes in unequal power relations that allow some individuals to get away with destructive, export-oriented logging, slum evictions to build commercial offices, and a host of other beggar-thy-neighbour activities. As the industrialised nations have shown, power allows some to get away with destroying someone else's backyard or source of livelihood and with exploiting the labour of the desperately poor. Example after example can be cited to show how the rich and powerful either directly caused environmental destruction or forced low-income individuals to live in a situation of great environmental vulnerability or hazard and thus to participate in the destruction of their own livelihoods.

In the past, such destruction has been accepted by most governments, donor agencies, and opinion leaders as necessary to economic development. A questioning spirit is a flame in Asia and the Pacific, however, as large numbers of women's groups, indigenous people's organisations, grass-roots movements of many sizes and shapes, and even the occasional spiritual leader call for a redefinition of development as inclusive, integenerational, ecologically sensitive, and based on a vision of shared creativity and removal of deprivation. Such visions see economic growth as a global anachronism. Economic development is an imperative for low-income communities and nations as it will improve the quality of life for all.

History is far from over. The drama of social and environmental change has more acts. On the one hand, it can be an exciting challenge; on the other, it can lead to despair and alienation. What is certain, however, is that the future is unpredictable. There will be change: some ideologies are dying, people are restless in their exclusion, and awareness is growing of the implications of continued environmental deterioration.

Preparation of *Sustainable Development in Asia* has had its discouraging times as the dead weight of error committed in the name of "development" bore down as the heaviness of pessimism. From beginning to end, however the burden has been lightened by the excitement engendered by success stories of Asia-Pacific people's struggles to halt environmental deterioration and social destruction and to return some measure of self-esteem and creative power to society's excluded.

Consumption, Production and Distribution

What is critical to sustainable development is the pattern of growth. East Asia has examples of broad-based economic growth that had clearly positive impacts on quality of life for many of its citizens and saw rapid declines in absolute poverty. Such a broad-based growth pattern (now largely abandoned in countries such as the PRC) is exemplary. Basic needs and basic security were spread largely throughout society, although the process was often a violent one. No country, however, has come close to managing a pattern of growth that has not dislocated large numbers of people and destroyed lives, health, and livelihoods through environmental destruction, even though attempts have been made to compensate for losses.

Sustainable development requires consideration of consumption, production, and distribution. Technocratic preference, however, is to focus on production and thereby hope to somehow reduce environmental impacts through tinkering with economic and technical efficiencies. It will not do. The numbers of people in Asia and the Pacific are too great to seriously contemplate their consuming at OECD levels using OECD technology. To argue otherwise is to be lost in Panglossian wishful thinking.

First, people must radically restructure their consumption patterns to emphasise basic needs for all and reduce conspicuous consumption. The change is partly a question of values and social mores and partly a question of political choice regarding investments in transport, urban and regional planning, and environmental awareness and education.

Sustainable Development in Asia emphasises consumption and thus immediately engages in the contentious realms of values, ethics, and the constitution of happiness. It is rough terrain because economics as the ruling ideology presumes the market can determine what is best for people. It argues that what is best is a matter of value and that economics should be celebrated as a tool for rational calculation rather than as a substitute for social ethics and political decision making.

As market and State have, to an extent, drained communities of autonomy, self-reliance, pride, and integrity, modern hierarchies based on material consumption have prevailed. One consequence has been demand for goods embodying high energy and material inputs. It is the extraction, conversion, transport, and use of these goods that overburdens local and global ecosystems. This chapter postulates new consumption patterns based on old values and attitudes that emphasise creativity, inclusions, and social maintenance over greed, competition, and ostentation. No predictions are proffered, but the options seem clear.

Second, we envision two great production revolutions in the early 21st century. A new industrial revolution will radically transform reductionist, problem-oriented science, technology, and industry into a holistic, system-design perspective that mimics nature's cyclical resource patterns. A green revolution will similarly move beyond the wonders of high-impact monocropping to a holistically designed "natural" agriculture of high productivity and low impact.

Sustainable Development in Asia goes beyond current attempts to foster clean production's or eco-efficiency's incremental improvements to reducing energy and materials throughputs in production processes. It argues for an entirely new approach that begins with needed services, takes a holistic-systems look at minimising waste and pollution, and leapfrogs to zero-emissions service provision. Calls by management and production experts in the industrialised nations for a new industrial revolution are echoed by the report's observation that the advantages are with Asia to actually implement the new industrial revolution.

In a similar vein, it is recognised that the very issue of

sustainable development is critical to Asia partly because of the astounding success of the green revolution in transforming agriculture and society. The costs of that transformation give impetus to the call for the greening of the green revolution by eschewing more myopic and unidimensional solutions to a perceived production crisis and adopting holistic and diversified approaches emphasising quality, livelihood stability, and maintenance of soil and water.

Sustainable Development in Asia sketches a 12 part programme for rural regeneration that puts stress on (i) legal rights to organise politically and to access land and other productive resources; (ii) redefined research and development and extension services that emphasise sustainability, diversity, stability, and learning from traditional ways; (iii) forms of cooperation that can make smallholders competitive in today's markets; and (iv) the State helping smallholders gain and maintain access to land, common property resources, irrigation water, agricultural inputs, and markets. It is a vision that challenges some of globalisation's fundamental precepts, but it is also a vision that offers hope for poverty reduction and environmental improvement.

Finally, equitable distribution is a keystone to sustainable development. Equitable sharing of resources (land, water, air, minerals) will allow all to meet their basic needs. It will reduce absolute poverty to a memory. It will stop the segregation of the poor in environmentally hazardous or fragile places. It will allow women and children to breathe clean air, be relieved of the extreme drudgery of today's household tasks such as carrying fuel and water, be accorded respect by transport planners, and receive proper nutrition, education, and health.

The most ubiquitous theme is the potential of mobilising individual and collective energies. Self-help, empowerment, social action, social capital formation, civil society's resurgence—whatever the name, all are measures that recognise that markets are imperfect and limited in scope and the State cannot fill in all the gaps. The recognition creates the space for many agents of change acting locally while being supported (not directed) by governments.

Mobilisation does not occur in a vacuum. Unequal power relations, whether within households, communities, or nations, produce both conflict and cooperation. The conflict can be violent and unpleasant, but it can also be creative and transformative. It is necessary for sustainable development that creative conflict take place within a framework of socially recognised and legally enshrined rights, that people and groups be able to assert and practice these rights, and that they have recourse to due process and transparent judicial and administrative procedure.

Governments have much to say about rights and much power over the equity of access. If poverty is largely about limited access to land, information, capital markets, water, education, and public services in general, then governments must take seriously the need to broaden access as an integral component of sustainable development. Ignoring land reform, encouraging enclosure of the commons, subsidising elite preferences, and repressing moves to organise the socially excluded can only lead ultimately to more of the same—pro-rich, anti-environment growth.

Communities are mobilising themselves to do the following:

- Demand their rights to life and health when faced with severe urban environmental hazards.
- Demand access to land, water, and other services when forced to make way for infrastructure projects, logging and mining concessions, and privatisation (or nationalisation) of what used to be common property resources.
- Form user groups to sustainably manage common property resources.
- Bring together individual, household, and community

resources for environmental improvement with the support and cooperation of government.

- Share information and resources with other groups about common environmental and political concerns such as globalisation, toxic hazards, and new technologies.

- Pressure industries to clean up and hold businesses accountable for their resource-using practices through access to information, processes of accountability, and monitoring of practices.

- Increase group empowerment through microcredit, land-sharing schemes, tree-management projects, and water selling.

- Pressure governments and developers to take seriously the rights and needs of women, children, low-income residents, and the socially excluded when planning and building infrastructure.

The challenge is mobilisation as creative power—mobilisation that manifests a view and asks (i) what positive energies and resources people can contribute to development rather than what they lack as the passive poor, (ii) what can be done to redistribute knowledge to serve the interests of the excluded, and (iii) what the possibilities are for redistribution of physical and financial assets to better serve the interests of sustainable development. While this, mobilisation must come from people in struggle to better their own lives and to exhibit their own values, it demands support from reinvigorated governments that can promote more equitable access to resources, protect the environment, support the risk-taking of small farmers and entrepreneurs, deliver public goods such as health care and education to all, participate in co-management of common property resources, and sponsor research on and development of technologies and techniques for a regenerated agriculture and a zero-emissions industry.

Sustainable Development in Asia thus recognises the

essential role to be played by governments—governments supportive of social mobilisation and characterised by transparency and accountability to the public gaze. In a similar vein, this report recognises the possibility of market forces having a progressive character, if corporate governance can be assured through State and civil-society vigilance. The corporate view that sustainability means sustained access to cheap and docile labour, cheap resources, and a regulatory-free environment, must give way to a conception of corporate responsibility that welcomes competition, accountability, internalisation of external social and environmental costs, and transparency to the public gaze. The public must gaze with vigilance and determination. As the public is, ironically, both the cause and solution to the problem of sustainable development in Asia, this report advocates its key role in the process.

The international environmental policies and institutions together constitute a diverse body of global environmental governance. If traced from an evolutionary perspective of sustainable development, the Earth Summit and Agenda 21 have laid the foundations for the advocacy of global environmental governance within the wider concept of global governance. According to these foundations, there is no single model, form, or institution of global governance, nor is there a single structure or set of structures. However, recognizing the systemic nature of the issues with which it deals, it promotes systemic approaches to dealing with major global concerns. The aims of global governance include reforming and strengthening the existing system of intergovernmental institutions, and improving its means of collaboration with private and independent groups. Among other things, global governance will strive to subject the rule of arbitrary power—economic, political, or military—to the rule of law within global society.

I argue elsewhere (Mohammed Salih, 1997a) that global environmental governance operates within the confines of, and consistent with, the principles laid down in global governance legal instruments, conventions and international environmental policy proclamations. *Our Global Neighborhood* (1995:216) indicates that global environmental governance emphasizes the need: (1) to put into action global legal, intellectual, and institutional groundwork for a concerted effort to achieve sustainable development; (2) to establish a Trusteeship of the Global Commons (TGC) and to be made responsible for acting on behalf of all nations, including the administration of environmental treaties; to enact an Earth charter for world endorsement, pending the outcome of the global efforts exerted be the Earth Council and Green Cross to achieve this endeavor.

Considering the ultimate association between environment and development, it has become obvious that one of the most conspicuous outcomes of the Earth Summit is that the stage has been set for global governance aided by diverse trends of globalization to become the dominant paradigm and the most influential actor on the global scale. Global environmental policies, according to Rich (1994:273), have evolved around the premise that Global environmental management can work. The project as it emerged out of Rio has two principal approaches—a growing body of international environmental treaties among nation-states and increased foreign aid for environmental protection and management as well as poverty alleviation, channelled and managed mainly through the Global Environmental Facility (GEF) and other financing arms of the World Bank.

Notions such as global environmental policies imply not only that the natural economy has already been rendered subject to global capital operations, but also that sustainable development has been defined according to the logic of global capital operations and that of the dominant global governance institutions that support it. Seven years after the Rio Conference proclaimed Agenda 21 (1992) as the guiding principle for global sustainable development, the question remains as to why contradictory Northern political discourses have converged to agree on the assumption that what is ecological is by necessity global. Erroneously, however, that which is ecological is global, but that which is global concerns a socially, economically, and politically differentiated humanity. Global environmental governance has therefore been an integral part of the economic, social, and political processes responsive to Agenda 21 and other international environmental policy proclamations, conventions and treaties.

The question that continues to beg for an answer is whether such grand global projects as environment and sustainable development, free trade, and even globalization are reconcilable within the new global context of development. The global environmental movement is explicit about the need to establish a global resource management regime responsible for protecting the global commons from abuse by irresponsible nation-states or greedy corporate interests. Managing the global commons therefore requires global environmental policies, respected and implemented by all nation-states. Neo-liberal globalization, on the other hand, is premised on the need for trade liberalization and opening up new markets and reaching out for new consumers.

The global environmental conventions, treaties, and laws, which resulted from the deliberations of multilateral environmental forums and negotiations, have contributed to the consummation of sustainable development as a global ideal. As I have mentioned earlier, sustainable development advocates the need to integrate environment and development in decision-making. In my view, sustainable development meets free market environmentalism half way in defending decentralized private choice of the market as a superior economic management system to the command and control approach. According to Eckersley (1995:15–16), free market environmentalism asserts that bureaucratic regulations are inefficient and open to corruption in many environmental regulatory regimes concerned with the management of forests, water rights, and public lands. It also argues for the removal of government subsidies and intervention in the form of externality taxes to correct market failures.

Because free market environmentalism has much in common with the current drive towards economic policy reforms (deregulation, free trade, and the market liberalization and open door economic policy), not surprisingly it argues for rolling back the state and assigning it a minimal role in environmental protection. Hence, as part of the core values of the global environmental agendas agreed upon by states (Agenda 21, 1992) and other international conventions, it advocates growth as an engine of sustainable development and hence environmental protection.

More than the good-will of global finance institutions that try to integrate the environment into their investment operations, the protection of the global environment will depend on the capacity of strong states to implement economic policy instruments capable of harnessing/mitigating or abating the consequences of economic growth on the environment. Legal instruments or command and control policies, although important, will not be in a position to deliver results without persuasive socio-economic incentives.

The current environmental policy principles developed for OECD countries and applied in the developing countries have been summarized by Opschoor and Turner (1994:4) as follows:

(i) The polluter pays' principle: *i.e.,* the polluters pay the cost of meeting socially acceptable environmental quality standards.

(ii) The prevention or precautionary principle: this explicitly recognizes the existence of uncertainty (environmental and social) and seeks to avoid irreversible damages in relation to the imposition of a safety margin into policy; it also seeks to prevent waste generation at source, as well as retaining some end-of-pipe measures.

(iii) The economic efficiency/cost effectiveness principle: this applies both to the setting of standards and the design of the policy instruments for attaining them.

(iv) The decentralization principle: to assign environmental decisions and enforcement to the lowest level of government capable of handling it, without significant residual externalities.

(v) The legal efficiency principle: this seeks to preclude the passage of regulations that cannot be realistically enforced.

Reflections on these environmental policy principles and their practice in various parts of the world have produced mixed results, even in their proponents view.[17] Business and international trade operators often misuse economic policy instruments, including market-based instruments such as (a) taxes on emissions and tradable emissions permits and (b) resource use-permits. My reasons are as follows:

(i) Environmental taxes keep down the cost of compliance since the market determines that those who can most afford to act do so, and they deal with the total amount and distribution of the problem.

(ii) Environmental taxes act as a continuous irritant to the polluters, who therefore have a continuing incentive to avoid the financial cost and taxes by introducing cleaner technology.

(iii) The price of polluting products will tend to be higher than the price of clean products, and thereby the consumer will encourage producers to choose the latter.

(iv) Environmental taxes can be used in a fiscally neutral manner to reduce other distorting taxes in the economy.

(v) Reinforcement of environmental standards and the 'polluter pays' principle. If the influential regional trading blocs (EU, ASEAN and NAFTA) adopt reasonable environmental standards and adhere to the 'polluter pays' principle, they may be able to ensure that pollution control and environmental costs are internalized into enterprise costs and product prices.

However, it is doubtful given the current variations in levels of economic development within and between states that the affluent ones would agree to sacrifice affluence for the sake of global environmental gains. In this respect, developing and small industrial countries seem fearful of the implications of implementing global environmental protection policies. On the other hand, enforcing compliance with global environmental legal instruments such as trade restriction may encourage non-co-operation in global environmental protection. However, without global environmental co-operation, international environmental laws are ineffective regulatory instruments.

Obviously, this discussion illustrates that social scientists are at the forefront of attempts to understand the forces behind globalization and environmental destruction, as well as attempts to contribute to the policy debate. In the process, social scientists have become more aware of the intricacies that may hinder the advancement of firm conclusions, such as those of the natural sciences.

Essentially, the globalization-environment debate has questioned the ability of disciplinary boundaries to withstand the complex nature of environment and development and their multi-layered consequences on the totality of the human condition. The debate also integrates theoretical-philosophical policy and activists research. As lamented by Redclift and Benton (1994:7–8), the relationship between structure and agency became more focused and there is hardly any contribution that can be described as purely theoretical or philosophical in nature. This is particularly true even for contributions from environmental ethics and environmental philosophy, which are defined as practical philosophies that engage the environmental consciousness of individuals and groups to restructure their relationship with the environment. The social sciences have more than ever before been confronted with a myriad of data collected on a global level and that has little to say about the socio-economic and environmental conditions of the societies from which it has been collected.

While some social sciences (*e.g.*, economics) can generate

data on a global scale, others are more concerned with the local consequences of globalization, better known as the global-local nexus. Although globalization, environment, and development are not entirely new subjects, the intensity and complexity of their interaction pose new and complex questions that have structurally forced disciplinary social scientists to abandon their earlier hard-nosed attitudes towards interdisciplinary research. The globalization in its various manifestations, including sustainable development, are difficult to answer within the confines of any angle social science discipline. Disciplinary approaches unconscious of their own limitations (and those of the social sciences as a whole to integrate development and the environment outside the policy realms) have not succeeded in hindering our understanding of the complex relationships linking powerful and over-loaded concepts, such as globalization and the environment. As the current debate illustrates, the uncertainty that has evolved around the future of development has also manifested itself in the uncertainty about our environmental future.

REFERENCES

Axford, B. (1995), *The Global System: Economics, Politics and Culture*, Cambridge, Polity Press.

Beck, U. (1995), *Ecological Politics in an Age of Risk*, Cambridge, Polity Press.

Bierstreker, T.J. (1996), "The Triumph of Liberal Economic Ideas in the Developing World." In Stallings, B. (ed.) *Global Change and Regional Response: The New International Context of Development*, Cambridge, Cambridge University Press.

Blaikie, P.M. and Brookfield (1989), *Land Degradation and Society*, London, Methuen.

Brenton, T. (1994), *The Greening of Machiavelli, The Evolution of International Environmental Policies*, London, The Royal Institute of International Affairs.

Brundtland Report (1987), *Our Common Future*, Oxford, Oxford

University Press. World Commission on Environment and Development..

Clark, L. Gordon (1995), "Global Competition and Environmental Regulation: Is the Race to the Bottom Inevitable?" In Eckersley, R. (ed.) *Markets, the State and the Environment*, Basingstoke, Macmillan.

Commissions on Global Governance (1995), *Our Global Neighbourhood, Report of the Commission on Global Governance, Oxford*, Oxford University Press.

Daly, H. (1996), *Free Trade, Capital Mobility and Growth versus Environment and Community*, The Hague, Institute of Social Studies.

Dieren, Wouter v. *(ed.)* (1995), *Taking Nature into Account: A report to the Club of Rome*, New York, Copernicus.

Eckersley, R. (1995), "Markets, the State and the Environment." In Eckersely, R. *(ed.) Markets, the State and the Environment*, Basingstoke, Macmillan.

Ehrlich, P. and Ehrlich A (1996), *Betrayal of Science and Reason: How Anti-Environmental Rhetoric Threatens our Future*, Washington DC, Island Press.

Ekins, Paul (1995), *Harnessing Trade to Sustainable Development*, Oxford, Green College.

Engels, Frederick (1940), *The Dialectics of Nature*, New York, International Publishers.

Giddens, A. (1996), "Urbanism, Globalization and Environmental Politics." In Goldblatt, D. (*ed.*) *Social Theory and the Environment*, Cambridge, Polity Press. The Group of Lisbon (1995), *Limits to Competition*, Cambridge, Mass, and London, the MIT Press.

Hannigan, J.A. (1995), *Environmental Sociology: A Social Constructionist Perspective*, London and New York, Routledge.

Hirst, P. and Thompson, G. (1996), *Globalization in Question: The International Economy and the Possibility of Governance*, Cambridge, Polity Press.

Mohammed Salih, M.A. (1999), "Introduction", Mohammed Salih,

M.A., and Tedla, S. (*eds.*) *Environmental Planning, Polices and Politics in Eastern and Southern Africa*, Basingstoke, Macmillan.

Mohammed Salih, M.A. (1997a), "Global Ecologism and Its Critics. In Thomas, C., and Wilkin, Peter (*eds.*) *Globaliszation and the South*, Basingstoke, Macmillan.

Mahammed Salih, M.A. (1997b), "Natural Capital." In O'Hara, P. (*ed.*) *Encyclopaedia of Political Economy*, London and New York, Routledge.

North, R.D. (1995), *Life on a Modern Planet: A Manifesto and New York*, Manchester University Press.

Opschoor, J.B. (1999), "Foreword," Mohammed Salih, M.A., and Tedla, S. (eds)., *Environmental Planning Polices and Politics in Eastern and Southern Africa*, Basingstoke, Macmillan.

Opschoor, J.B. and Turner, R.K. (1994), "Environmental Economics and Environmental Policy Incentives: Introduction and Overview." In Opschoor, J.B., and Turner, R.K. (*eds.*), *Economic Incentives and Environmental Policies: Principles and Practice*, Kluwer Academic Publishers.

Redclift, M. (1984), *Development and the Environment; Red or Green Alternatives*, London.

Redclift, M. and T. Benton (*eds*). (1994), *Social Theory and the Global Environment*, London and New York, Routledge.

Rich, Bruce (1994), *Mortagaging the Earth: The World Bank, Environmental Impoverishment and the Cripis of Development,* London, Earthscan.

Sachs, W. (ed.) (1993), "Introduction," *Global Ecology: A new Arena of Political Conflict,* London and New Jersey, Zed Books.

Shiva, V. (1993), "The Greening of the Giobal Reach; Global Environment or Green Imperialism:" In Sachs, W., (ed.,) *Global Ecology: A New Arena of Political Conflict*, London and New Jersey, Zed Books.

South Commission (1990), *Challenge to the South,* The Report of the South Commission, Oxford, Oxford University Press.

Taylor, Annie and Thomas, C. (1999), *Global Trade and Social Issues,* London and New York, Routledge.

Thomas, C. (1992), *Environment in International Relation*, London, Royal Institute of International Relations.

Tolba, M.K. and El Kholy, O. (1992), *The World Environment 1972–1992: Two Decades for Challenge,* London, Chapman and Hall (United Nations Environmental Program).

Tylor, G.R. (1970), *The Doomsday Book: Can the World Survive?,* London, Thames and Hudson.

Welford, R. (1997), *Hijacking Environmentalism: Corporate Responses to Sustainable Development*, London, Earthscan.

Wilson, G.A. and Bryant, R. (1997), *Environmental Management; New Directions for the Twenty-First Century*, London, University College London.

World Bank (1993), *Environmental Briefs,* Washington DC, World Bank.

CHAPTER 2

Major Challenges for Sustainable Development

Human Health: A Barometer of Sustainable Development

The number of people without access to basic health has grown dramatically as the world's population has increased. So, too, have the range of health challenges. Since 1900, humans have introduced more than 100,000 previously unknown chemicals into the environment. Many are harmful to human health, but little is known about the environmental and health effects of the majority of these substances. Human health is affected as well when natural resources are degraded, air and water are polluted and habitat destroyed.

For example, the global HIV/AIDS crisis is likely to have originated in species that live in forests where people have only recently entered. Health is a basic human need and right. Efforts to promote sustainable development during the past half century have advanced global health tremendously: life expectancy has increased, child mortality has been reduced and diseases have been checked. But for millions around the world, basic health remains a distant dream. Persistent diseases like malaria and tuberculosis are all too common in the world's poorest countries. Women and children die from diseases that could easily be prevented with known, relatively inexpensive vaccines and technologies. Hundreds of millions of people do not have access to the health care services they want and need to plan their families.

In short, global health is a barometer of sustainable development. Healthy people can create a healthy future.

The Environment and Health

- Environmental conditions contribute significantly to communicable diseases, especially infectious, parasitic and respiratory diseases, which account for 20 to 25 per cent of deaths worldwide.
- An estimated 1.5 billion people do not have access to potable water, and 3 billion – half the global population – lack sanitary facilities such as a sanitary latrine, covered waste water drain or flush toilet. Diseases associated with dirty water kill between 5 and 12 million people a year, mostly women and children.
- Well-known and relatively inexpensive treatments could prevent about 60 percent of the global disease burden related to acute respiratory infections; 90 per cent of diarrhea; 50 percent of chronic respiratory infections; and 90 percent of malaria.
- Air pollution kills three million people annually, 90 per cent in developing countries. More than two-thirds of these deaths are associated with indoor air pollution, which comes chiefly from burning fuel indoors for cooking and therefore affects mostly women and girls. Such burning is also closely associated with the incidence of respiratory infections, lung diseases and low-birth-weight babies.
- Cancer-causing agents like lead, mercury and cadmium are widespread in the environment from growing human consumption of heavy metals in industry, transportation (*e.g.*, leaded gasoline) and other activities.

Reproductive Health

- Scientists now regard certain chemicals such as PCBs, DDT, dioxins and at least 80 pesticides as "endocrine disrupters" that may interfere with normal hormone function.

They may undermine intelligence, disease resistance and reproduction. As research continues, concern is also growing about their role in certain cancers, declining sperm counts, infertility among women, miscarriages, and early puberty in girls.

- Several chemicals are associated with childhood development problems, pregnancy failures and cancer in women—breast, ovarian, cervical, uterine and vaginal.

- Quality reproductive health care requires adequate supplies of clean water.

- Women's traditional roles (gathering fuel and water) contribute to general ill-health, infection and diseases that make them much more vulnerable in pregnancy and child birth. As natural resources are depleted, women must work ever harder to obtain the necessary materials, putting their health at greater risk.

Promoting Global Health

UNFPA helps developing countries, at their request, improve access to and quality of reproductive health care, particularly family planning, safe motherhood, and prevention of sexually transmitted infections (STIs) including HIV/AIDS. Priorities include:

Reproductive health and family planning

UNFPA works for universal access to reproductive health services, including voluntary family planning, for all couples and individuals by 2015, the goal set at the 1994 International Conference on Population and Development.

HIV/AIDS prevention

As a UNAIDS co-sponsor, UNFPA helps people learn ways to avoid infection and obtain appropriate services; protects pregnant women against infection; and ensures condom availability for HIV/AIDS prevention.

Young people

UNFPA programmes help adolescents and young people obtain accurate information and non-judgemental counseling services to prevent unwanted pregnancy and STIs, including HIV/AIDS.

Safe motherhood

To reduce the 500,000 preventable maternal deaths per year in developing countries, UNFPA promotes wider access to skilled delivery assistance and emergency obstetric care.

Reproductive Health Supplies

UNFPA provides logistic support and commodities to help countries improve people's access to affordable and high-quality methods of contraception and STI prevention, including condoms.

Response to Emergencies

The fund helps ensure that women displaced by natural disasters or armed conflict have life saving services available, such as assisted delivery and prenatal and post-partum care. It also works to reduce displaced women's vulnerability to HIV infection, sexual exploitation and violence.

Strategy for the European Union

Life expectancy has increased sharply due to better hygiene, nutrition and medical care. In most respects therefore, our standards of living now are higher than they have ever been. Growing economic interdependence resulting from the single market, globalisation, and new communication technologies provide a strong spur to efficiency and increased productivity, and offer new opportunities at all levels. But these positive developments should not blind us to a number of potential threats. Indeed, not everyone is equipped to take advantage of these new opportunities. There is a real risk that some will fall behind and be unable to catch up. There is also a growing awareness that we are putting increased pressure on the carrying capacity of our planet. A number of worrying long-term trends have emerged.

Main Challenges for Sustainability

Severe weather events may become more frequent if we do not act to avert climate change. Rising sea levels threaten the very existence of some small island states, and we should not forget that a large part of the European population lives at or below sea level.

Recurrent, persistent, poorly understand threats to food safety, rampant antibiotic-resistant strains of bacteria, the unexplained emergence of toxic algal blooms: these are all warning signs that we are interfering with our environment in unforeseen ways. Unresolved, these and other menaces to animal and human health threaten our very survival.

One in every six Europeans—more than the population of all but the largest Member States—lives in poverty. Income disparities are widening in some Member States. Our social systems are failing to deliver on a large scale, and are ill-equipped to deal with the ageing of the population.

We are failing to secure the long run viability of our natural environment. Recent decades have seen very significant losses in bio-diversity. A high percentage of existing species is at risk of extinction. Fish stocks in European waters are close to collapse.

In major cities, transport congestion has been rising rapidly and is approaching gridlock. This has major social, economic and environmental costs which fall largely, though not exclusively, on the three-quarters of the European population who live in urban areas. Enlargement will intensify the challenge of achieving economic and social cohesion.

The Community's Responsibility

The EU Member States share a significant number of common values and aspirations, together with a similar sense of what constitutes progress and how our societies should develop over the next generation. The aim of a European sustainable development strategy should be to give substance to this vision, and to map out what needs to change if we are to make this vision a reality. Moreover, the growing institutional, economic and social interdependence of our countries requires us to work together to meet these challenges. In a number of economic sectors, moves towards sustainable development can only be achieved by action at the EU level. Clear examples arise where the Community has exclusive competence because of internal market regulations. or where integrated European markets mean that uncoordinated action by Member States is likely to be ineffective.

However, achieving sustainable development will also require action at national, regional and local level, as well as from business and citizens. For this reason, in identifying and analysing the main challenges to sustainability facing the European Union, the Commission services have not confined themselves to subjects for which the EU institutions have an exclusive or shared responsibility. Moreover, the EU strategy should look beyond the present borders of the Union to be relevant for all the countries that will join the Union in the coming years. Economic and social disparities will be wider in an enlarged Union, and many of the problems identified in this paper are faced to a greater or lesser extent by the future Member States. Our common future demands a common European approach.

The International Dimension

EU policies in areas such as international trade, foreign direct investment, development co-operation and immigration influence prospects for sustainability far beyond the borders of the Union. This is very obviously the case for issues such as global poverty or climate change, where the EU and Member States are only part of a much wider picture. Furthermore, as a number of developing countries industrialise and approach European levels of economic development there will be a gradual increase in global environmental pressures. Sustainable Development is therefore a global objective that the EU cannot achieve by itself.

Tackling these problems will require a coherent international approach by international organisations. However, to provide credible and effective leadership in this global context, the EU has to show it can make progress at home towards sustainable development, as well as meet its international commitments. This chapter therefore focuses squarely on policy reforms needed within Europe to enhance sustainable development. It will nevertheless be important to consider whether any of the measures that we might take in Europe to move towards sustainable development might put at risk the prospects for sustainable development in the rest of the world.

The role of the EU in helping to achieve sustainable development on a global scale will be dealt with much more comprehensively by our preparations for the Rio + 10 Summit in South Africa in 2002. This work has already started, as described in a recent Commission Communication "Ten years after Rio: Preparing for the World Summit on Sustainable Development in 2002".The EU also has an important role to play in international organisations, such as the World Trade Organisation and the upcoming UN Conference on Least Developed Countries. Our influence in this wider context will be all the greater if we can demonstrate that we are putting our own house in order and thereby improving prospects for global sustainability.

The Political Context of This Communication

Sustainable development was put on the global political map by the 1992 United Nations Earth Summit in Rio de Janeiro, following the report of the World Commission on Environment and Development (the "Brundtland report") in 1987. At the Rio + 5 follow up conference in 1997 the EU and other signatories of the Rio Declaration committed themselves to drawing up sustainable development strategies for the Rio + 10 World Summit on sustainable development in South Africa next year. The Amsterdam Treaty, which came into effect in 1999, makes sustainable development one of the core tasks of the European Community. Article 2 of the EC Treaty states that "The Union shall set itself the following objectives ... to promote economic and social progress and a high level or employment and to achieve balanced and sustainable development, in particular through, the strengthening of economic and social cohesion".

Against this background, the Heads of State and Government asked the European Commission at Helsinki in 1999 to draw up a European sustainable development strategy and submit it to the European Council at Gothenburg in June 2001.

This consultation paper is the first step in this process. It sets out the analytical basis for the EU sustainable development strategy. It gives the Commission services' initial views on sustainable development, and the challenges and opportunities it presents. More specifically, it identifies some persistent trends that pose a threat to sustainable development in Europe, and analyses the causes of these problems. Finally, it presents a policy toolkit to put Europe on a more sustainable path.

Comments on this paper are invited from all stakeholders as the Commission finalises its proposals for the Gothenburg European Council.

Interpreting Sustainable Development

The most widely quoted definition of sustainable development is that in the Brundtland report. It defines sustainable development as "development that meets the needs of the present without compromising the ability of future generations to meet their own needs." In essence, ensuring a better quality of life now and for future generations.

There are many alternative interpretations of sustainable development and even with the definition above it is clear that different views are possible on what is meant by the term "needs". Nevertheless, there is a broad consensus that, at a minimum, sustainable development captures two important ideas:

- That development has an economic, a social and an environmental dimension. Development will only be sustainable if a balance is struck between the different factors that contribute to the overall quality of life.
- That the current generation has an obligation to future generations to leave sufficient stocks of social, environmental and economic resources for them to enjoy levels of well being at least as high as our own.

Because of its origins in the environmental movement sustainable development used to be dismissed as a "luxury" that should not be bought at the expense of economic growth. But sustainable development is much more than a purely environmental concept-it poses the fundamental challenge of combining a dynamic economy with a society offering opportunities to all, while improving resource productivity and decoupling growth from environmental degradation.

Although sustainable development has a very wide scope it should not be seen simply as a convenient way to bundle loosely together a collection of social, economic and environmental problems under a new label. Instead, a comprehensive perspective is needed that ensures that policies—both sectoral and horizontal–are mutually supportive rather than working against one another. Achieving this in practice will oblige policy makers to ensure that economic growth is not bought at the expense of a social divide and environmental deterioration, that social policy underpins rather than undermines economic performance, and that environmental policy is based on sound science and is cost-effective.

The Opportunities of Sustainable Development

While sustainable development will require changes to individual business and consumer behaviour to avoid some negative consequences for society as a whole—present or future—it also offers great opportunities. Indeed, many of the more far-sighted businesses have already realised that sustainable development offers new possibilities and have begun to adapt their operations and investment plans accordingly.

It is now increasingly recognised that stringent environmental policy need not put a brake on economic growth even as conventionally measured. (Current statistical measures of economic performance, such as Gross Domestic Product (GDP), are valuable indicators, but are limited in many ways. For example, GDP does not take into account the costs of pollution or put a value on unpaid work.) While environmental regulation can impose a one-off cost in terms of economic output, these costs are at least partly offset by a boost to employment and revenues in eco-industries providing cleaner technologies and services. Moreover, the evidence shows that the long run growth rate depends largely on the rate of technological progress. Policies for sustainable development could increase economic growth by boosting our rate of innovation, and may eventually lead to goods that are cheaper to buy and use than their "dirty" predecessors.

In addition, many of the more concrete policies needed for sustainable development are likely to have a positive impact on economic growth. For example:

- Policy making in the last quarter century has tended to underexploit the potential of the labour market and overexploit natural resources. The inefficiencies in present tax systems means that there is scope to price labour back into the market and pollution out of it.
- Removing unnecessary or harmful subsidies will bring direct financial benefits to tax payers and improve the efficiency of the economy. Market reform to get prices right will create new business opportunities to develop services and products that ease pressure on the environment, and that fulfil social and economic needs.
- Policies to reduce poverty and extend opportunity to all can help avoid the waste of resources and individual talent that are implied by social exclusion and unemployment, while lowering the costs of social support.
- Better pricing and new technologies can break the trend of increasing congestion on our roads by encouraging greater use of other modes of transport and more efficient use of infrastructure. This will prevent gridlock and save time and other costs for business and the general public.
- Enhancing economic and social cohesion by helping lagging regions to exploit their full productive potential should benefit the Community as a whole.
- Encouraging the research, development, and innovative use of new, cleaner and more efficient energy technologies

will not only have a positive impact on the environment and possibly employment, but also on the security of European energy supply.

Creating the Opportunities

These examples show that there are many "win-win" situations. A sustainable development strategy should seek to identify and exploit these opportunities, fostering economic efficiency, employment growth and environmental friendliness. The EU has an industry with a rich potential in the application of efficient and environment-friendly technologies. This is one of Europe's most promising assets. To exploit this potential, policy must provide Europe's industry with a better framework for innovation and technological development.

More generally, policy makers should create the conditions in which citizens and businesses are encouraged to integrate environmental and social considerations in all their activities. Although this will be beneficial for society as a whole, some policy changes create clear winners and losers. In such cases, we need to ensure that we pursue policies that are in the general public interest, while making sure that those who have to adapt to changes in policy are treated fairly and do not suffer unnecessary costs. Sustainable development therefore has an important institutional dimension. It cannot be achieved without good governance and active public participation. (These issues will be dealt with in much more detail in the Commission's forthcoming White Paper on Governance.)

The EU sustainable development strategy will need to build on the foundations of several processes rooted in Treaty provisions which already guide European economic, social and environmental policy-making. The Broad Economic Policy Guidelines, and the economic reform process initiated at the Cardiff summit in 1998, provide a solid framework for economic policy co-ordination. Employment and social policy co-ordination has given rise to guidelines for employment and labour market reform and to co-operation between Member States in modernising social protection and promoting social inclusion. Environmental policy has its own process for the integration of environmental concerns into other sectoral policies (the Cardiff process), while at the beginning of this year, the Commission proposed the 6th Environmental Action Programme setting out a 10-years perspective for EU environmental policy.

At Lisbon in March 2000, the Heads of Government and State decided to bring various social and economic initiatives together in a single annual review, geared towards making Europe *"the most competitive and dynamic knowledge-based economy in the world capable of sustainable economic growth with more and better jobs and greater social cohesion".* As there is some obvious overlap between the scope of the Lisbon review process and the sustainable development strategy, the Commission has proposed in its report to the Stockholm European Council to complete the Lisbon process by integrating an environmental dimension, and suggested that to ensure consistency between the two the mechanisms to review progress should be dovetailed.

In order not to duplicate the work contained in other policy reviews the EU sustainable development strategy should focus on a small number of themes where a cross-cutting approach provides new insights by taking into account the spillovers between decisions in different sectoral policies. The sustainable development strategy can also add value to existing initiatives by putting stronger emphasis on the long term. As the following sections of this document show, many of the trends that threaten sustainable development are the consequence of past choices in production technology, patterns of land use and infrastructure investment, and are difficult to tackle in a short time frame. The decisions we take in the near future will also have long term effects over many decades on our patterns of development—and their social, economic and environmental consequences. It is therefore important that we address our current problems as a matter of urgency.

Focussing on the Most Important Issues

By its very nature, sustainable development is an inclusive approach to policy making. Its scope covers almost any issue with an important social, economic or environmental component. This very wide perspective has both advantages and disadvantages- these is a trade-off between breadth of coverage and depth of analysis. The Commission services have deliberately limited the scope of this consultation paper to a small number of issues that in their view pose the greatest threat to sustainable development.

Choosing a set of topics to include implies making judgements. The criteria that we have used to judge whether a topic should be covered in the EU sustainable development strategy are:

* *Severity* – Do current trends pose a significant threat to our quality of life or threaten to significantly reduce our stocks of social, environmental and economic assets? Are the costs of doing nothing likely to be high or unevenly distributed?

* *The time dimension and irreversibility* – Is there a "slow burn" problem that worsens only gradually but that may be very costly or impossible to put right if action is left to a very late stage? Is there a significant inter-generational aspect?

* *A European dimension* – Is the problem identified common to a number of EU countries, or are there spillover effects between countries? Are policy responses likely to have implications going beyond national boundaries?

Based on these criteria the Commission services propose the following six topics as priorities for inclusion in the European sustainable development strategy:

- Climate change and clean energy
- Public health
- Management of natural resources
- Poverty and social exclusion
- Ageing and demography
- Mobility, land use and territorial development.

Clearly, each of these topics covers a very wide range of issues and we cannot hope to provide a comprehensive picture here. Moreover, within each broad heading, there are some problems and policy dilemmas that are much more acute than others. Within each topic, we have therefore again narrowed our focus by applying the criteria above, in order to identify those trends that pose the most serious threat to sustainable development:

Climate change is a global problem which can only be solved by widespread international co-operation. While its impacts are difficult to predict precisely, they could include changes in agricultural patterns, land use, disease zones, water supplies, increased risk of natural disasters and flooding, and resulting labour migration. These would have enormous economic and social consequences. Decoupling economic activity from emissions of greenhouse gases—notably carbon dioxide—requires a major shift to *clean energy* use, which will not be achieved quickly or easily.

Severe threats to *public health* are posed by the growth in antibiotic-resistant strains of some diseases, which reduce the effectiveness of existing treatments. We also do not yet know enough about the longer-term effects of the thousands of chemicals currently in use. Health problems related to sedentary lifestyles or poor eating habits are often passed from parents to sedentary lifestyles or poor eating habits are often passed from parents to their children. All Member States face the challenge of delivering high standards of health care without excessively burdening public finances.

Our *management and use of natural resources* has implications for the well-being of future generations. Loss of bio-diversity and the resultant reduction in genetic resources are irreversible. Restoring fish stocks to sustainable levels will not be achieved unless the severity of the problem is recognised and traditional management attitudes change. The volume of waste—some of it hazardous-is rising inexorably.

Poverty and social exclusion are problems common to all Member States. The severity of the issue can be judged from the fact that one European in six is poor (with much higher concentrations in some groups such as one-parent families), and poor health, low educational attainment and deprivation tend to be passed from one generation to the next. Moreover, rapid changes in technology raise the threat of a "digital divide" and a two-tier society.

All European countries face similar challenges due to the *ageing* of their populations. This will place considerable stresses on the funding of pensions. Ageing populations may also place higher demands on health care services and on long-term care, though much will depend on whether people enjoy relatively good health in old age. The structure of the population alters very slowly over time: those who will be pensioners at the start of the second half of this century have already been born, as has a substantial part of the future population of working age.

Current patterns of *mobility* cause severe pollution and congestion throughout Europe. Emissions of greenhouse gases from transport are growing more rapidly than from any other source, and in many urban areas traffic seems to be grinding gradually to a halt. Transport infrastructure is one of several factors influencing *territorial development* and *land use*. In turn, concentration of economic activities can give rise to congestion, but also has economic benefits such as the creation of business networks and fluid labour markets, and can allow new solutions to emerge such as the provision of urban public transport systems.

Each of the topics touches to a greater or lesser extent on each of the economic, environmental and social dimensions of sustainable development. Each topic is relevant for a number of existing Community and national policy areas. Moreover, each is linked to some of the others. For example:

- Addressing climate change should have beneficial impacts on natural resource use, on mobility and land use, and on public health.
- Poverty can lead to poor health. Poverty is also closely related to educational underachievement.

- The degree of social exclusion is influenced by urban planning and land use policies: low-income families tend to cluster in cheap housing, often on out-lying suburban estates. In such areas investment in transport infrastructure and other facilities may not be economically viable, so uncontrolled spatial development can aggravate segregation and social disparities.

Climate Change and Clean Energy

Human activity is affecting the planet's climate system. Available scientific evidence shows that the accumulation of *greenhouse gases* in the atmosphere due to human activity is causing global warming. The current central estimate is that temperature will increase by between 1 to 6°C by 2100[5]. Significant geographical variations are expected, and temperature extremes may be even more susceptible to change.

Climate change is likely to have severe and unpredictable consequences, such as higher mean temperatures and radical changes in weather patterns and rainfall. Higher temperatures may mean that dry regions become drier and wet regions wetter. Rapid temperature change may cause more extreme weather events (hurricanes, floods) with severe implications for infrastructure, property, social systems and nature. Changes in agricultural patterns, land use, water supplies and the migration of labour will have knock on effects on the economy and society. While some of these may be beneficial, major diseases such as malaria are likely to extend their reach as temperatures rise, with major implications for public health.

Climate change is a global problem that the EU alone cannot solve, as all countries emit greenhouse gases. In 1992, the United Nations Framework Convention on Climate Change (UNFCCC) was agreed. At present, 186 nations have ratified this convention and are legally bound by it. This Convention explicitly recognises the problems posed by climate change, and sets an "ultimate objective" of stabilising "greenhouse gas concentrations in the atmosphere at a level that would prevent dangerous anthropogenic (human-induced) interference with the climate system." However, the text does not specify precisely what this level should be—it remains a subject of scientific research and political debate.

The Kyoto Protocol to the UNFCCC, agreed in 1997, was an important additional step, committing developed countries to emission reduction and limitation targets for greenhouse gases. The EU agreed to cut emissions by 8% relative to 1990 levels by the years 2008-2012. However, the Kyoto Protocol has not yet been ratified by most signatories, and in particular none of the industrialised countries, and is therefore not yet legally binding. Moreover, the Intergovernmental Panel on Climate Change estimates that to stabilise CO_2 concentrations at even around twice the pre-industrial atmospheric concentration would require cuts in *global* emissions of around 50 to 70% over the next 100 years. This implies that implementing the Kyoto Protocol will only be a first step.

At present, the developed world has far higher emissions per capita than developing countries (the EU accounts for around 14% of global CO_2 emissions, but about 6% of world population, while the rest of the OECD has about 35% of emissions and 11% of world population). This raises important questions about how to reconcile the need to cut global emissions with economic growth and development in poorer countries. However, it also needs to be borne in mind that greenhouse gas emissions from less developed countries are expected to surpass those of industrialised countries in the next 15 years. Thus any long-term solution to climate change needs to include all nations of the world.

Major Concerns and Driving Forces

Global greenhouse gas emissions have increased seven-fold during the 20th century. This has largely been the result of increased use of fossil fuels for energy as economies have grown. The main facts and figures for the EU are:

- The dominant greenhouse gas produced by human activity is CO_2 released from consumption of fossil fuels which accounts for around 80% of emissions. The remaining

20% are due to other gases, such as methane, nitrous oxides and the fluorinated gases (HFC, PFC, SF_6).

- Some greenhouse gases have bigger effects on global warming than others. In order to put different gases on a comparable basis the emissions figures for non-CO_2 gases are usually converted to tonnes of CO_2 equivalents. The table below gives 1990 total EU-15 greenhouse gas emissions by sector on this basis as well as projected growth to 2010.

Table 2.1: Projected growth of greenhouse gas emissions between 1990 and 2010

Mt CO_2 eq.	*1990*	*Baseline 2010*	*growth 2010/1990*
Energy Supply	1421,7	1276, 6	-10,2%
Industry	757,1	686,1	-9,4%
Transport	753,1	1098,2	45,8%
Households	447,5	440,0	-1,7%
Private and Public Services	175,6	188,9	7, 6%
Agriculture	417,0	397,6	-4,7%
Waste	166,4	137,3	-17,5%
Total	4138, 3	4224,8	2,1%

Source: "Environment 2010: Our Future, Our Choice," 6th Environmental Action Programme of the European Community, COM (2001) 31 final, p. 25.

- EU Member States use large amounts of energy, but they tend to use it relatively efficiently; energy use and CO_2 emissions per unit of GDP are low compared to most other countries. However, emissions *per capita* from fuel combustion in the EU are around twice the global average and about four times the average for developing countries.

Due to the legacy of central planning the accession countries emit several times more CO_2 per unit of GDP than the current Member States.

- Some countries have also managed to make significant improvements in energy efficiency over time. For example, between 1985 and 1998, the GDP of the EU has grown by 35% while energy-related CO_2 emissions grew only by 4%. This is partly due to a move towards less energy-intensive sectors. In addition, a substantial part of this de-coupling has to do with one-off events, such as the switch from coal to gas on a large scale as a source of energy supply.

The main driving forces behind emissions in the EU to date have been:

- A high level of economic development linked to a dominance of fossil fuels in energy supply. Around 80% of our energy needs are supplied by fossil fuels. Our current heavy reliance on fossil fuels results from past investment decisions that were made without adequate attention being paid to the long run environmental impacts.

- Low energy prices: prices in real terms of oil, natural gas and coal have been relatively low throughout the 1990s and much of the 1980s. Coal prices declined by almost 50% between 1990 and 2000 in real terms. The low price of fossil fuels has reduced incentives for households, industry and the transport sector to invest in and use energy saving technologies.

- Rapidly increasing demand for mobility, being met largely by increased road transport and aviation. Between 1970 and 1998 passenger transport demand (measured in passenger kilometres) increased by over 100%, as did freight transport (measured in tonne kilometres). These trends are likely to continue. At present, emissions of greenhouse gases from transport are growing much faster than any other source.

- Emissions of non-CO_2 greenhouse gases such as methane from landfills and fossil fuel extraction, methane and nitrous oxide from agriculture, as well as fluorinated gases from industrial processes.

Policy Issues

At the EU level the only current instrument specifically aimed to reduce CO_2 emissions is the voluntary agreement of European, Japanese and Korean car manufacturers to improve the average fuel efficiency of new cars by 25% by 2008/2009. However, some other measures will reduce greenhouse gas emissions. These include the Landfill Directive (which will reduce methane emissions from landfill sites), a proposed Directive that aims to encourage energy from renewable sources and a Directive on Integrated Pollution Prevention and Control.

Some policy instruments are best applied at the national level, whereas others may require international co-ordination to be effective. A number of questions arise concerning the appropriate balance between policy developed at the EU level and policy at the national level. At present, the Commission is working with stakeholders in the context of the European Climate Change Programme (ECCP) in order to identify the building blocks for possible European-wide initiatives to implement the Kyoto commitment. Major issues to contend with are the following:

- Meeting the requirements of the Kyoto Protocol means achieving a reduction in greenhouse gas emissions of 8% compared to 1990 levels by 2008 to 2012. The costs of reducing greenhouse gas emissions vary from sector to sector. Critical questions therefore are what policy mix is best suited to implementing a cost-effective approach, and on which areas or sectors most attention should be focussed.
- Making the deep cuts in CO_2 emissions and other greenhouse gases needed to help stabilise atmospheric concentrations in the long term will require major investments. For example, in the power generation sector much of the current plant will reach the end of its operating life during the next 20-

30 years and there is a continuing technological and political debate about the future contribution of various energy sources, including nuclear energy and renewables, to electricity supply. Investments in energy supply, transport infrastructure, housing and industrial installations are long lived. It is therefore vital that consideration is given to what instruments are needed to ensure that these investment decisions take into account these long run effects.

- The costs of reducing emissions are likely to be significantly lower if cost effective instruments are put in place in good time. A first step would be removal of subsidies that encourage inefficient use of energy and are a significant drain on the public purse. An important question concerns the speed at which subsidies should be withdrawn, and how major adverse effects on particular sectors might be limited.

- Energy taxes related to the CO_2 content of fuels would be a cost-effective way to reduce CO_2 emissions. Higher taxes would increase costs in some sectors, but the revenue could be used to cut other taxes. Any disruptive effects of energy taxes on the competitiveness of energy intensive sectors could be minimised by having EU wide co-ordinated tax measures. The European commission proposed an EU wide carbon-energy tax in 1992, as well as a Directive setting a framework for taxation of energy products in 1997. However, neither of these initiatives has been accepted by the Member States, and progress would require a significant increase in political will.

- The Kyoto Protocol includes a number of flexibility mechanisms that allow emissions reductions to be achieved in a more cost-effective way, such as emissions trading schemes. Starting from a target for total emissions, this instrument allows firms flexibility to reach this joint target in a cost-effective way. Some Member States are considering introducing emissions trading, and in this context an important issue is whether it is best to arrive at European and international emission trading schemes by linking national trading schemes, or through a more centralised design.

- The liberalisation of energy markets will improve operating efficiency in the sector and lower energy prices. However, this will increase energy demand in the absence of any offsetting measures. Consideration needs to be given to what flanking measures might be appropriate. Liberalisation has the potential to allow new suppliers to enter the market (such as renewable energy sources), provided steps are taken to ensure that they are granted fair access to the transmission grid.
- While it is uncertain what climate change will bring, it is fairly certain that some climate change will take place. The damage that climate change causes will be lower if we can reduce the rate of change and help nature and human habitats to adapt. Efforts to reduce emissions are necessary, but it is also important to consider now how our societies can best adapt to climate change as it occurs.

Public Health and Sustainable Development

A healthy population is crucial for the well-being of our societies, and is therefore a prerequisite for sustainable development. A safe environment and decent health care are basic elements of social and economic progress. How a society cares for its most fragile members is also a measure of its own health and sustainability. Good health is important for our economic and material prosperity: sick or unhealthy people can't work and are dependent on those who do.

In general terms, the health of the Community population has never been better. Infant mortality has fallen sharply. People are living longer: between 1960 and 1999 average life expectancy increased by 8 years for men and women. Nevertheless, in recent years new potential threats to health have emerged. A number of major public health issues which threaten social and economic development are set out below.

Major Concerns and Driving Forces

Potential threats to our health come from the substances and products we are exposed to through the air we breathe, the water we drink and the food we eat.

- Major health problems and causes of premature mortality, such as cancers, cardiovascular diseases and road accidents, are related *to lifestyles*. Poor nutrition, lack of exercise, tobacco use and misuse of alcohol, for example, impose a considerable burden of disease and give rise to substantial costs for individuals and society. Health problems caused by lifestyles can have significant and long-lasting effects, as parents may pass bad habits on to their children. Obesity is a rapidly growing problem in many developed countries, and poor diet generally is a feature of others.

- Poor health is also related to *social and economic inequality*. Various studies have shown that relatively disadvantaged populations have lower life expectancy and higher burdens of morbidity than higher socio-economic groups. For example, in the early 1990s in England and Wales, unskilled men aged 20-64 were almost three times more likely to die from coronary heart disease than professional workers. Moreover, the difference in death rates had been widening over the preceding twenty years.

- The emergence of Bovine Spongiform Encephalopathy (BSE) and its transfer to humans as new variant Creutzfeldt-Jacob Disease (nvCJD) have heightened concerns about *food safety* and drawn attention to the incentives facing farmers and the food industry. According to a recent Commission report, by guaranteeing high prices over decades, agricultural policy contributed to increasing the quantity of food produced, but had negative effects on the quality of some food products. In addition, agricultural policy has paid too little attention to its effect n diet.

- Various types of *environmental pollution* from agriculture, industrial activity and transport also cause ill health. Indeed, some studies have suggested that *transport-related air pollution* is a bigger killer than traffic accidents, though the impact on life expectancy is generally less than 12 months, as many of those affected are chronically ill from other causes. Importantly, emissions of "conventional" air pollutants such as sulphur dioxide, nitrogen oxides and small particles are declining due to new pollution controls, and this trend is expected to continue, significantly reducing their impact on health. Nevertheless, high levels of pollution may still occur in some areas. Agricultural runoff, waste water discharges, and atmospheric deposition are the main sources of nutrients in the marine environment which are suspected to lie behind the unexpected appearance in several coastal waters of toxic algal blooms, an emerging threat to public health.

- *Chemicals* (especially in the form of pharmaceuticals) make an important positive contribution to public health, but there is widespread use of chemicals whose properties and risks are poorly understood. There are gaps in our knowledge about the toxicity or otherwise of the tens of thousands of chemicals in use in Europe today. While many of these are surely harmless, recent studies linking chlorine in the atmosphere in indoor swimming pools to asthma illustrate the range of our ignorance of the effects of chemical substances. The increasing incidence of allergies, which now affect one in three Europeans, has also been linked with exposure to toxic chemicals, though other factors are also important. The effects of allergies go beyond their direct impact on health: they are the major cause of days lost from school and so may lead to poor levels of educational achievement.

- The substances of most concern are those that are *persistent pollutants*—that is, they break down only slowly—and are "*bio-accumulative*"—that is, they build up in the body—so that continued exposure to even small doses can have chronic effects on health. For example, dioxins –by-products of some industrial and combustion processes–are a continuing cause for concern. Despite large and sustained falls in emissions of dioxins, a recent commission study[14] indicated that many individuals' average daily intake of dioxins was likely to exceed the World Health Organisation recommended maximum intake. Higher levels of dioxin exposure are also related to diet, since dioxins accumulate in fatty foods. Some chemical products have been identified as actual or potential causes of cancer or physical deformities. Endocrine disrupters, substances that may interfere with human and animal reproductive systems, are especially disquieting.

- *Communicable diseases*, particularly the re-emergence in a more virulent form of diseases thought to have been conquered, continue to threaten the health of the population. The recent rise in tuberculosis encapsulates the dangers. Increasing levels of *resistance to antibiotics* damage public health: infection that cannot be treated quickly spreads, and is more likely to be fatal. It is the older and less expensive drugs that are in more widespread use which tend to become ineffective as their targets develop and mutate. If we cannot master this trend, we risk undoing much of the social and economic progress that has been achieved on the back of improved health care. *Much of the problem is due to "mis-and overuse of antibiotics" for the treatment of illness of both humans and farm animals.* The remaining four antibiotics still allowed for use as growth promoters and as additives in animal feed are planned to be phased out by 2006. The Community's Scientific Steering Committee has also recommended changes in animal husbandry as an additional way to maintain animal health and welfare, and reduce use of antibiotics.

- Delivering high quality *health services* is a further challenge. The *costs of health care systems* are high and rising, and now absorb an average of around 8% of GDP in Member States. Much of this money might be better spent preventing disease by encouraging healthier lifestyles. The high cost of many modern treatments, the high rate of technological innovation—which makes available treatments for previously incurable conditions—and rising demand for improved healthcare, place new pressures on the financing of public care services. The impact of the *ageing of the Community population* puts further strain on health care costs and could cause public expenditure on health care to rise by 3% of GDP.

- The most important challenges of an ageing population, however, are the need for *better understanding and management of diseases which particularly afflict the elderly,* and for health services to adapt to provide patterns of care particularly suited to meeting the needs of frail, elderly patients, while also meeting the needs of the healthy aged. These new patterns of care will require substantial change in the nature of public health care systems, particularly as extended family networks become less common.

Policy Issues

- Specific Community competence in the area of public health only dates from 1993. Nevertheless, a wide range of policy areas affects health, so Community action to address health issues dates back much further thanthis. For example:
- A directive on the classification, packaging and labelling of dangerous substances was adopted in 1967, and has been updated on many occasions. The Commission Communication on Endocrine Disrupters listed some thirty Community legislative measures relating to environment and health impacts of chemical products; several of these measures were directed at improving food safety by reducing chemical use in farming. The White Paper on a new Community Chemicals strategy has the overriding goal of sustainable development. It aims to protect human health and the environmentation will raise many important practical questions.

- In the area of environmental policy, measures taken under Community legislation to reduce pollution from large combustion plants, and vehicle emissions technologies have contributed to the substantial and continuing improvements in air quality. Nevertheless, much research work remains to be done on assessing the impact of some pollutants on health, particularly the effects of small particles.

- Four EU action programmes on health and safety at work have been implemented since 1978. They have led to Community measures to protect workers against dangerous substances and situations, and to improve the working environment.

With Member States responsible for the organisation and delivery of health services and medical care, the new *Community health strategy* aims to develop a coherent approach to health issues across all EU policy areas. Ifs core objective will be to *identify all policies and actions* which might have an *impact on health* (including healthcare systems) and to find ways of assessing the health impact of these policies. This will require better policy co-ordination (a "joined up approach") to address inter-sectoral issues such as enlargement or social exclusion, and emerging health problems.

The proposed *public health action programme* will focus on three main strands of activity, intended to address many of the issues raised above.

- A first objective is to *improve health information and knowledge*. A comprehensive health information system will be developed to provide information and data on health status, health determinants and health systems to policy makers, health professionals and the general public.

- A second priority will be to *monitor and respond rapidly to health threats,* for example from communicable diseases. This could include attention to antimicrobial resistance, work on hospital infections, vaccine policy, and communicable diseases such as HIV/AIDS.

- Finally, the new public health action plan will address *health determinants*. It will include actions aimed at tackling the underlying causes of ill health, including lifestyle and environmental causes, by promoting health and preventing disease.

As many risks to health result from individual lifestyle choices, giving accurate information to the wider public and improving understanding at all levels is critically important. Food safety is paramount in this respect. In recent years, the credibility of public authorities in the management of food safety has been severely damaged by the perception that they were more concerned to protect the economic interests of producers than the health of consumers. Assessment and regulation of food safety that is independent of the economic sectors concerned is thus essential to improve public safety and to restore public confidence.[21] In addition, clear labelling of the health and nutritional properties of foods is long overdue, given the importance of diet and nutrition to health and well-being.

Management of Natural Resources

Natural resources underpin sustainable development. They provide essential life support functions such as foods and habitats, carbon storage and water catchment, and provide essential raw materials. Although small changes in most stocks of natural resources pose little immediate threat, a persistent decline is of great concern for resources that are difficult or impossible to replace, such as bio-diversity.

We can distinguish broadly between those natural resources that are renewable if carefully managed (such as fish stocks and fresh water) and those that are non-renewable (such as oil and mineral resources). There, we have concentrated on those where the long run trends are of most concern (bio-diversity, waste generation, fish stocks).We also include the question of exhaustion of non-renewable resources such as minerals and coal, although on current consumption rates stocks may last for decades or even centuries.

Major Concerns and Driving Forces

There are a number of general problems that undermine the efficient and sustainable use of natural resources. Different forms of industrial and agricultural activity affect many natural resources. When natural resources are part of a shared "commons" and access to their use is open to all this means that there is often little incentive for individuals to conserve and use them in a responsible way. Overexploitation can be the result. Poorly defined or disputed rights of ownership or access to resources weaken the incentives to conserve and use natural resources in a sustainable way.

Bio-diversity

At present we are failing to secure the long run viability of our eco-systems. Despite measurement problems, there are indications that recent decades have seen very significant losses in virtually all types of eco-systems at EU level. A high percentage of existing species within the EU are at risk of extinction. In recent decades the trends has been persistently in the wrong direction, and this poses a serious long term threat to the natural resources on which our economic and social system depend.

Changing land use is an important factor. Although measurement is difficult and imprecise, data for the period 1980-1990 for 11 EU countries indicate that close to 14% of land previously considered to be part of natural cover was lost to urban development and housing. In addition, between 1980 and 1998 there was an 11% rise in amount of land taken by road networks in Member States. A large percentage of all nature conservation sites in Europe can be considered at risk from new infrastructure development. Although policy at present tends to pay some attention to preserving particularly important habitats or sites of interest from development, the average level of protection is much lower.

Agriculture also profoundly influences the pattern of land use. The scale, the scope, and the nature of production techniques can have substantial impacts—good and bad—on the landscape and on natural habitats. Intensive aquaculture in sensitive marine areas is one of the driving forces for the appearance of toxic phytoplankton which can kill fish, seabirds and mammals. Intensive farming practices seem particularly prone to cause negative effects. These include "monotonous landscapes, the abandonment of traditional management methods, the use of large areas of wetland, moorland and natural rough pasture, pollution of ground water by increased use of pesticides and fertilisers, and reduction in biological diversity." Another European Commission report noted that intensive farming had "taken little or no heed of its impact on the environment."

However, it would be too simplistic—and wrong—to conclude that agricultural practices do nothing but damage the countryside. Many landscapes and site-specific environmental amenities reflect a farming heritage. Particularly in remote or mountainous areas, agriculture can play a crucial role in preserving attractive landscape features and ecological diversity. Abandonment of land or of traditional land management practices in such areas would be bad for bio-diversity and would reduce the environmental and amenity value of these areas. Public policy therefore has a potentially important role in setting the right incentives to encourage the management of bio-diversity and rural sustainability.

Water Resources

At the global level, the problem of water shortage will prove one of the major challenges over the next few decades. However, at the level of the EU there are few water shortage problems, with the important exception of parts of southern Europe, where over exploitation of water has led to drying out of some areas and to salt water intrusion in aquifers around the Mediterranean coast. It is a cause for concern that in some areas current extraction is tapping water tables that will take centuries to replenish.

Pollution of water resulting from agricultural, household and industrial activity is a more widespread phenomenon in Europe. Water pollution causes damage to aquatic life and imposes sizeable costs in terms of the treatment needed to supply clean water to agricultural, household and industrial users. The spread of built-on land, including into natural flood plains, highlights the links between water management and land use planning. Absence of an integrated approach to these issues is causing increased damage from floods.

Fish Stocks

Fish represent an important renewable resource that provides a livelihood for those in the fishing industry and an important food source. There is strong evidence that existing rates of harvesting of fish stocks are unsustainable and threaten the viability of major fishing areas. The International Council for the Exploration of the Seas has persistently warned that EU waters are being over-fished. The same is true world-wide. Stocks of hake and cod in EU waters are at crisis point, and catches of all fish are falling rapidly. Landings of fish in the mid 1970s were nearly twice as high as in 1998.

Collapse of stocks is potentially disastrous for those who derive their livelihood from the industry and has important consequences for marine eco-systems. The collapse of the Canadian cod fisheries in the early 1990s devastated local fishing communities, leaving them few long-term prospects. The EU industry is characterised at present by over capacity, falling employment, and low profitability. Lack of recognition that radical adjustment is needed has also tended to delay the introduction of effective adjustment measures, aggravating the problems of those in the industry.

Since 1983 the EU has Regulated Fishing under the Common Fisheries Policy (CFP). The CFP has offered, and still offers important benefits, such as a legal framework for regulation and enforcement, and a mechanism for restricting access to the main fisheries. On the whole however, the pllicy has serious shortcoming:

* The setting of total allowable catches year-by-year has led to a neglect of longer term conservation and management. Member States have regularly postponed difficult decisions because of the short-term costs of the stringent measures needed for stocks to recover.

* As a result, the quotas that each country is allowed for catches of fish are too high, and are difficult to reduce by negotiation as each country would prefer others to make cuts. Member States have until recently lacked the political will to act decisively.

* The financial instruments used in the sector under the CFP have tended to work against each other. The effects of measures to reduce capacity have been partly offset by subsidies to modernise and improve fleet technology. Other operating subsidies, such as exemption from fuel tax for fishing vessels, encourage over-fishing.

* There are technical problems in the scientific measurement of stocks, and in controlling the impact of fishing on growing fish and other species: finding a way to reduce "discards"— fish that are caught and then through back into the sea – is a major problem.

* There is evidence that enforcement of regulations on the part of Member States has been too lax and very uneven, which has reduced confidence in the CFP as a viable policy.

Current policy has failed to secure sustainable exploitation of fisheries resources, and will need to be changed if it is to do so. In the future, the Community fisheries sector will have to be significantly smaller than it is today, if it is to survive. The Common Fisheries Policy is to be reviewed between now and 2002. Unless there is meaningful reform the costs in long-term economic damage to fishing communities, as well as to the marine environment, will be high. The recent Commission Green Paper puts forward options for a change of approach towards subsidies in the fisheries sector.

Non-renewable Resources

Extraction of non-renewable resources such as coal, oil and minerals may have significant impacts on landscape and bio-diversity if appropriate measures for waste management and restoration are not undertaken. A balance clearly has to be struck between exploiting these resources and protection of nature.

In addition, there has been a long running debate about whether certain non-renewable resources that are valued mainly for their commercial potential, such as iron ore, coal and oil deposits, are running out. Conventional indicators such as trends in prices don't suggest a rapid increase in scarcity of these resources, and measured reserves for many assets run into decades. Moreover, rising prices in themselves stimulate the development of alternative technologies that reduce resource use. In many cases, we can more than compensate for reductions in stocks of resources by providing other forms of wealth for future generations, such as technology and infrastructure or by developing substitutes for the resource being used up, such as renewable energy sources.

However, despite little apparent evidence of scarcity there is still a question of whether we are using these resources up too quickly, leaving little for future generations. It is of course true that these resources are essentially finite, and so our current use erodes the stocks available in the future. We therefore should therefore aim to use these resources responsibly and more productively wherever possible.

Waste

Every person in the EU generates on average 3.5 tonnes of solid waste each year. In recent years, waste volumes have grown faster than GDP. Similar growth rates over the longer term could significantly increase pressure on the environment and adversely affect public health. To date, the pressure to improve resource efficiency and reduce waste has come largely through commercial pressures to cut costs and from regulation by pollution control authorities. However, regulation can be expensive if it forces unnecessarily rapid adjustments to existing technology, rather than being designed to allow cheaper improvements to develop over time. As in other policy areas, the phasing in of new measures therefore has to strike a balance between the costs and benefits of early introduction.

A number of industrial sectors, such as the paper, glass, and metal industries have made significant improvements in resource efficiency in recent years, either through restructuring their activities towards higher value added products, or through raising process efficiency. There has also been a reduction in the use of hazardous substances in products, thus helping their management as waste. These are welcome developments, and there are other innovative approaches being adopted in the business community to improve resource efficiency. Policy needs to facilitate an active approach from the business sector that stimulates long-run improvements in resource efficiency if we are to decouple growth of waste and GDP.

The major challenge that cuts across almost all resource issues is how to revise incentive structures in such a way that non-commercial considerations are given adequate weight by those managing and exploiting natural resources. The diversity and complexity of natural resources makes this difficult. A particular concern is how to reform policies that have an unacceptably high impact on natural resources (such as over-fishing and agriculture) without unacceptable socio-economic costs. In particular, how support and subsidy regimes can be reoriented to generate an interest in effective long-term management. Water shortages and water pollution are both due to failure to provide adequate incentives to encourage more responsible water use.

In the farming sector, first steps have been taken in broadening the focus of the Common Agricultural Policy towards taking account of wider economic, environmental and social objectives. These have had some success. Reduced levels of price support contributed to less use of inputs such as chemical fertilisers and pesticides. "Agri-environmental" measures have contributed to preserving bio-diversity and led to lower levels of water pollution. Taking land out of production ("set-aside") has been shown to have beneficial environmental effects, provided it is properly managed. However, at present the goal of sustainable rural development remains subsidiary to the narrower objective of supporting farmers' incomes.

An important prerequisite for improved long run management of our natural resource base is improved information on the current state of our natural resources, such as the measurement of bio-diversity and levels of fish stocks. Such data are essential for ensuring that consumption does not exceed the capacity of the resource to regenerate. The difficulties in measuring stocks of some resources and how they are evolving means that trends are not picked up as quickly as they should be.

In order to decouple economic growth from the use of resources and the generation of waste there is a need for effective instruments to shape the awareness of business and consumers and provide steady pressure for a long run increase in resource efficiency throughout the economy. Greater efficiency in our use of resources should reduce pressure on the environment, preserve large amounts for future generations, and allow more time for the development of substitutes.

Poverty Social Exclusion

Poverty and social exclusion are closely related but different. Exclusion is a broader idea than poverty as it implies the idea of "access" at all levels, and this can be interpreted very widely. We do not propose to expand on the differences here, and for short hand we simply use the term poverty. Reducing poverty is central to sustainable development. Although it is not a new phenomenon, it has an enormous direct effect on individuals in terms of ill health, suicide rates, persistent unemployment, and potential exclusion from the mainstream of society. The burden of poverty is borne disproportionately by single mothers and older women living alone. Poverty also has a strong tendency to repeat itself, often remaining within families for generations. This has a high social cost, particularly the waste of human talent and energy implied by unequal opportunities. A well-designed set of integrated policies to reduce these social costs would improve both fairness and efficiency. Poverty is a problem with long term consequences and requires a long-term approach.

Poverty can arise for a whole range of interdependent reasons. Major factors are differences in family background and wealth, differences in access to education and jobs, effort and luck, the effects of tax and benefit systems on redistributing wealth, and the direct provision of some services by the state (for example, health, policing, social services). These different effects can offset or reinforce one another, so small initial differences can sometimes have big effects. This complexity also explains part of the difficulty in arriving at a satisfactory definition of poverty.

The willingness to accept different forms of deprivation depends on our social and political values. These inevitably vary from Member State to Member State, but there is also a shared commitment between countries of the EU to forming a more cohesive society and the fight against poverty and social exclusion is acknowledged to be a major element in the value systems of Member States.

Current pattern of poverty within the EU are diverse and evolving. This section provides an overview of important trends drivers of change, and emerging risks:

- The measurement of poverty depends on the definition used, but on one common definition *(relative) poverty*[32] averages 17% in the EU (excluding Finland and Sweden). *Vulnerability* is more widespread: 32% of Europeans experience at least one annual spell of low income over a period of three years, while 7% of the population – around 25 million persons – experience persistent poverty during this period. Persistent income poverty ranges from around 3% in Denmark and the Netherlands to 12% in Portugal.

- There are significant *income inequalities* which threaten social cohesion. At EU level, the poorest 20% of the population receives less than one-fifth of the income of the richest 20%. Social benefits reduce the proportion of poor people in all Member States but to very differing degrees, the reduction ranging from around 10% in Greece and Italy to over 60% in Denmark.

- Income gaps *between women and men* remain significant, with women's earnings almost one-quarter below that of men. This gap increases the risk that women will fall into poverty, since social security benefits and pension entitlements are often related to previous earnings.

- Many *cities* have serious pockets of poverty and social exclusion. Unemployment rates can vary significantly between districts, being up to 10 times higher in the worst affected parts than in the least affected.

- There is a *high level of early school leavers*: more than one in five of those aged 18-24 leave the education system with only lower secondary education at best. This is a particular worry, as there is a possible vicious intergenerational circle between childhood poverty, low educational achievement and poverty in adult life.

- Significant proportions of the *adult population fail to attain the literacy levels* considered as necessary to cope with everyday life in advanced societies, though the Nordic European countries in particular have made significant progress in resolving this problem.

- *Rapid change in the labour market is posing a risk to those unable to adapt to change.* Organisational and contractual changes present risks for vulnerable individuals.

- There is also some concern over the risk of a *technological divide*. Persons in the high-income groups use the Internet three times more frequently than lower income groups. Older people have scarcely any access to the Internet (1/7) of the youngest group). There is a significant gap between men and women as regards access to information and communication technologies. Moreover, there are significant differences across the Union in access to the Internet, with a clear North-South divide. In Greece, Spain, Portugal and Italy, the rate is half the EU average, while in the Nordic countries it is considerably higher.

- *Changing family patterns and household structures are increasing vulnerability for particular groups in society.* Household sizes are declining. Around one in twelve people live alone, an increase or 50% over the last 20 years. The proportion of dependent children living in one-parent households (mainly single mothers) has increased by 50% since 1983. Around 13% of all dependent children in the EU are living with just one parent. Three out of four single parent families are facing financial difficulties and the probability of living in poverty is twice as high for these children.

- *Ageing populations* raise new concerns about social exclusion and poverty among the elderly. Provision for retirement income needs to reflect the prospect of increased life expectancy, with many living perhaps 30 or 40 years after retirement. This will be a particular problem for the very old if their pension income fails to keep pace with price rises. Changing family patterns may reduce the amount of support and care given by families.
- Immigration flows make *global poverty* a domestic EU concern. The persistence of *racism, xenophobia,* and of social and economic *discrimination* make it difficult for immigrants to be effectively integrated.

Policy Issues

Economic and technological developments offer new opportunities and more choices to individuals to fulfil their potential. At the same time, these developments increase competitive pressures and carry the risk of creating a "two-tier" society where the more vulnerable members find themselves unable to keep up with fast-moving changes.

At the Lisbon European Council in March 2000, the EU set out a new strategy to strengthen employment, economic reform and social cohesion. Modernising social protection and combating social exclusion were identified as essential elements of this strategy. Tackling the sources of unemployment and poverty is central to its success. This means enabling greater access to quality jobs, in particular through increased opportunities for education and training for all ages, to encourage flexibility and the capacity to adapt to the requirements of a rapidly changing labour market. Equally important, tax and benefit systems must be reformed to make them more employment friendly and to remove poverty traps, particularly those which deny women the opportunity to take up paid employment.

The Nice European Council gave further substance to the objectives set at Lisbon by approving the European Social Agenda. To take full advantage of this momentum for change, social policy must be placed in its wider context of the European Union Sustainable Development Strategy: many other policies (such as education and training, transport, housing, health) have an impact on social exclusion. In addition, we must look beyond the 10-year horizon of Lisbon:

- Poverty is a persistent problem that is often transmitted from one generation to another. Eradicating poverty will take more than a decade. It is especially important to limit the passing of problems –such as lack of education or poor housing and living conditions—from one generation to another.
- Strategies to tackle poverty and social exclusion require a balance between targeted initiatives and general social measures. There is a particular need to avoid the risks of an underclass within which poverty replicates itself. This may require specific action for groups at risk (such as children, early school leavers, minority groups, disabled, elderly) or for some geographical areas. Community support comes from the European Social Fund and a specific programme on social inclusion.
- Financial integration and the increased mobility of the tax base are putting more pressure on tax and benefit systems. While private markets have the potential to ease this pressure by delivering some services more cost-effectively, their use must be carefully designed to ensure that universal access to basic entitlements such as decent health care, good education and core social services is maintained. Modernising social protection means building an active welfare state, not dismantling it.

Ageing and Sustainable Tourism

The population of the European Union and of the accession countries is ageing, in contrast with trends in most developing countries. Migration flows into the EU have occurred in recent years and this has offset some of the effects of the ageing of the Community population. Nonetheless, recent Eurostat projections show that the old age dependency ratio (those aged over 65 as a percentage of the population aged 20-64) will double between 2000 and 2050. By the middle of the century, there will be one person aged 65 or over for every two aged 20-64. These demographic changes will have profound economic, budgetary and social implications.

An ageing population puts into question the financial sustainability of pension schemes and public health care. Under plausible assumptions pension expenditure (now reported to amount to 10% of GDP on average) would increase by 3-5% of GDP in the majority of Member States between 2000 and 2040. Spending on health care could increase by a further 3% of GDP over the same period. At the same time, the shrinking labour force will lead to a lower rate of economic growth, unless it is offset by increased productivity.

Public pensions in the EU are either provided by governments, using revenues from taxation, or by the social partners, based on contributions of employers and employees. Many pension systems are funded on a "pay as you go" basis, where today's workers support today's retired. Because demographic change occurs slowly and is largely predictable, there is a strong temptation to put off difficult political choices when problems lie in the distant future. This raises the prospect of threats to fiscal stability, or a significant reduction in entitlements for future pensioners. A long-term approach is essential to prevent the occurrence of a social divide between generations and widespread poverty among the elderly.

Some options for reform to existing pension systems would put more emphasis on today's young people to provide for their own retirement. For example, moving towards a "funded" system in which individual build up their own pension provision over time, often with state support. This may have some advantages in terms of transparency about who pays for what, but funding would not overcome the structural tension between the length of working life and pension needs in retirement. Moreover, a rapid shift from pay as you go to a funded system would mean that the current workforce would pay twice—once for pensions for the current aged, and once to build up provision for their own retirement. A wider range of policy options must therefore be explored.

Mobility, Land use and Territorial Development

Mobility, land use and regional development are tightly interwoven in modern societies. In the short run, the demand for increased mobility depends on incomes and prices for using different modes of transport. In the longer run, it also changes according to patterns of land use—the location of people, homes, factories, offices, farms and shops. This spatial pattern is in turn a function of factors such as local planning rules, availability of infrastructure, the price of transport services, and personal preferences about where people want to live. The relationship between spatial patterns and transport thus runs in both directions.

Mobility, for both work and leisure, is important to our continued economic and social well-being. However, mobility is not an end in itself, but a means to access different goods and services. It may enhance business, employment and education opportunities as well as allowing for a wider range of leisure activities and lifestyles. However, increased mobility has important side effects, like emissions of greenhouse gases, air and noise pollution, the use of land, and congestion, effects which reduce quality of life. Emissions of greenhouse gases from transport are growing more rapidly than from any other source. Congestion costs are rising, while damage to eco-systems and bio-diversity are major concerns. More than 40,000 people are killed and over 1.7 million injured every year on European roads.

Encouraging people to live close to work and avoiding low-density development ("urban sprawl") can reduce the need for mobility and land take. Better pricing different modes of transport and policies to improve the quality of life in urban areas can limit the desire for long-distance commuting and would help encourage less transport-intensive living patterns. However, high-density living implies less living space, as well as more congestion and urban stress if not supported by effective urban infrastructure and public transport. Striking an appropriate balance between urban and rural areas is therefore not solely a transport issue, but also a matter for rural and urban policy.

There is also a complex link between mobility and regional development. At present, the picture of the EU is one of a richer, more densely populated core and a poorer, less populated periphery. The second cohesion report.[39] identified a group of central regions covering just one-fifth of the Union's area, but which contain over two-fifths of the population and account for half of EU GDP. However, several prosperous regions lie outside this area. The uneven distribution of population and economic activity will be more marked in an enlarged Community. Improving transport links can be important to give regional economies access to wider markets, but it is not a panacea for regional underdevelopment and the costs and benefits of new infrastructure need to be carefully weighed. A region also requires a range of other infrastructure and services to support a centre of economic activity.

Major Concerns and Driving Forces

Higher mobility and greater land use for building and infrastructure are above all driven by economic development and increased affluence. Recent decades have seen very rapid growth in distances travelled by other freight and people, as incomes have grown and prices of some modes have fallen or remained flat in real terms. The key facts are:

- Over the last thirty years freight transport demand has persistently grown faster than GDP and has doubled since 1970, with much of the increase coming in road transport. Air freight transport has grown even more rapidly. Passenger transport, particularly by car, has followed a very similar pattern. On average, almost one European in two now owns a car.

- These trends are predicted to continue in the immediate future. Freight transport in expected to grow by around 40% between 1998 and 2010, with road transport accounting for most of this increase. Passenger transport is expected to grow more slowly, mainly due to the rising costs of congestion on the roads, slow population growth and lower growth of car ownership as it approaches saturation in some countries. Air travel is expected to grow by a remarkable 90% over the same period.

- Change in vehicle emissions technologies have significantly reduced emissions of some atmospheric pollutants over the last decade, improving air quality. To some extent these improvements have been offset by growth in traffic volumes, but despite future increases in traffic, air quality is expected to improve significantly over the next 20 years. Greenhouse gas emissions on the other hand, are rising very rapidly due to the continued increase in transport overall.

- Congestion and inefficient use of infrastructure have large economic costs, perhaps as much as 2% of GDP. As well as wasting time, congestion raises costs for business and prices in shops for consumers. In Amsterdam, if current trends continue, rush hour public transport will move at little more than walking pace by 2005. One-tenth of the trans-European road network suffers from capacity constraints, causing congestion. The costs of congestion will rise rapidly as infrastructure increasingly reaches capacity.

- Over three-quarters of the European population live in towns and cities, which play a vital role as providers of services ad centres of economic activity. Traffic congestion affects above all urban areas, which are also challenged by problems such as inner-city decay, sprawling suburbs, and concentrations of acute poverty and social exclusion.

– In aggregate terms, the Community has been able to maintain a rough balance between the rural and urban communities. At present, the population of rural areas is increasing, and in recent years, their employment levels have grown faster than the Community average, though the picture varies from region to region. However, this may change after enlargement of the Union. Structural change in the new Member States could lead to a collapse in rural areas and rapidly growing pressure on urban infrastructure.

– In some Member States income inequalities between regions are worsening, though at the level of the Community the gap between richer and poorer regions has narrowed somewhat in recent years. Nevertheless, the differences remain substantial, and can be expected to be greater still in an enlarged Union. In the EU15 the richest region has an income per head 6 times that of the poorest; if the accession countries were included in the calculation the ratio would be more than ten to one.

– Relatively low levels of spending on research and development in some lagging regions may hamper their ability to catch up, though this is only one of very many factors influencing economic performance.

The factors that lie behind these problems include:

– The affordability of travelling by road and air improved relative to other modes over time. The price of private motoring and aviation travel as a percentage of average wages has fallen as cars have been produced more cheaply and efficiently and airlines have raised productivity, while the price of public transport has tended to keep pace with wages over time. For distances of more than a few kilometres, road transport—whether of people or freight—offers the convenience of "door-to-door" service that other modes find difficult to match.

- The completion of the internal market has boosted trade flows, but the resulting pattern of transport activity has been unbalanced due to an absence of corresponding improvements in the pricing structure for different modes. In addition, liberalisation of freight transport by road has been achieved across the Community but only a few Member States have opened rail freight to competition, so rail freight markets remain fragmented and closed. This uneven pace of reduction in the costs of different modes of transport has had adverse environmental effects.

- Local planning regulations also affect transport demand. "Urban sprawl"—in particular low-density housing –drives people into private cars. The growth in car use is closely associated with an increased degree of urban sprawl, and the availability (or not) of public transport. Transport-related noise and poor air quality in urban areas can encourage migration of people and enterprises from cities to suburbs and create a vicious circle.

- Transport policy has generally sought to match the increase in demand for road and air transport by significant public investment in infrastructure, both from national budgets and the Community structural funds. Extension and improvement of the road network has significantly increased the flexibility and speed of road freight and the speed and convenience of cars. This has underpinned the rapid growth in freight transport and use of private cars.

Patterns of mobility and land use are also linked to the balance between rural and urban communities. Access to good transport and communication infrastructure is an essential part of preserving the viability of both rural and urban society. Poor infrastructure and lack of access to services such as information and communication technologies may discourage private sector investment in rural areas, limiting employment opportunities. However, while better transport links can support the rural economy by expanding markets for local produce, they also tend to increase commuting and rural house prices and have environmental impacts.

Policy Issues

In recent decades transport demand has risen broadly in line with GDP. While further growth in activity is expected, this trend is not sustainable. There is clearly a longer term need to decouple transport growth from GDP and to limit the economic and environmental costs of transport growth that does occur. The Commission is preparing a review of the EU's Common Transport Policy, to be published in a forthcoming White Paper. This will set out the broad thrust of Community policy over the next ten years or so. Although the time horizon for the Sustainable Development strategy will go beyond this, it will be important to ensure that the two are consistent. An accurate appraisal of the policy issues is needed:

* At present the relative prices of using different transport modes do not reflect their full costs of use, in terms of additional congestion, damage to infrastructure and to human health and the environment. As a result there is inefficient use of existing infrastructure, and the balance between modes is distorted. For example, aircraft fuel is at present not taxed, unlike other fuels. The need to develop better pricing of different modes has been recognised in a number of commission documents but progress has been slow.

* New developments in intelligent traffic management systems, such as a the use of global positioning systems that track the movement of vehicles, and electronic fee collection systems for road pricing, have the potential to improve the use of infrastructure and reduce congestion costs. In addition, successful technology would be a world leader and could be exported widely. Improvements in communication technologies offer a potential alternative to transport. Distance working using modern communications may provide one way of reconciling demands for distance living with reduced mobility. It will be important to consider how best this potential can be exploited.

* Improvement in use of infrastructure can reduce congestion, and new infrastructure—when it is proved to be necessary—can fill important gaps in the network and increase capacity. Local planning rules also affect the location of economic activity and the development of new infrastructure and resulting transport flows. Planning decisions in the past have often not properly accounted for the effects of new development on the natural environment, congestion and other impacts, and policy needs to take these issues into account in the future.

* Development of housing, business, and new transport infrastructure also has implications for the relationship between town and countryside. Attention is needed to ensure that policy does not actively undermine the balance between the rural and urban economies.This means ensuring that urban areas do not develop ruban sprawl that fractures communities and destroys the distinctiveness of the countryside, while ensuring that rural policy provides active support for a living countryside. This cannot be a matter for transport policy alone, but also requires more coherent rural and urban policies.

* The rural economy also continues to depend to an appreciable extent on farming and the Community's Common-Agricultural Policy has been geared to maintaining farm incomes. The recent shifts towards more sustainable rural development—which aimed to improve the competitiveness of agriculture while enhancing its social and environmental functions—and still modest. Agriculture is still associated with high levels of pollution, and has damaged many of the aesthetic and ecological qualities of the landscape it once helped to create. This in itself undermines the attractiveness of the countryside as a place to live. There is therefore potential for agricultural policy to provide more support for a sustainable rural economy.

* Community structural funds have made sizeable investments in physical and social capital in the less developed regions

of the Community and Ireland's phenomenal economic growth in recent years shows the possibilities for territorial development if Structural Fund assistance is used within a coherent policy framework. In addition, measures such as the Trans European Networks (TENs) have aimed to improve links between peripheral and central regions of the Community. One of the main objectives of the TENs in the future will be the completion of a rail network that will encourage a shift from road to rail

* Enlargement is likely to bring with it new and more acute challenges. The new Member States will in general be poorer and have a much larger agricultural population. Their infrastructure has suffered from many years of under-investment. Closing the gap with the Union will need a major investment effort. Since these investments will shape their future transport and land use patterns for many years ahead it will be crucial to integrate economic, environmental and social issues into planning and infrastructure appraisal to ensure that all costs and benefits are taken into account.

* Many of these issues are identified in the European Spatial Development Perspective. This aims to offer Member States, their regions and cities a non-binding framework for co-ordination of policies with significant impacts on regional development, without, however, seeking to impose it on them or on other policy areas. This approach reflects the fact that solutions to many of the problems relating to the interactions between mobility, land use and territorial development can only be implemented at regional and local level, while others may benefit from a national or Community approach.

To make a decisive step from awareness to action, and to put in place an effective response to the issues raised in this section, two important questions must be answered. First, are there any common causes to these long-term social and environmental challenges? Second, why have we not done more to deal with them? If, as argued in earlier greater social and environmental responsibility is not an obstacle to long-term economic development, why have Member States and the European Union failed pursue sustainable development more vigorously?

In order to develop a general answer to these two questions by identifying the main obstacles to creating a more sustainable society and economy. Following from this diagnosis, we then lay out the main tools we can use to achieve the specific goals of the European sustainable development strategy which the Commission will propose to the Gothenburg meeting of the European Council.

Common Problems

Many of the problems identified in the previous section have common roots. They are characterised by complex interdependencies between sectors. Several are long-term in nature, with problems building up gradually. Firms and citizens often face poor incentives to produce and consume in a sustainable way. They may be ill informed about the wider effects of their actions, or about alternatives. And institutional obstacles make it difficult to respond effectively to these failings. This section looks at these issues in more detail, and shows how they have contributed to the problems identified above.

Wrong Incentives

Individuals and companies often face incentives which encourage them to behave in ways which, while individually rational, have negative impacts on others. Market prices for the use of goods and services which do not properly reflect the true cost to society of providing them lead to too much consumption of those goods and services and too little of others. For example, when we drive we generally slow down the progress of other road users. Since this cost is not incorporated in the price we pay to drive we do not take it into account in deciding how and when to travel. As a result, there are enormous inefficiencies in the way we use road space. High taxes on labour income act as a disincentive to participate actively in the labour market, while poorly designed tax and benefit systems can generate poverty traps.

Incorrect prices are also a major source of many environmental problems. In general, the market prices for goods and services do not incorporate the costs of pollution. Consequently, producers have little incentive to find and adopt cleaner methods of production, and consumers are not encouraged to seek out cleaner products. Worse, in some cases the most polluting industries benefit from significant subsidies that encourage the production of dirty goods and discourage consumers from switching to cleaner options.

Sectoral Policy Inconsistency

Both at national and Community level, individual policies generally concern specific sectors of the economy such as coal and steel or particular areas such as trade or competition. These policies are normally developed by separate administrative departments which have specialised knowledge of their own sectors, but are less concerned with how their policies affect other parts of society and the economy. This narrow, sectoral approach to policy making has led over time to some significant problems:

- Due to a high level of interdependence between some sectors the solutions to some problems lie in the hands of policy makers in other sectors. Environmental policy increasingly requires action by other policy areas such as enterprise, energy, transport and agriculture. Transport policy depends on taxation, research and technology, and land use planning policy. Social policy instruments acting in isolation will not solve problems of social exclusion. In many cases these spillovers between sectors are not fully taken into account, so policies in different sectors pull in opposite directions. This undermines their effectiveness and wastes resources.

- The narrow sectoral approach makes it easier for interest groups representing a particular sector to obstruct reforms which would benefit society as a whole but would have negative consequences for them. This uncoordinated focus on sectoral impacts rather than on the wider interests of society means that reform in practice is attempted in a piecemeal and inconsistent way. Measures that have clear winners and losers are fought over one by one, rather than being seen as part of a wider package that could benefit all.

- The Community dimension adds extra potential for inconsistent policy making. Both responsibility (the extent of "Community competence") and the way in which decisions are taken (unanimity or by weighted majority) vary from one policy domain to another. The sequence in which new policy initiatives are taken, both at EU and national level, can also lead to undesirable outcomes.

- Problems of co-ordination are compounded by a proliferation of new policy initiatives and multi-annual programmes at EU level. There are currently over 60 multi-annual initiatives described s "strategies". The different initiatives are rarely synchronised. The Agenda 2000 time frame runs from 2000 to 2006, the Single Market Strategy from 1999 to 2005, the next Framework Programme for Research from 2002 to 2006 and the new Environment Action Programme from 2001 to 2011.

Clearly, there are limits to the extent to which policies in different sectors can be reformed simultaneously. The Agenda 2000 reforms involved changes in particular to agricultural, structural, and external policies. Undertaking a similar exercise for an even wider set of policies would pose severe practical problems. Attempting to review all Community policies at the same time would lead to institutional paralysis. Measures to improve coherence should instead focus on linking together policies where the gains from co-ordination are expected to be greatest. In addition, if the design of sectoral policy attempts to take wider considerations than the interests of the sector into account, improving policy consistency should not mean that all policies need to adopt identical time tables.

Short Termism in Policy Making

A striking example of the possible effects of a short-term perspective is our inability to manage renewable natural resources sustainably. The Community has been unable to agree cuts in fish catches that are essential to preserve stocks for the future because of the short-term costs. This is despite the substantial long-term economic and ecological benefits in preserving stocks from collapse. Short termism has been a particular problem for environmental policy as many environmental problems are not immediately visible, but it is also true in other policy areas. When spending must be reduced to balance the national budget the first item to be cut is usually investment. This is because cuts in everyday services are immediate and painful, whereas the deterioration of public infrastructure takes time and is not immediately noticeable.

A root cause of short termism in the design and implementation of policy is the nature of the political cycle. The gap of at most four to five years between elections naturally limits governments' time horizons. In addition, one group that does not have a voice in these political choices is the future generation. In the absence of a coherent long-term vision, policy priorities may be influenced too much by short-term events. Policy responses then take the form of "quick fixes", which themselves may make the problem more acute, or cause difficulties in other areas.

Problems of short termism are likely to be worse when the costs of doing something are upfront and highly visible while the benefits are difficult to quantify and spread over several years. Moreover, costs and benefits may be unevenly distributed: costs of change often fall on particular groups of producers or citizens, while benefits are more widely spread. As a result, the "winners" from a policy change usually do not make themselves heard, whereas the "losers" do. Short termism can therefore be compounded by a highly sectoral approach to policy making.

At Community level, the regular six-monthly change in the Council Presidency induces a short-term perspective. New initiatives are often launched to take advantage of a political window that becomes available while a particular Member State holds the Presidency. A Member State's running of the Presidency tends to be judged by he amount of activity it generates—the number of regulations or directives adopted—rather than the quality of those measures.

Policy Inertia

The hardest innovation in policy-making is to stop old practices. Some unsustainable trends result from a failure to change or cancel policies which are past their "sell-by date." These are measures which made sense when they were introduced, but which have not been changed in response to changing circumstances. For example:

* When state pensions for all were first introduced life expectancies were much lower, and working lives typically much longer than today. Early retirement schemes and the tax and benefit system have resulted in biases that favour early withdrawal from the labour market, leading to a fall in the average retirement age. Both need reform today, when skill shortages are emerging, and the shrinking working age population and increasing numbers of pensioners threaten the sustainability of public finances.

* Town planning rules which imposed rigid separation between the location of housing and industry made sense when much industrial activity was very polluting. Now that industry is cleaner and services play a more important role in the economy these zoning laws may no longer be justified. More than this, together with rising levels of private car ownership they worsen traffic congestion.

* Our energy supply infrastructure is currently heavily dependent on the use of fossil fuels. This reflects investments made in the past when the impacts of burning fossil fuels on human health and the global climate were not as well understood. Changing our sources of energy supply is now a slow process as the infrastructure is long lived.

* Public policy as well as case law and political processes can, often for very good reasons, move much behind the pace of technological progress in areas such as genetically modified organisms, genetically modified food, and other innovations.

The paradox of having both policy inertia on the one hand,

and short termism on the other, is more apparent than real. Both problems essentially arise from an excessively sectoral approach to policy making. This enables sectional interests to prevail over the wider concerns of society, by preventing necessary reform to outdated policies needed to orient them towards the longer term.

Limited Understanding

We have a poor understanding of the causes and likely effects of several of the problems identified in above. For example, the definition, causes and consequences of poverty are complex and controversial. There are competing explanations for why disparities in the distribution of income are widening in some places, and for changes in family structures and birth rates. There are large information gaps in many other areas such as the measurement of changes in bio-diversity and their potential long-run effects.

We face similar uncertainties about the precise impact of many policy responses. In addition, in many cases inadequate attention has been paid to whether existing policy has actually been effective. Frequently, it is assumed that spending money on a problem is the same as successfully tackling it. In practice, we have often failed to assess whether a policy has achieved its objectives, how much it has cost, and what its positive or negative spillovers on other areas have been. This is complicated by the fact that policy objectives are not always well defined. In consequence, we often have an insufficient basis on which to assess what reforms might be necessary.

Inadequate Communication and Dialogue

Arguably, many of the existing failures to tackle unsustainable trends reflects a policy process that is too fragmented, technocratic and distant from the real concerns of people. Alienation from the political process can also result from a perception that policy making is excessively influenced by vested interest groups, to the detriment of the population at large. Whatever the truth of these views, it is undeniable that there is at the very least a strong belief that the average citizen has little scope for direct input into the political process, and that policy making has become disconnected from their daily concerns. This is reflected in rising abstention rates at elections for all levels of government. These issues will be examined in more depth in the Commission's forthcoming White Paper on Governance.

Scientists and policy makers often communicate poorly with the public and with each another, and misconceptions are common on all sides. As a result public awareness of the long-term consequences of different policy options, consumption patterns and lifestyle choices is also limited. In part, this may arise from the increased complexity of the modern world and the corresponding complexity of policy responses. Recent health scares—such those relating to BSE or phthalates—demonstrate the fragility of public confidence in the integrity of science and scientific advice about risks. This confidence is further undermined by the perception that the interpretation and dissemination of research results is sometimes subordinated to commercial pressures.

Common solutions for Sustainable Development in Europe

The previous section identified some common problems which have led to the emergence of the unsustainable trends described in section 2. This section suggests how we can go about solving them.

The analysis in section 3 shows that better policy integration is needed at all levels, so that different policies complement each other instead of pulling in different directions. Policy integration should start at the outset of the policy making process. Sustainable Development should become an underlying principle in all areas of EU activity. However, joined-up thinking in policy-making is not enough on its own. Better co-ordination and greater dialogue will not improve things if policy does not make full use of the right tools and ideas. Accordingly, this chapter not only sets out some ways to improve policy coherence, but also describes the most important tools that can and should be used as the building blocks of a strategy for sustainable development.

A Common Basis for Policy Design and Implementation

One of these building blocks is the principle that the costs and effects of all policies should be examined more systematically. This analysis should try to include not just the impacts in the area targeted by the policy, but also its spillovers – good and bad – onto other policy areas. Identifying spillovers and sharing of expertise between different departments of government is important if we are to create the conditions for "win-win" policies and improve the coherence of policy making. Inevitable though, in some cases we have to make trade-offs between changes in economic, environmental and social assets. Careful assessment of the costs and effects of different policy options and their distribution is vital to ensure that these trade-offs are made in the interests of society as a whole, and that mechanisms are put in place to enable business and citizens to adapt to change.

Good policy design should also consider the different instruments available to meet the policy objective. The aim should be to give policy makers as full an assessment as possible of the costs and effects, the advantages and disadvantages of the different options, so that we can reach our desired objectives, whatever they may be, at least cost. This does not mean going for the cheapest or "do nothing" option. It means doing things efficiently and effectively. This helps us get the most we can out of the available resources by avoiding waste and inefficiency.

Climate change provides a very good example of the importance of cost effectiveness. Some policy measures – such as gradually removing subsidies for the use of fossil fuels – can reduce greenhouse gas emissions while actually raising economic performance. Still, meeting the targets in the Kyoto Protocol is likely to have some economic costs. However, the size of these costs and how they are distributed will depend very much on what policies are used. The Commission services have estimated that a policy of equal percentage reduction targets for different economic sectors would be nearly three times more expensive than a policy that encourages the biggest savings in sectors where emissions can be reduced at relatively low cost.

Long Term Targets and Intermediate Milestones

Sustainable development is a framework for policy that focuses on long-term management rather than short-term quick-fix solutions. Identifying concrete, ambitious, achievable long-term objectives are necessary to give substance to policies for sustainable development, and to develop popular understanding and support for these policies. These objectives should lead to the establishment of clear – and preferably measurable – targets. Intermediate milestones allow us to judge our progress. When the policy target can be expressed in very precise terms, it may be possible to meet targets agreed at the European level through Member States applying their own, cost-effective solutions. Clear long-term targets also provide other important advantages:

– Sustainable development means leaving an adequate legacy to future generations. Long-term targets are required to limit the scope for short termism and to ensure this obligation is met.

– Uncertainty and instability in the policy regime generate their own costs. Clear long-term signals can help companies and individuals plan better. This is particularly important as the capital stock of an economy turns over only relatively slowly. Investment decisions have long lasting effects and are costly to reverse.

– Provided targets can be clearly defined, it can make sense to delegate responsibility for meeting targets to those most closely involved with particular policy areas, or to an independent authority free from short-term political pressures. The latter is the case of the European Central Bank, which has been given responsibility to provide stable prices. However, not all policy objectives can be defined in such clear terms, and there are limits to the extent to which it is desirable to devolve power to unelected, unaccountable bodies.

– Implementing new policy measures gradually can reduce the costs of change considerably by allowing adequate time for businesses and individuals to change their patterns of production and consumption. For example, companies that have to adapt to new technologies to remain competitive generally have much less trouble adjusting if these changes can be made as part of the normal investment cycle. Taking a gradual approach avoids the unnecessary creation of unemployment and gives workers time to acquire new skills.

A few policy initiatives have shown that it is possible to gather consensus around gradual but steady adjustment to long-term targets, which smooth the transition to sustainable policies. An example is the ten-years perspective for reform of economic and social policy agreed by the European Council at Lisbon.

Creating Markets and Getting Prices Right

"Getting prices right" so that they better reflect the true costs to society of different activities would give everybody the right incentive to integrate the effects their behaviour has on others into their everyday decisions about which goods and services to make or buy. It is therefore one of the most important tools available to policy makers.

There are many different ways of changing the prices or other incentives that companies and consumers face so as to underpin sustainable development. Direct methods include the creation of tradable property rights (such as emission permits) that allow markets to set a price for pollution, eco-taxes that discourage over-use of environmental resources, and legal liability regimes. Governments can boost markets for sustainable products and services through their public procurement policies.

Clearer definition of property rights can also play a useful role in improving the management of natural resources where there is a risk of over-consumption. Subsidies can be an effective tool in some cases where behaviour has positive spillover effects. For example, there is some merit in the idea that companies should be paid a temporary subsidy to take on the long term unemployed, as the social costs of long term unemployment on individuals, their families and the public sector finances are very significant. Any proposal made in this respect would have to comply with the principles of EC and Member States' legal systems.

The *user pays principle* is an important first step in improving incentives. It means simply that under normal circumstances those that benefit from the use of something should pay for it. This reduces wasteful consumption, and gives those who use a resource the right incentives to behave responsibly. Evidently, the user pays principle cannot be applied indiscriminately – there are very legitimate exceptions to its application in modern societies, not least in aspects of social provision through the welfare state. Public subsidy is often necessary and justified. However, the user pays principle is an important reminder that the rationale for subsidies should be clearly set out to avoid wasteful use of resources.

The *polluter pays principle* is an important extension of the user pays principle to environmental policy making. The underlying philosophy is that polluters do not have an inherent right to pollute. The polluter pays principle has been defined in various ways, but the most important interpretation is that the polluter should pay for the costs his pollution imposes on others—for example through a tax on polluting emissions. This provides an added incentive to look for reductions in pollution. A more limited interpretation would be that polluters should pay only for the costs of any pollution control measures required by law.

The polluter pays principle is already part of the EC Treaty, but it is not yet widely enough applied at either EU level or in Member States. A much more rigorous and consistent approach is required. Significant improvements in both economic and environmental performance could be achieved without increasing the overall tax burden by gradual reform of existing tax structures and subsidy regimes, so that the prices paid by producers and consumers more accurately reflect the costs and benefits their activities impose on other members of society.

Part of the difficulty in applying the polluter pays principle is that it can be difficult to define who the polluter really is, as both producers and consumers bear some responsibility for the environmental impacts. For practical purposes therefore the responsibility for combating pollution should be assigned to those who are in the best position to reduce pollution at relatively low cost. In recent years a number of initiatives by Member States have aimed to encourage producers to design products that are easier to deal with in the waste phase by making them responsible for the environmental impacts of products throughout their life cycle. Some recent Commission proposals have also been based on this idea of extended producers responsibility.

Sectoral Policy Coherence

In order to try to redirect policy in individual sectors away from a narrow set of objectives there have been several efforts at Community level to "integrate" broader concerns into the conduct of sectoral policies, such as employment promotion, regional development and environmental protection. The current efforts to integrate environmental concerns into other sectoral policies (the Cardiff integration process) have shown that some progress is possible through such initiatives.

The Cardiff process has increased understanding of the issues and helped develop new policy approaches. However, there are also limits. Improved dialogue does not in itself solve all problems when there are unavoidable trade-offs between competing interests. Moreover, this type of policy integration is itself a sector by sector approach, so it is unable to guarantee that different integration initiatives take a consistent approach. It is therefore unlikely to produce the best overall balance between the interests of consumers, citizens and producers.

Practical improvements to the sectoral integration approach would result from greater transparency—that is, a clearer presentation of the economic, social and environmental costs and benefits of different policy options. Consistent and rigorous evaluation should be conducted jointly and openly to ensure that the different objectives are given their appropriate weight in each sector. Improving our understanding of causes, effects and inter-linkages between sectors is therefore critical to designing and implementing policies for sustainable development.

Beyond Integration: Improved Coordination in Community Policy Making

Sustainable development implies a society-wide approach to policy design. Sustainability must be placed at the core of the mandate of all policy makers. This means more than tagging on environmental and social objectives to existing policies. Achieving these objectives should be as relevant to judging the success or failure of a policy as its sectoral targets. Otherwise integration and sustainability risk becoming buzzwords to which policy-makers pay lip service only. Integration must mean something more than minor adjustments to "business as usual" if sustainable development is to move from rhetoric to reality. This needs political commitment and leadership.

As one part of the current internal reforms, the Commission has established a Strategic Planning and Programming function to help improve co-ordination between departments. In addition there is a need throughout the Community institutional structure for a practical political mechanism to arbitrate in a consistent and rational way across sectors when competing interests are at stake, and to provide clear long-term policy objectives. Moreover, consideration could be given to creating a "council" for sustainable development with no direct stake in the policy process. Such a body may be better placed to provide objective critical reviews of existing policies. Several Member States have already established independent councils in order to advise their governments on sustainable development issues.

Regular Policy Reviews

Regularly and systematically evaluating policies to ensure that they are meeting their objectives, bringing benefits to society as a whole and are consistent with the overall objective of sustainable development should become a core element of policy making. Such reviews should be undertaken in an open manner so that the views of all stakeholders can be taken into account. In addition, more use should be made of "sunset clauses" in legislation that provide for it to be automatically ended or reviewed after a number of years. Not all policy measures need to last forever but it is a rare –and brave! – regulator who will voluntarily declare that s/he is no longer needed.

Technology at the Service of Society

In the context of sustainable development, technology can be a double-edged sword. Technological progress has enormously increased our material wealth and improved our quality of life in every area, from communications and transport to new foods and health. They can also offer major opportunities for more efficient use of resources through changes in production techniques and the way services are delivered. Moreover, technology can help us ease potential trade-offs between competing ends. New technologies can often reduce pollution or risks for health and safety at work at much lower cost than adjusting existing technologies. Without further advances in technology and its wider use, the most challenging environmental problems, such as climate change, can only be tackled through painful changes in production and consumption patterns. Technology will therefore be at the heart of moves to sustainable development.

However, technology also brings its own challenges, particularly when change is rapid. New technologies and working methods can increase competitive pressures and can force difficult adjustments. Emerging technologies create new opportunities but sometimes also new risks and in some cases – such as genetics – new ethical questions. The enormous effect of technology on the material productivity of our societies also raises the prospect that we increase the scale of output and consumption more rapidly than we can reduce pollution per unit produced, thereby increasing overall pressure on the environment over time – the "rebound" effect.

This means that technological progress has to be actively harnessed in the interests of sutainable development. The challenge for policy is to influence innovation so that the solutions chosen by markets are "winners" for sustainable development. Market-based approaches that "get the prices right" are important to stimulate the development of new and environmentally safe technologies and their rapid take-up. Public policy can also help to accelerate the diffusion of new technologies by benchmarking, demonstration projects and removing non-market barriers to their use, including regulations that unnecessarily hamper innovation.

A clear, long-lasting commitment from governments to pursue sustainable development as a core policy objective will strengthen the signals coming from prices. This will help to give companies assurance about the stability of the policy framework and encourage a pro-active approach by business during a time of rapid structural change. Credible long-term policy commitments will give companies time to develop new techniques and adapt smoothly to the transition to sustainability. As well as aiming to provide the right framework conditions, public authorities can also fund basic and essential applied research where it is too costly or too risky for an individual company.

Improving Knowledge and Understanding—Sound Science, Risk and Transparency

Science and scientific research does not take place in a vaccum. The results of research can have important effects on the direction of public policy. This inevitably raises doubts about the objectivity and completeness of the research methods and results when commercial interests are at stake. To remove or at least minimise such suspicions research results should be reported in an open way. New research should be carefully peer reviewed to ensure its credibility. Confidence in the use of scientific information would also be enhanced by independent synthesis of the evidence so that it can be communicated to and understood by a wider public.

Given the speed and complexity of technological innovation, independent scientific research is essential to help us evaluate the opportunities and risks of new production techniques and new products. Risk is sometimes a necessary part of social progress—risk takers and innovators are essential for a dynamic economy. However, many risks are undesirable and have to be actively managed. For example, in the development of new medicines a balance has to be struck between the potential benefits that the treatment offers, and the risk that it may turn out to have damaging side effects. Similarly, the risk posed by new synthetic chemicals have to be weighed against their benefits in use. Therefore in the context of sustainable development dealing with risk means carefully evaluating the economic, environmental and social effects of innovations and taking a balanced view of the likely positive and negative impacts.

Inevitably, in some cases we do not yet have enough information about the existence or scale of a risk to properly assess its real importance. However, lack of proof that a risk exists does not provide an adequate excuse for ignoring it. This simple truth is at the heart of what is commonly known as the "precautionary principle." But the precautionary principle in itself provides little practical guidance about how to manage risk and uncertainty. Risk management decisions are inevitably a trade-off between the level of protection desired, the costs of reducing risk, and the weight of evidence that the risk is real. This is ultimately a matter for political judgement and responsibility.

During the course of the last few decades many commonplace risks have been eliminated or reduced, thanks to improvements in systems of social protection, environmental and health improvements and higher standards of living. However, recent years have seen the rapid emergence of new problems many unforeseen or unforeseeable. This calls for new institutional responses. We need to improve our capacity to respond speedily to emerging risks, to speed up scientific assessment of risks (such as the risks posed by persistent pollutants or biotoxins) and to improve our capacity for dealing with crises. Most importantly, decisions on how to tackle risks that we face as consumers and citizens must be made transparently, in an accountable manner, and with the public interest at heart.

Better Information, Education and Participation

Improved information for producers and consumers is important to enhance the effectiveness of policies that seek to encourage changes in behaviour. Consumers can respond better to price signals and other incentives if they have relevant information, such as the cost savings they can expect from using more energy-efficient domestic appliances or the health improvements they can expect from better diet. Information gaps can undermine the effectiveness of policy. Moreover, if we are to exercise our personal freedoms wisely and take an active part in civil society we need information about the wider effects of our choice of lifestyle on matters such as our health and on traffic congestion.

The process by which policy is made should be transparent. An open dialogue about the costs and benefits of different options will help test the arguments that underlie different policy proposals. Establishing a dialogue between stakeholders can be time consuming, but is essential to building mutual trust and understanding and may increase the chances of finding mutually acceptable solutions. The current European Climate Change Programme is a good example of a more open policy process. Sustainable development can thus become a way to revitalise the democratic process by involving citizens in decisions that affect their daily life and generating a real debate on society's priorities.

Access to high quality education and training for all ages will enable citizens to take an active party in democratic society. Our behaviour as individual citizens is not determined exclusively by strictly financial considerations. It also reflects a sense of belonging to society, of sharing a common set of social values. Providing better information not citizens about the goal of sustainability and its importance is a way of strengthening this social capital and encouraging sustainable behaviour by all.

Measuring Progress: Indicators

Indicators provide the basis for assessing progress towards the long-term objective of sustainable development. Long-term targets only have meaning as policy goals if progress towards them can be assessed objectively. This requires targets expressed in precise terms. Careful measurement will also improve our ability to identify interactions between different policies and deal with possible trade-offs. There are some cases when improvements in one area can only be achieved at the expense of deterioration in another. Such trade-offs are already a part of policy-making, but the advantage of measurement is that they are made explicit and transparent. This does not mean that everything must be quantified. Quantified and measurable targets are important, but must not become the exclusive focus of policy. Indeed, some elements of sustainable development are intrinsically hard to quantify. Not everything can be turned into numerical data. This is particularly true of some environmental and social assets. We cannot easily measure the value of bio-diversity or the quality and quantity of social relationships. To avoid neglecting them we must devise better qualitative indicators.

Identifying an appropriate set of measures and indicators, both quantitative and qualitative, will not be easy given the scope of the issues addressed in this paper. Inevitably, not all the desired data will be available. It is a persistent temptation to measure what is easiest to measure rather than what is important. This has to be avoided if we are to develop robust indicators that provide accurate signals. It is more important to be roughly right (with imperfect indicators of what matters) that precisely wrong (with perfect indicators on developments of little importance).

The first stage in the preparation of an EU strategy for sustainable development. In it, the Commission services have set out their views on the challenges and opportunities which would be presented by making sustainable development the overarching priority of Community policy. This approach is underpinned by a belief that to provide leadership in a global context the EU has to meet its international commitments and reform its internal policies so as to make progress towards sustainable development. Of course, the EU also has to play its full role in international organisations, such as the UN, the IMF and World Bank and the WTO, as these bodies have an important contribution to make towards sustainable development.

CHAPTER 3

Globalization and Dimensions of Gender

All development affects livelihoods. It creates new opportunities while posing a threat to some traditional occupations. In order to be sustainable, development must offer, to those whose jobs and occupations are at risk, opportunities which they can recognise and convert to their own advantage. For the urban poor in low-skill, marginal occupations, livelihood has several critical dimensions. Rapid economic changes in response to changing market currents may place not just individual livelihoods but entire livelihood categories under threat. Such vulnerable groups in urban areas must be provided with appropriate security nets, opportunities for developing new skills, appropriate entrepreneurial skills and social welfare programmes for basic survival.

Sustainable development, especially in the urban based sectors, demands urgent and strong policy measures to safeguard the livelihoods placed at risk by the forces of liberalisation, privatisation and globalisation.

Programmes of skill and versatility development, backed by support for promoting small-scale entrepreneurship, management and marketing must be developed for those whose occupations and livelihoods are at risk.

Basic education for function literacy, livelihood skills and responsible citizenship is a precondition for sustainable development. Such education must be appropriate to the social, economic and environmental context, must be of the highest quality possible within that context, and must be available to every child and youth as a fundamental right. Facilities for each child to acquire such education without being discriminated against on the basis of economic class, geographical location or cultural identity, are a must.

Changes in the global political economy since the 1980's have had a dramatic effect on the lives of women, who have become increasingly integrated as players in the world's production and consumption processes. Women have been affected by globalization in the most diverse aspects of their lives and in the furthest reaches of the world. The effects have been multiple and contradictory, inclusionary and exclusionary. (Afshar and Barrientos, 1999:1)

This is the opening paragraph to Afshar and Barrientos's anthology *Women, Globalization and Fragmentation the Developing World*. The tone in the first line—*a dramatic effect*—indicates that something radical has been happening in the lives of women since the early 1980s. These radical changes in the lives of women can be traced back to changes in the global political economy; they are comprehensive and contradictory and either exclude or include women. But women have also become players in global production and consumption processes; players in a game that is played on a global level, according to the authors. The question that immediately surfaces is what the influence of globalization processes for women is. In this chapter, the relationship between globalization and gender is studied more closely. There will be an analysis on the basis of the multidimensionality of gender concerned with how this relationship takes shape in the current debates on globalization. This is followed by a discussion on how to avoid the pitfalls that have been noticed in the debates on globalization using this analytical gender model. Furthermore, we will explore the application of this analytical model on the debate on gender and globalization. In doing so we hope to initiate a discussion on the applicability of this model to the debate on globalization in general.

This will be done according to the following steps. First, there will be a brief exploration into the way in which globalization is given meaning in the literature. The heterogeneity of standpoints within globalization literature is the starting point for shaping our thoughts on globalization and gender. The question as to whether it concerns homogenization, heterogenization, or creolization cannot be answered unequivocally and demands a method of analysis different from that usually used to analyze globalization processes. We must therefore consult women's studies and the way thinking about gender and difference has been shaped there. This discussion exposes not only the dichotomous way of thinking, but also the power of attributing meaning. Here ingredients are supplied for a different approach to the category of women. It is discussed how theories on 'the layeredness of gender' are an integral part of an analytical and methodological approach that can be helpful in analyzing the relationship between globalization and gendering in a less common way. This perspective will then be used to study the way in which globalization and gender has been shaped within development issues. The question is whether or not this new discourse on globalization and gender will reproduce the same dichotomies and stereotypes. It will be answered through an analysis of the discourse on the feminization of poverty and personal research into female-headed households in Botswana. In the last part of this article the consequences of the alternative approach for future research will be discussed. Personal research into women and political representation in Mexico will be used to this end. The effects of inclusion and exclusion are again discussed with the difference that women have now become players in a more complicated game in which they not only produce and consume, but in which they also give and appropriate meaning.

Globalization and Localization

Before it is possible to state ideas on the relationship between globalization and gender it might be pertinent to address briefly what characterizes globalization. We are mainly concerned with how globalization as a phenomenon is given meaning in the scientific discourse. This has made us think and has made us challenge it. There are different thoughts on globalization, which is demonstrated by Schuurman's taxonomy elsewhere in this book. In this taxonomy there are nine possible movements or positions that can be identified with regard to globalization. These positions are so varied that they move from a Utopian to a nihilistic vision. As a common denominator of the different positions one could say that globalization is, at the very least, about an increasing interconnectedness of the world through technology and flows of capital, commodities, people and culture. Exceptions to these views are of course those in which there is no such thing as globalization in the first place and where it is assumed that there is at best a degree of regionalization.

The question into the meaning of globalization, how linear the process is, and if it causes actual changes on a global scale has to do with the way in which different authors give meaning to these changes. Where one author is clearly within the bounds of modernistic thinking when it comes to an analysis of globalization, another is trying to break that very pattern of thinking (Albrow, 1997). This is best expressed in the way in which one author sees globalization as no more than a continuing homogenization of the world according to the Western model .

Whether globalization is seen as a process of homogenization, heterogenization, or creolization depends largely on the perspective of analysis. It has been noticed that many analyses, including analyses that move within the field of development studies, adapt a macro-economical perspective. The dominant way of thinking about globalization within development studies is characterized by this macro-economical vision in which globalization is mainly seen as a process that, though complex and set in many fields, is still unilinear. The unilinearity of that complex process is then largely determined by a neo-liberal logic based on a modernistic way of thinking. Even when authors are critical of this neo-liberalization the pattern of thought is always within the bounds of a linear process.

Globalization hereby comes first as a process that is set in a global context, without problematizing that context. It occurs as an 'out there' process, but what does that context envelop and who does it concern? Global from whose perspective and according to which process? Only in a neo-liberal and then in an anti-liberal range of thought does globalization get its meaning. This means that globalization acquires a very specific meaning, with an emphasis on macro-political and macro-economical interconnectedness. Within gender and development literature a comparable development seems to be taking place. Recent gender and development literature is mostly *reactive* when it concerns macro-political and economic questions (cf. Pearson & Jackson 1998:9–10).

Literature that refers to topics such as the influence of structural adjustment programs, internationalization of the job market, and the position of women within the global economy largely reflects a pessimistic vision (Sen, 1997; Wichterich, 1998). They are approaches in which changing macro-economical relations and their alleged negative effect on local circumstances are central. The image that is put forward by these analyses is that women are victims of neo-liberal processes.

Some speak even about the economistics turn among academics specializing in gender and development and find this turn to be a historical and ignoring potential socio-political dimensions of restructuring (Marchand, 1996:580). Even those who criticize this development as such seem only to want to reproduce the occurrence of globalization as a neo-liberal logic. Within this literature the economic worldwide restructuring in the form of one global capitalism in turn has an often-assumed influence on international governments and on households and families (Connelly *et al.* 1995; Spike Peterson, 1996:5). We will come back to the supposed character of this influence later.

Here the observation that a link is made between global, national, and local processes will suffice. The question is, however, what the nature of these connections is and what results it has for nations, groups, families and individuals. The next question is whether the linkages point in the direction of homogenization as a linear process. Many of the globalization thinkers make globalization synonymous with Westernization, either viewed positively from a Utopian standpoint or negatively, critical of cultural imperialism.

We believe the process of interconnectedness as described above moves within the field of tension between homogenization and heterogenization, and thereby follow authors such as Appadurai (1996) and Hannerz (1987). The intellectual exercise needed to go beyond globalization as a homogeneous, unilinear, and macro-process should reflect the changed meaning of space and time as a part of globalization. Flows of capital, commodities, culture, and people are no longer bound to space in the sense of territory. Capital has no loyalty towards its native soil, as Tomlinson so eloquently puts it.[2] The speed with which flows of capital travel across the globe due to digitalization and the shift from trade in commodities to trade in knowledge seems to influence and alter the mechanisms of the market.

Not only are flows of capital no longer bound to territory or time, but flows of culture are also less often bound to time, place, and space. In this respect the concern is not only with time in the sense of speed, but mostly that time in relation to distance is less and less an inhibiting factor. Distance matters ever less, because people can travel more easily.[3] People are also able to be at several places in the world at the same time, in a virtual sense, through video, the Internet, satellites, and other means of communication. Due to intensified migration and flows of refugees the formation of, for example, the Iranian culture is no longer a matter restricted to Iran, but it also takes place.

This means that time and space will no longer be a buffer in an exchange of cultures the way it was before. The question that presents itself is whether the disappearance of the buffers of time and space will lead to a slow but steady homogenication of the world. We tend to agree with Appadurai that globalization will result in a continuous field of tension between homogenization and heterogenization, with a multiplying of differences rather than the emergence of a homogeneous world culture. According to Bauman (in Tomlinson, 1996:32–33), there is a worldwide (international) spreading of modernization, but not to a universal degree. Even where modernization seems to strike in the form of the often-mentioned McDonaldization, this modernization takes on a more hybrid form on a local level than the growing sales figures of, for example, a product such as the Big Mac seem to indicate.

As far as the reaction to the spreading of modernization is concerned, there are various tendencies to be observed. For example, an acceptance of, resistance to, and creolization of cultural patterns that seem to accompany products like Coca-Cola can be observed. A well-known example of acceptance but not of acculturation can be found with the Mayas in Chiapas in Mexico. They have incorporated Coca-Cola into their religious rituals as a sacred potion. Coca-Cola can be seen as a symbol of modernization on a global level in a dominant Western discourse, but the Mayas have not adapted or recognized this symbolic meaning. In other words, Coca-Cola as a commodity can be found all over the World but it does not have the same connotation everywhere.

An important aspect of this example is that Coca-Cola as a symbol of modernity can also have an entirely different meaning that is virtually unimaginable in a Western discourse. Coca-Cola is a potent symbol of a modern commodity. The Western perspective of global, however, is entirely different from that of the Mayas. And although that perspective was at a safe distance until now, a part of the former colonies, of exotic faraway places, these kinds of perspectives are drawing ever closer due to the continued interconnectedness of the world.

The changes that can be observed under the influence of globalization with respect to time and distance in cultural (and political-economical) differences are breaking away from very set dichotomies within Western thinking about the artificially created cultural other. Memmi (in Hartsock, 1987) in his work *The Colonizer and the Colonized* has already eloquently described how time and distance are utilized by the colonizer in creating so-called actual differences between the colonizer and the colonized. The differences between colonizer and colonized were made into absolute and actual differences by the way the colonizer placed the colonized outside the course of history.

The colonized were lazy, backward, and everything that the colonizer was not. These characteristics of the colonized were subsequently made absolute by rooting them in time and geographical distance. The colonized were after all what they were and that would never change. The colonized was subsequently placed outside a possible opportunity of change, evolution, and finally history. Geographically these differences, where possible, were rooted in distance. The distance between the slave quarters and the house of the master on plantations is an example of this. What is in fact a social difference is hence mad into a biological and metaphysical difference.

These dichotomous categories are exactly those subject to change due to globalization. These changes not only occur in reality, but also in reflection upon reality, such as in art and science. Where the post-modern crisis of thinking questioned these dichotomies on the level of the scientific discourse these same dichotomies are in practice the subject of discussion due to the large flows of migration, means of virtual communication, and intensification of international flows of capital. The cultural other is no longer far away, different, vague, exotic, backward, repressed and underdeve-loped, but a very concrete neighbor. The fact that the distance between people and commodities matters less means that the dividing lines that were considered to be matter-of-fact from an enlightenment and modernization point of view can also be breached practice. However, this does not mean that people are casting off their historical, cultural, and contextual roots and connections. The connections with culture and history are sometimes apparent from a clinging to dichotomies. In the extreme, religious fundamentalism and nationalism are well-known examples.

To be able to analyze mechanisms of inclusion or exclusion it is necessary to identify on which levels these processes of inclusion and exclusion take place. To grasp global and local flux and closure requires us to dismiss the idea that the world is a collection of nameable groups. As Geschiere and Meyer state: "In order to develop concepts which are suited to grasping flux, social scientists have to struggle hard to get away from the intellectual habit of fixing practices, spaces and countries into a map of static differences" (1998:6). It is the production of differences that is the point here. Thinking in divisions, in other words, the dichotomous way of thinking that has a prominent place in modernistic thinking is subject to discussion here (cf. Alexander, 1994). This means that a different attitude towards differences and the way differences are produced under the influence of globalization is required. But how can we look upon differences differently? We consider it analytically helpful to look at the multidimensionality of the concept of gender and the multidimensionality of difference that is linked directly to it. The discussion about differences, that started with criticism mostly from black women on the white Western middle-class perspective which dominated theories within women's studies, forced feminists to alter their perception of women as belonging to an homogeneous category (cf. Lazreg, 1998; Mohanty, 1991). This was a tough problem for feminism because loyalty between women, considered a fact, came under attack and with it feminism as a political project, as it had been formulated up to that point (Davids and Willemse, 1999). An important point of criticism on the Western middle-class perspective was that being a woman was always, but not exclusively, concerned with gender. Gender is also made up of ethnicity, class, religion, and sexual proclivity, to name but a few markers, In order to give these markers a place and to do justice to differences and diversity among women gender is used as a layered concept (Harding, 1986; Scott, 1989).

Referring to gender in layers is not new within women's studies in the Netherlands, but which layers are being referred to here?[6] As such we prefer the term dimensions to layers or levels. Layers and levels both hold connotations of above and below, higher and lower, which could again lead to statements on dichotomous positions, something that must be avoided. Dimensions of gender may be analytically different, but in practice these are interwoven in a constant dynamic interaction.

To start with, a symbolic dimension may be attributed to this process; the dimension of symbolic order, in which representations of masculinity and femininity obtain their substance, sometimes solidifies into very persistent cultural texts. An example of such a cultural text is that women are more emotional than men and men are more rational than women. This is the dimension of symbols, representations, ideal images, and stereotypes. It is the dimension in which the discursive elements of discourse manifest themselves. Differences between men and women are articulated as absolute differences in this dimension, as differences between *the* man and *the* woman. Dichotomous categories are being articulated here that have a lot more nuance in practice.

The second dimension that can be distinguished within this process is the structural or institutional dimension, the dimension that shapes the symbolic within a socially institutionalized practice, such as the division of labor, education, health care and marriage. This representation creates its own subject position and categories, for example in the Netherlands the category of *bijstandsmoeder* (mother on social security) where there is no legal category *bijstandsvader* (father on social security). Within this dimension the structural differences between men and women become apparent. As stated above, it becomes clear within this dimension that men and women differ on the grounds of class, ethnicity, age, sexual proclivity, etc. Within this dimension in which the differences of the symbolic dimension presented as absolute obtain meanings in the daily practice of different groups of people, does not suggest that these groups are homogeneous. One *bijstandsmoeder* is not the same as the next.

This takes us into the third dimension of gender, the dimension of the individual subject. This is the dimension in which individuals shape their identities. Although the second dimension referred to the differences between men and women as well as among men and among women, the third dimension also concerns the differences within men and women. This dimension refers to the process of identification of individuals with the multiple identities or aspects of identities that are handed to them. Notions of the self and the others are also internalized and no longer refer to differences between the self and an actual other, but also to differences within the self. The variation in the way in which individuals assume those subject positions is precisely the result of the space for negotiation that they have. This space for negotiation is not only limited by structural positions and a symbolic attribution of meaning, but also by personal endowments. This space for negotiation is also known as the strategic space or 'room to manoeuvre.[9] This room to manoeuvre has its limitations in discourses that may have solidified.

The different dimensions of gender are in constant interaction. This means that the actors must always relate to these different dimensions. Within this figurative negotiations is the space that individuals have to exert power and influence upon each other. Although this was referred to as the subversion of the male bastions in the 1970s, this was counteracted by the empowerment of actors and individuals in the 1990s. The concept of empowerment no longer refers to 'liberation' as a reversal of power positions, but to a process. Being able to give direction to one's personal life is central in empowerment. It is in that sense not the power *over* but the power *to*. Power *to* centralize one's own subjectivity as a response to dominant definitions of feminity and masculinity (Davids and van Driel, 1999).

The daily living environment is structured by discourses, were claims to truth are no longer questioned. If we are even aware of them, they present themselves as clichés. Truths that create a certain notion of feminity and actually force women to relate to certain subject positions. This is exactly where the effect of power of the dominant discourse lies. Subjects are not victims of this effect of power, however, but are an active part of it. As Wieringa argues with regard to empowerment, this is one of the major sides where the transformative potential of the empowerment approach should be located. The construction of a collective self for women should enable them to see themselves as vocal subjects, able to define and defend their gender interests in order to critically and creatively reshape their worlds (Wieringa, 1994:834). In the next section we will take a closer look at the extent to which the new debate on gender and globalization considers women as vocal subjects.

Globalization and Dimensions of Gender

The discussion on gender and globalization will here be analyzed further using the above-mentioned multidimensional gender model. How do mechanisms of inclusion and exclusion take place in the current scientific debate on feminization of poverty? Which discourses dominate this debate, what are the mainscripts, what are the subscripts, and what are the new subscripts?

As has been indicated above, the result that appears on a global level is not the result of a unilinear process: "Global processes are composed of webs of practices that emanate from international, national, regional and local spheres (Villareal, 1994:2)." In other words, macro-processes occur in and are transformed into daily life practices. This applies not only to entities such as the state or the market, but also to households and families. The latter two are also constructions that are transformed into living reality by acting subjects who respond to outside changes and impulses. However, what is considered globalization within this process by scientists for the most part consists of the global dimension of this process and only to a lesser extent the interaction with the daily life world. The danger of essentialists generalizations is close in this case.

Generalizations, and especially essentialist generalizations, are in danger being stereotypical. Different as according to race, class, sexuality, locality, historical background, and age are central elements of deconstruction, as we have stated in the paragraph on gender. The rejection of an essentialist position, however, should not result in the opposite extreme, that is, the perpetual emphasizing of differences among and diversity of women, as a result of which nothing exists but differences. However, generalizations made on the basis of the supposedly common characteristics of the position of women, which are relevant to theory and policy, should be possible and should not be confused with taking an essentialist stance (Martin, 1994:644, 646, 648). Generalizations are necessary for a political agenda, for policy, and for a research agenda because otherwise there would only be difference and no possibility of a scientific or political debate (van Driel & Deuss, 1997; van Driel, 1997).

The debate on the feminization of poverty as a result of globalization does, in our opinion, have essentialist traits on the basis of preconceived generalizations. This occurs especially when the debate on the feminization of poverty focuses on female-headed households as an expression of that same feminization of poverty. The reasoning is as follows: Through globalization feminization of poverty takes place[10], this poverty can mostly be found in female-headed households. The step to the claim that households headed by a woman are poor is one that is easily made. The final conclusion in this reasoning, then, is that globalization leads to an increase in the number of poor female-headed households. This reasoning subsequently is used nationally as well as internationally to justify attention to women in policies.

The result is that female-headed households appear as a uniform category and that they are poor and require support. This statement has an implicit economic connotation concerning poverty as well as an implicit and explicit gender connotation. What is implied is that female-headed households are poorer than male-headed households. The question that is not asked, however, is whether women are better off in male-headed households. By making male-headed households the norm important contradictions vanish within these households, and so does the possibly unbalanced economical and social position of women compared to men (cf. Sen, 1990). Here female-headed and male-headed households appear as two objective categories placed on opposite sides of a poverty scale. When deconstructing the category of the female-headed household and its assumed poverty the question is whether the above-mentioned statement holds water. This reconstruction is carried out in brief below, and there the relationships between the concepts of globalization, feminization of poverty and female-headed households is central.

Feminization of Poverty and Female-headed Households Deconstructed

In one of our researches we took up the tasks to deconstruct the growth in female-headed households as an expression of the feminization of poverty (van Driel, 1994; 1997, see also Mencher & Okongwu, 1993 and Chant, 1997). In Botswana, where the research took place, the number of female-headed household is currently 50 percent. The central question of the research was why Botswana has so many female-headed households (and unmarried mothers). The answer to this question is complex and revealed historical aspects and conceptual and methodological problems. At the conceptual level the definition of households and headship and, thus, of female-headed (or women-headed) households are problematic.

To stay with the latter female-headed households can reveal a highly diversified group of women. Female-headed households mean lone-mother households, comprising a mother and her children. But these households, again can differ considerably in marital status (divorced, separated, never married, widowed), stage in the life-course (age, labor burden, access to resources), class position (financial means, social mobility), race (stigmatization, discrimination) and juridical status (*de facto/de jure* status, rights). Female-headed households can also mean female-headed extended households, lone-female households and single-sex/female-only households. Grandmother-headed households and embedded female-headed households can also be distinguished (van Driel, 1994; see also Chant, 1997:10–26; Rogers, 1995). Hence, the concept of female-headed households presents a highly diversified picture.

It might be obvious that these conceptual problems of definition cause methodological problems. Ideological and social aspects influence the data garnered and, thus, the outcome of censuses and surveys. Which households are represented in, for example, census figures and can these figures which are collected in different places at different times be compared? For some regions of the world figures are not available since distinctions between different types of household are not even made. The impact of the period in which we have been studying changes in household/family compositions is of considerable importance, too, as figures on the occurrence of female-headed households in Brazil in the 19th century indicate. In 1802, 45 percent of all households in Sâo Paulo were headed by women, partly because the sex-ratio was heavily feminine; 75 men to 100 women. In 1836 the percentage was 39, while in the interior of Brazil 25 percent of the households were estimated to be headed by women. In the 1980s the figures for the whole of Brazil were around 14.5 percent (Moore, 1994:8; Chant, 1997:730). Apart from the conclusion that female-headship is not a recent phenomenon and that problems of definition make data difficult to compare, these data indicate that the numbers of female-headed households can fluctuate over time and that specific causes have to be analyzed for different periods.

In the case of Botswana the changes in gender relations and in the composition of households over a period of 100 years were studied. During the pre-colonial time female-headed households were a contradiction in terms: households were, by definition, headed by men. During the colonial time (1885–1966) the phenomenon of the 'femme sole' emerged, which developed after independence into the phenomenon of female-headed households. It was found that due to Christianization changes at the symbolic level emphasized the importance of marriage and women's roles as mothers and housewives and men's roles as breadwinners, supporting their female kin. This ideal of the role of women as housewives and mothers replayed the ideal of the central role of women in agricultural production. At the level of gender structure the sexual division of labor did not change. Women maintained responsibility for subsistence production, whereas men's participation in trade and wage labor gave them access to an independent economic life. As a result, the dominant norms and values at the symbolic level and the actual gender structure clashed at the individual level.

As in the past, women are still food providers, whereas men have been able to escape their economic role. The dominant discourse of women as social minors survived but the ideology of the male breadwinner did not materialize, resulting in diverging interests of men and women, instead of political and economic interdependency between women and men, as in the past. Due to the introduction of wage labor, men no longer need women as food providers to the same extent. Hence, changes at the symbolic level and in both the reproductive and productive sphere have had their own dynamic, but they have also had mutual reinforcing effects, which have produced the category of female-headed households over a period of 100 years (van Driel, 1994: 204–220). Thus, a direct link between globalization as a recent phenomenon and the increase in the number of female-headed households seems disputable. And although, according to research such as that carried out in Botswana, the number of female-headed households seems to be increasing in certain regions, caution is needed with the interpretation of the data (see also Chant, 1997:69–87).

A second important conclusion is that female-headed households are not poor by definition and that poverty in economic terms is not necessarily reflected in social-cultural and psychological terms. An independent position might be preferred or even chosen. In other words, many subject positions are possible in which the meaning of women as the head of a household can fluctuate greatly through time. After all, households are not static units, but change with time, willingly and/or unwillingly. A lower income may even be preferred over a position of dependence and domination.

The research in Botswana has for example shown that female-headed households can be an expression of self-determination; that women can choose a position as a female head. The research also showed that female support networks could be much more important, also in economic terms, both in female-headed and male-headed households. These gender aspects do not however occur in the poverty angle, which is concerned with the economic positions of households, income, and access to resources. Not a trace can then be found of the above-mentioned dimensions of gender. Gender is considered to be one-dimensional, almost an economic calculation.

The Production of a Global Discourse

Within the discussion on feminization of poverty a process of exclusion takes place; only economics seem to matter, quantified and objectified. The reproduction of simplifications, especially concerning the feminization of poverty therefore leads to certain clichés that are untrue. This is Marcoux's response to the assumed progress of the feminization of poverty. The author states that no scientific study documents the oft-repeated statement that 70 percent of the world's poor are women. The author calculates that if adequate data were available, the average proportion of women among the poor would be lower than 55 percent. Moreover, although women-headed households do seem more vulnerable to poverty than men-headed households, when comparable data are available, the actual difference in poverty incidence is not very great. However, he states that the gender bias in poverty seems to be real and growing, although very unequally across countries and places (Marcoux, 1997:1–8).

Baden and Goetz (1998:23–24) even refer to "Lies, Damned Lies and Gender Statistics": when it concerns the feminization of poverty and female-headed households. A UN employee stated this under the *assumption* that was what gender imbalance looked like Jackson (1998) analyses how women are made into the instrument of the fight against poverty on the basis of such clichés, both nationally and internationally. This means that policy maker and scientists unthinkingly adopt statements on the feminization of poverty in that they are being reproduced and are thereby given credence that is no long based on reality.

What is more problematic than this one-dimensional concept of gender in the long run is that the space to act is vanishing. The empowerment of women, which is the concern in most cases, is hereby made into a meaningless slogan. After all, the processes on a macro-level that are said to lead to the feminization of poverty should be reversed and women have no power over that; on the contrary, they are victims of it. An envisaged gender policy is hereby replaced by an anti-poverty policy. The New Poverty Agenda of such multilateral oranizations as the World Bank and the UN are also no longer concerned with gender out with how the lives of poor people can be improved in a sustainable way.

This is an implicit reproduction of the ideal of the male breadwinner principle and it is solidified into a cultural text, even in scientific work. The household with the breadwinner father and the domestic and caring mother is the norm. The fact that education and care also labor is thereby moved into the background (cf. Pearson, 1998: 178). Female-headed households are not compared to male-headed households in which the male-head does not have a partner and takes on the educational and caring tasks. By not questioning this norm it is logical that the thought that female-headed households are not always poor by definition but that they are at a greater risk of being poor takes hold.

Gender is reduced to a problem of poverty within the debate on the feminization of poverty. This also means that the unbalanced position of woman is made into a problem of poverty and that gender disappears out of the back door (cf. Jackson, 1998). The question here is what is the main script, but the sub-scripts should also be taken into account, the scripts that are about to be crushed by the force of the main scripts. We would here refer to the above-mentioned argument on the socio-cultural and psychological significance of these households and the implicit norm of the male-headed households. The economic main script not only dwarfs the gender subscript, but even makes it vanish.

Two processes of exclusion take place here. First, the exclusion of gender analyses, which are now apparently unimportant in the fight against poverty. The questions of whether these households are poorer and what the causes of this poverty could be are only addressed in economic terms. As a result, an exclusion of women as acting subjects with their own identifies and concerns takes place. Thus the structural and individual dimension of gender falls from view. The definition of female-headed households, produced on a symbolic level, is said to be found in practice; in other words, practice is here being adapted to the symbolic dimension. It then depends on the chosen analytical perspective to which degree women in a specific local and historical context, as in Botswana, relate to this globally produced definition of female-headed households.

What is implied above is that a process of inclusion and exclusion not only takes place on an empirical level but also on the level of production of knowledge. In connecting female-headed households in a linear way to the feminization of poverty and by characterizing the latter as a result of globalization and as a global phenomenon, a semi-global scientific discourse is presented. The result of this global discourse is that female-headed households are defined as poor and thereby as a problem. The infinite diversity of reasons for this fact thereby disappear from sight, while at the same time the demand for the meaning of those households for women themselves also disappears. Female-headed households appear as an objective category of households in which the subject positions of the female head vanishes completely as does the socio-cultural and psychological meaning that their status has for them personally.

This is complicated even further when we have to look simultaneously at the global processes on the one hand and the local processes on the other. Within the debate on the feminization of poverty two processes are unthinkingly reduced to a global phenomenon. When this happens, the global phenomenon only has meaning in terms of a linear way of modernization thinking.

In that sense the debate on the feminization of poverty seems to fall in line with the above mentioned theoretical positions in which globalization is seen as a homogenizing process. Women who are at the head of a household are thrown together and reduced to a poverty problem and thereby appear as a category on a global level. But, what has happened with women as vocal subjects? In the above approach to the feminization of poverty women seem to have lost their capacity to politicize their interests. An approach that considers women as vocal subjects needs a different angle towards differences and dichotomies. This is further elaborated below.

Research into the way in which women attempt to politicize

their interests will, we consider, require diverse dimensions. These diverse dimensions will be discussed by taking one of our researches into women and political representation in Mexico as an example (Davids forthcoming). In order to fall in line with international democratic principles and global discourses on the empowerment of women, a local process of attribution of meaning takes place and will be deconstructed in the example. This deconstruction highlights that the meaning of motherhood is essentialized to such an extent that the ideal of private motherhood is extended to the public political arena (see also Willemse, forthcoming). From this example it can be concluded that ideas and meanings surrounding motherhood in the Mexican national political context often figure as subtexts in political discourses. Symbolically the image of *La Virgen de Guadalupe* serves as an archetype for motherhood and femininity. Even though the meaning given to this symbol, being a suffering and self-sacrificing mother, is comprehensible all across Mexico different meanings of this symbol of motherhood are articulated differently in the various (party) political discourses. When we look at the structural institutional dimension we, for example, recognize to a dominant image of the woman as mother within the right-wing liberal discourse, whereas this image not only has a different meaning within left-wing discourses, but is also articulated with the image of the woman as feminist.

For all of these discourses the definitions of feminity mark the boundaries of 'the accepted' and the matter-of-fact assumptions with reference to feminity on the basis of which women can enter into the political arena. The constructed definitions are then ultimately linked to inclusion and exclusion mechanisms. Within the rightwing liberal discourse for example being a woman is essentialized into motherhood in a symbolic dimension, and made into *the* difference between man and woman. According to this interpretation women are mothers first and foremost. This idea is elaborated below using an example of how this discourse on femininity is shaped within the righting liberal opposition party, the Partido Action National (PAN).

In their political program women are not explicitly mentioned:

it is much more the family and a woman's role within the family that PAN addresses in its program pamphlets. PAN promotes itself as the party that guarantees change. It promotes a new nationalism according to a more modern and civilized society. It depicts itself as a movement against governmental corruption and a protector of civil rights. The family is looked upon as a breeding-place for moral principles setting the guidelines for the public conduct of civilians. In this way PAN presents its politics, the political always being presented as close to the private, to the personal and domestic sphere. This results in a sharp contrast with the ruling party Partido Revolutionario Institutional (PRI), where the personal life is displaced by public issues (Barrera, 1993:89, Massola, 1993, Venegas, 1993).

To what extent modern and political meanings can be given to the role of the woman as mother depends on the space that each woman is able to create besides motherhood, and without losing the essential function of the mother. Actions by women in the public and political arena are thus justified from the position of women as mothers. Women are expected to be able to combine a professional and a political career with the essence of their womanhood, that is motherhood. In the literature on Latin America the extrapolation of motherhood from the private sphere to the public sphere is described as the production of the symbol of *supermadres*. This clarifies within a symbolic dimension how women are' 'othered.'

One could expect such as discourse in reality to be exclusive rather than inclusive for women who aspire to a political career. In practice women are better represented in a right-wing liberal opposition party such as PAN than they are in other parties, especially when looking at high positions. This could be for several reasons that are related to different dimensions of gender. Through a symbolic dimension it is clear that a moral, political, and gender discourse come together here. Within the right-wing liberal political discourse these values of femininity are again articulated with a certain morality that is especially formulated in opposition to the governmental party, the PRI. Women ore seen as morally purer than men and therefore less capable of corruption because of the values connected with motherhood and on the basis of their symbolic motherhood, as it were. It is especially important to emphasize this for the members of PAN who like to portray themselves as morally pure in contrast with the corrupt members of the PRI.

Another aspect is the space this discourse offers for connecting this image of motherhood with modern meanings, such as professionality and international democratic principles, like a balanced political participation by women, which was briefly touched upon before. This is possible by being a *supermadre*. When we focus on the institutional structural dimension it becomes clear that the opportunities for women to realize this ideal of the *supermadre* is very different for women of different classes and backgrounds. Within an institutional structural dimension it becomes clear that many of the women that are active at a high level within PAN are able to do this because they are part of an elite, highly educated and financially capable of combining a professional career with the role of motherhood. This therefore constitutes an elite discourse, in a manner of speaking.

However, this does not mean that all women that are active within PAN are mothers or that they use being a mother as a strategy to be a respectable woman as well as a politician. In an individual subject dimension it is possible to identify the different strategies that women develop to create this space for themselves. This is concerned with the way in which women secure a position within this discourse. For example, one of PAN's most successful female members of parliament was not a mother but a single woman who lived alone while she was in office. This is a slightly unusual pattern for Mexico where most women marry from home, even if they have a university degree. Nonetheless the woman was able to develop rhetorical strategies in which she identified with this ideal of the *supermadre*. In her strategy she was able to elevate motherhood to moral motherhood. On that basis she was able to justify her own position within politics and to give her presence as a woman politics meaning.

Women are therefore not the victims of such a discourse, but are a part of it. This also refers to the dynamics that signifies those discourses. Women are forced to relate to the symbolic dimensions. In that capacity they are forced to negotiate the dominant discourse and in doing so they slightly change its meaning. It is in the dynamics of the interaction between the different dimensions of gender that the possibilities of change lie. The opportunity to determine one's own gender identity critically and creatively also lies therein. When we look at the political participation of Mexican women and of Latin American women in general, from a historical perspective we notice that women at various points in time have given professional and modern meanings to motherhood in various different ways.

Dimension of Inclusion and Exclusion

The discourse on motherhood does not always have to have a repressive or exclusive effect on different groups of women. Women in different Latin American contexts have been able to capitalize, within a gender and moral discourse, on an ideal of motherhood as the original domain of the home and the family. One of the best-known examples from a critical political discourse point of view is that of the mothers of the Plaza de Mayo in Argentina.

What is noteworthy in this case is that motherhood is made essential as it is in many such discourses. This mostly happens in the more politically fundamental discourses. this is not unique to Mexico or Latin America; in Nazi Germany and Nazi Italy this making feminity essential in the role of the mother was also put forward. De Ras (1984) also writes on how the image of Mary as a mother figure was part of the creation of a political fundamentalist movement in Germany at the bringing of the 20th century. Gender is often utilized in these cases as a boundary marker for an ethnic or national identity.

The interesting question is then whether this discourse is comparable as a symbolic dimension to other discourses in which a reaction of closure, of shielding the national, ethnic, or other identity from globalization can be observed. We may then ask ourselves whether such discourses lead to the same strategies on a local level. The conclusion that women may actually be excluded on the basis of this discourse is not one that should be drawn easily; as the example from Mexico shows, some women might be and some might not. Ambiguous meanings are articulated simultaneously within discourses, even when a discourse at first sight seems to exclude women. Globalization then emerges as a struggle for attributing meaning, which may have an entirely different content on a global or a local level. In terms of flow and closure gender can be deployed both globally and locally as a demarcation of a boundary; it is a marking point, as the example of motherhood and women in politics in Mexico shows. Gender then becomes a global and local ingredient of the construction of meaning.

It is important to ascertain how global such discourses are as far as the context and the symbols therein are concerned. How does feminity figure in such discourses? Which contexts are being referred to and which global scale is meant? These questions arise especially when globalization and that which is accredited to globalization, is reconstructed analogously to the concept of gender.

What does this mean for our future research, for the way in which we want to handle the questions on globalization and gender? For our research into 'engendering civil society in a globalization world' it means that we analyze the processes of change in a reconstructive manner. Globalization is then seen not as an 'out there' process, but as a struggle for attributing meaning that manifests itself on a local and global level. This 'global' aspect can be viewed only from a local context, whether this context envelops a national context, or a village, or family. (Our insights with regard to the relation between global and local in relation to the multidimensionality of gender have been sharpened significantly through our discussions with Karin Willemse, for which we extend our gratitude.)

The complication with the concept of globalization is that it does and does not exist. It is both virtual and real. The process globalization can only have meaning and in that sense become real in a certain geographically and historically specific context. As King (1991) also indicates it demarcates a boundary in our thinking' in the sense that the question from which (local) context the global is given meaning must always be asked. In other words, the question "whose global process is meant?" Always needs to be asked because this process always takes place within certain constellations of power. As has become clear from the last paragraphs it is more than even necessary to realize that knowledge must be considered as situated knowledge in discussions on globalization.

Because it was also stated at the start of the article that global is not synonymous with universal it cannot be assumed that there is such a thing as a global phenomenon that has the same meaning everywhere in a local context. As far as the global context is to be seen, it is not homogeneous or universal. There is not just one global context which has the same meaning for all those involved, even if it does cross national boundaries. This meaning is always rooted in national and local history. Where a global context in Mexico is the result of a history of Spanish rule and North-American dominance, this context is more likely to be one of British rule and South-African dominance in the case of Botswana.

In order to gain an insight into the multidimensionality of the so-called global, gender as a multidimensional concept is a useful analytical tool. It is through continued contextualization similar to the multidimensionality of gender that the global and the local are no longer two dichotomous positions, but are inextricably connected. The local remains crucial in the analysis of global processes, but has less of a static meaning. On a local level it not only concerns matters that are linked to a specific time and place, but in the local discourse the global discourse, especially, obtains its own meaning. This meaning is subject to constant change and leads to different realities.

To be able to analyze the floating dynamic of these processes a different way of thinking about sciences differences is necessary. The analytical gender model not only supplies us with ways to connect the global with the local, but also helps us gain an insight into the production of differences. The production of differences indicates how insight into the way in which boundaries are marked is crucial in processes of inclusion and exclusion. This means that one must not only think in terms of global flow and local closure. Flow and closure take place simultaneously on a local as well as a global level. This opens up diffent perspectives for the scientific debate on gender and globalization. In this chapter, we have attempted to show that the debate on globalization and gender has several pitfals that can be exposed using the multidimensionality of gender. Furthermore, we hope to have clarified how these pitfalls can be avoided using multidimensionality of gender.

In this chapter the power of attributing meaning is central in the discussions on gender and globalization. This power of attributing meaning is not limited to the theme of gender. In the debate on globalization, which was discussed in the first part of this chapter, when we refer to the taxonomy of Schuurman we actually come across the power struggle for attributing meanings. The same questions can be asked with reference to the positions mentioned in the taxonomy that were asked in reference to gender and globalization. We would therefore like to use this chapter to stimulate the discussion on the wider applicability of the analytically multidimensional gender concept as a pattern of thought and inspiration for the debate on globalization.

REFERENCES

Alexander, Jeffrey C. (1994), "Modern, Anti, Post and Neo: How Social Theories Have tried to understand the 'New World' of "Our Time,"" *Zeitschrift für Soziologie*, 23 (3), pp. 165–97.

Anderson, B. (1983), *Imagined Communities: Reflections on the Origin and Spread of Nationalism*, London, Verso.

Appadurai, Arjun, (1999), "Disjuncture and Difference in the Gloal Cultural Economy." In: Featherstone, Mike (ed). *Global Culture: Nationalism, Globalization and Modernity*, London, Sage, pp. 295–310.

Appadurai, Arjun (1996), *Modernity at Large: Cutural Dimensions of Globalization*, Minneapolis, University of Minnesota Press.

Braidotti, R. (1994). *Nomadic Subjects. Embodiment and Sexual Difference in Contemporary Feminist Thought*, New York Columbia University Press.

Chant, Sylvia (1997), *Women-Headed Households: Diversity and Dynamics in the Developing World*, London, MacMillan.

Chuchryk, P. (1994), "From dictatorship to democracy: the women's movement in Chile." In: J. Jaquette (ed.), *The women's Movement in Latin Americal: participation and Democray*. Boulder, CO: Westeviewer Press, pp. 65–108.

Davids, Tine and Driel, Francien van (1999), "Van vrouwenstrijd wereldwijd naar meerstemmigheid en diversiteit." In: Hoebink, Paul Haude, Detlev, and Velden, Fons van der (eds) *Doorlopers en breuklijinen: van globalisering, emancipatie en verzet,* Assen, van Gorkum, pp. 406–420.

Davids, Tine, and Willemse, Karin (1993), "Inleiding themanummer In het lichaam gegrift; feministische antropologenop opgrens van kennisoverdracht en representatie." *Tijdschrift voor Genderstudies*, Jrg, 2, no. 1, maart, pp. 3–14.

Davids, Tine (Forthcoming), *From Marias to Machas: Gender, Images and Political Representation in Mexico*, PH.D. Dissertation.

Driel, Francien van (1997), *Global Economic Developments and Changing Local Family/household Compositions*. Paper presented at the workshop Globalization and Development Studies, Nijmegen, 30 October—1 November, 1997.

Driel, Francien van, and Deuss, Marleen 1997), "Met vrouwen een andere ontwikkeling? Theorieen, strategieen en verschuivingen in debatten." In: Lieten, Krittoffel and Velden, Fons van der, *Grenzen aan de Hulp, Beleid en effecten van ontwikkelingssamenwerking,* Amesterdam, het Spinhuis, pp. 163–189.

Geschiere, Peter, and Meyer, Birgit (1998), "Globalization and Identity: Dialectics of Flows and Closures, Introduction, Development and Change," 29 (4), pp. 601–615.

Ghorashi, Halleh (forthcoming), *The Ways to Survive the Battles to Win: Iranian Women Political Activists in Exile*, Ph.D. Dissertation.

Hannerz, U. (1987), The World in Creolization.' *Africa, 57* (4), pp. 546–559.

Harding, Sandra (1986), *The Science Question in Feminism*, London, Cornell University Press.

Jackson, Cecile (1998), "Rescuing Gender from the Poverty Trap." In: Jackson, Cecile, and Parson, Ruth (eds) *Feminist Visions of Development, Gender Analysis and Policy*, London, Routledge, pp. 39–64.

King, Anthony D. (1991), "Spaces of Culture, Spaces of Knowledge, Introduction," In: King, A.D. (ed.) *Culture, Globalization and the World-System*, London, MacMillan, pp. 1–18.

Kirkwood, J. (1986), *Ser Pollitica en Chile*, las Feministas *y los Partidos*. Santiago de Chile: FLASCO.

Lareg. Marnia (1988), "Feminism and Difference: The Perils of Writing as a Woman on Women in Algeria." In: *Feminist Issues*, vol. 14, no. 1, pp. 81–107.

Mencher, Joan P. and Okongwu, Anne (1993), *Where Did All the Men Go? Female Headed/Female Supported Households in Cross-Cultural Perspective*, Boulder, Colorado, Westview Press.

Mohanty, Chandra Taipade (1991), 'Under Western Eyes: Feminist Scholarship and Colonial Discourses." In Mohanty, Chandra Taipade, Russo, Ann, and Torres, Lourdes, *Third World Women and the Politics of Feminism*, Bloomington, Indiana University Press, pp. 51–80.

Moore, Henrietta (1994), *Is There a Crisis in the Family*? United Nations Research Institute for Social Development (UNRISD), Geneva.

Pearson, Ruth, and Jackson, Cecile (1998), "Interrogating Developmnt: Feminism, Gender and Policy, Introduction", In: Jackson, Cecile, and Pearson, Ruth (eds) *Feminist Visions of Development: Gender Analysis and Development*, London, Routledge, pp. 1–16.

Peterson, V. Spike (1996), "The Politics of Identification in the Context of Globalization. In: Women's Studies International Forum," vol. 19, nos 1/2, 1996, pp. 5–15.

Rogers, Beatrice Lorge (1995), 'Alternative Definitions of Female Headship in the Dominican Republic.' *World Development*, vol. 23, no. 12, pp. 2033–2039.

Said, E.W. (1978), *Orientalism*, New York,Vintage Books.

Schuurman, Frans (1997), *Emancipatory Spaces in the Global Era*, Paper presented at the workshop Globalisation and Development Studies, Nijmegen, 30 October, 1 November, 1997.

Scott, Joan Wallace (1989), "De constructie van gelijkheid versus verschil. De bruikbaarheid van de poststructuralistische theorie voor het feminime." In: *Tiende jarrboek voor de vrouwengeschiedenis*, Nijmegen, SUN, pp. 96–112.

Sen, A. (1990), "Gender and Co-operative Conflicts." In: I. Tinker (ed) *Persistent Inequalities: Women and World Development*, New York, Oxford, Oxford University Press, pp. 123–149.

Sen, Gita (1997), 'Globalization, Justice and Equity: A Gender Perspective.' *Development,* vol. 40, no. 2, pp. 21–26.

Third World Centre (1999), *Research Programme 1998-2003, Globalisation, Governance and Development: Actors and Structures in Processes of Inclusion and Exclusion*, University of Nijmegen, 12 February.

Tonkens, Evelien (1998), "Gender in welke lagen? Kanttekeningen bij de gelaagde genderconcepten van Scott, Harding en Hagemann-White en hun toepassing in empirisch onderzoek." *Tijdschrift voor Genderstudies*, jrg. 1, no. 1, pp. 42–49.

Venagas Aguilera, L. (1994), Mujeres en la militancia blanquiazul. In: Massolo, A. (ed), *Los Medios y los Modos Paticipation Politica y accion colectiva de las mujeres*, Mexico D.F., El Clegio de Mexcio, pp. 45–78.

Villarreal, Magdalena (1994), *Wielding and Yielding: Power, Subordination and Gender Identity in the Context of a Mexican Development Project*, Wageningen, Ph.D. dissertation.

CHAPTER 4

Challenge to the Global Community Poverty and Rural Development

The World Summit on Sustainable Development (WSSD), Governments, U.N. institutions and development agencies are focussing on economic well-being by targeting poverty alleviation as the overriding concern to achieving sustainable development. This is both welcome and necessary, and the WSSD presents an opportunity to embed this firmly in the sustainable development agenda. However, the other two pillars of the sustainable development agenda also must be strengthened in the process. The World Summit on Sustainable Development is an important occasion for the world community to assess progress in addressing sustainable development and to agree priority issues for the future. Ten years ago, the U.N. Conference on Environment and Development (UNCED) called for sustainable development *"to ensure socially responsible economic development while protecting the resource base and the environment for the benefit of future generations"*. It is widely recognised that economic well-being, social development, and environmental stability must be addressed together if development is to be sustainable.

The drive to alleviate poverty brings with it the caveat that social development and environmental stability must be included as essential elements. This challenge is being issued by organisations which work within the sustainable development arena and is based on their practical experience. It is an appeal to build on previous analyses and conclusions, not least in the report of the Brundtland Commission but also in the considerable preparations to UNCED. Sufficient technical knowledge exists to implement sustainable development. Political will and appropriate incentives are now required to convert the ideals of sustainable development into practical action. As we move into the 21st century, human institutions, from local to global, are facing many economic, social and environmental challenges. Sustainable development is that which is economically viable, socially acceptable and environmentally sound. Development is not sustainable if it does not integrate all three elements. It implies long term synergy through changes in business practices and lifestyles, as well as the adoption of environmental and social standards to stay within the limits of available resources.

Economic Well-being and Poverty

The world is experiencing extremely rapid economic change, including powerful trends towards the use of market forces and market-based policies throughout the world; global economic integration driven by trade liberalisation; and increased economic interdependence among nation states and reductions in national economic sovereignty. At the same time, the disparity between rich and poor continues to grow, both within countries and between them. Pressures to develop and achieve economic well-being through a primary focus on financial, human and physical capital is driving short-term unsustainable exploitation of the natural resource base and eroding social capitical. This is occurring more rapidly and over larger areas than ever before.

Such resource exploitation, while providing immediate benefits to some, imposes both short-and long-term costs on many others. These "others" are often the poorest of the poor, who depend heavily on natural resource use and the maintenance of biological diversity. As a result, poverty reduction strategies are undermined by the breakdown of the social fabric and the loss of the environmental services upon which all life depends.

Social Development

Many countries are struggling with the strains of poverty, rapid population growth and migration, the replacement of a subsistence by a market economy, and massive environmental impacts. In many developing countries faced with a rapid decline of traditional value-systems, a major challenge is the need to enlarge, strengthen, and empower a stable civil society that will build the trust and public self-confidence which enables participatory governance. Democratic, culturally diverse, and socially inclusive societies are essential parts of modern sustainable development. High worldwide military expenditure is continuing to affect sustainable development. New instabilities, often linked to inter-ethnic tensions and the demand for the subdivision of existing states, are emerging. This situation has manifested itself in a large number of armed conflicts which current international mechanisms are unable to resolve. At the same time, social cohesion is declining in many societies. Societal and cultural dislocation, fuelled by globalisation of communications, is endangering the existence of many smal! cultures—especially those of indigenous peoples. One result is a decline in the sense of community, leading to social unrest and a weakening of environmental responsibility.

Environmental Stability

Environmentally, it is clear that much of our industrial, agricultural and other uses of renewable and non-renewable natural resources are unsustainable. It has been widely acknowledged, both during UNCED and subsequently by bodies such as the World Bank and the OECD Development Assistance Committee, that the current trends in environmental degradation are a major threat to the achievement of sustainable development. The on-going loss of biodiversity; decline of forest, freshwater, marine and soil resources; changing climate; loss of stratospheric ozone; and accumulation of toxic substances in soil, water, and living organisms, are all threats to the environmental goods and services upon which all human life depends for food, fodder crop production, and innumerable other goods and services. It is usually the rural poor who are the first to suffer when these systems fail, but not even the most insulated of city dwellers in the industrialised countries are immune from these effects. Poverty is often associated with degraded rural environments. Environmental degradation has many consequences, because a healthy natural environment sustains non-monetary economies and can be viewed as the "social security" of the rural populations. When the productive functions of healthy rural environments degrade or when people lose access to those productive environments, movement to cities in search of alternative livelihoods can excerbate urban poverty. Environmental degradation therefore undermines sustainable livelihoods and affects the rural poor by disproportionately affecting their health, livelihoods and security, and can aggravate poverty in already stressed urban environments.

A sound environment alone will not alleviate poverty, but attempts at poverty alleviation in isolation of the environment will sooner or later be undermined. It is evident today that the costs of past environmental mistakes are being borne by the current economy. Recent data have shown that natural disasters, exacerbated by the mismanagement of natural systems, have the greatest human impact on the poorest countries.

While governments are now well aware of the three pillars of sustainable development, the market economy has taken priority over social development and environmental concerns in recent decades. In many parts of the world, global economic integration has led to social and cultural fragmentation. Changes in land ownership and resource tenure, changes in agricultural policies, declines in government services, and economic disruptions all have a disproportionate impact on the poor. As old political systems are replaced by new democracies, and as economies are decentralised, social tensions are leading to a desire to build a sense of community through local sovereignty and separatist groups of various kinds. Perhaps the most disturbing form of interconnectedness is that linking environmental degradation, economic development, population growth, refugee movements, and violent conflict. It is clear that weakening in any one of the pillars leads to problems in the others. Addressing any of the pillars in isolation, without considering their interactive effects, can give rise to unanticipated consequences. For example, raising energy prices significantly to reduce energy emissions may disproportionately affect the urban poor, who often spend a greater proportion of their income on energy, thus increasing income disparities. And agricultural subsidies in food-surplus countries may ironically undermine food production by the rural poor, who are forced to sell their crops at an unrealistically low price. Such inequities contribute to social unsustainability, which may in turn be reflected in decreasing ability to design and implement sound environmental, economic and social policy. The end result is a failure of governance.

The Responsibility of WSSD

The WSSD presents an opportunity for the global community to re-affirm and strengthen the global view that sustainable development is the only option for a viable future. Sustainable development builds on the following principles:

- Effective actions must *deal with the causes and not only the consequences of poverty;*
- Poverty reduction, social equity and environmental security are mutually reinforcing;
- Environmental degradation has real economic and social costs that undermine long-term local, national and global sustainability;
- Access to information is an issue of economic, social, and environmental equity;
- Development-oriented research is essential to adapting to changing conditions;
- Mainstreaming sustainable development promotes a convergence of agendas at global, national, and local levels, so it must be addressed as a cross-sectoral goal;
- Cultural diversity helps communities adapt to locally-available resources. Effective linking of economic well-being, social development and environmental stability requires a good understanding of the state of the natural

resource base in a given area, the positive and negative pressures affecting that state, and the responses that society can bring to bear to reduce negative pressures and increase positive ones. Success in this quest for sustainability requires the joint efforts of three sectors:

1. National and local governments, supported by international instruments that provide standards, incentives, and regulations;
2. The private sector, whose new freedoms resulting from globalisation place the responsibility of informed stewardship squarely on their operations;
3. Civil society, whose pressure and support can ensure that the public interest is being well served.

The challenge ahe ad lies in enabling these three to work harmoniously together, each providing checks and balances on the others and recognising their muturally supporting roles in achieving sustainable development.

Toward Sustainable Agriculture

Efforts to tackle the twin blights of environmental destruction and inequitable and unjust distribution of assets should be restructured. They should be undertaken not by any one institution, but should be the result of multiple complementary changes that together can create just and sustainable rural communities. The stimulation of many rural centres of action interacting with the State and market will create the synergies necessary to fundamentally restructure rural development. *The Quality of Life in Rural Asia* (Bloom *et al.* 1999) proposes useful and practical recommendations for the promotion of sustainable development. The analysis and recommendations made here only complement them.

Whatever technological and natural limitations may constrain development in a particular area, change is vitally dependent on social relations. Change will inevitably cause conflict and shifts in the power positions of rural actors. Sustainable development requires altering social relations and recognising the intensely political nature of environmental change and poverty. It transcends economics because economics has failed to recognise the fundamental processes of nature, the commodification of nature, social struggles to claim rights over nature, externalities arising from the exploitation of nature and labour and the depreciation of nature by such exploitation. Only by recognising politics as a legitimate arena of discussion is it possible to effect positive and sustainable change.

Sustainable agriculture does not require merely curbing the more egregious excesses of high-input industrial agriculture controlled by marketing and input-supply cartels. It also requires scrapping the system itself and moving in a revolutionary direction toward a holistic or systems approach to agriculture.

Systems thinking revolves around social relations and nature. It seeks to affirm the power of a mobilised society and to establish a new, healthier balance among State, market, and society. Catalytic local institutions play an important role in creating the new balance, as does the revitalisation of democracy at all levels. Part of the process is recognition of human and political rights for all and of the cardinal importance of access to resources, especially land, to people's self-empowerment.

Rural Regeneration

Rural regeneration involves two major themes:

- Mobilisation of self-help and self-conscientised groups of the disadvantaged ("powerless") to improve their lot and their stake in nature's and society's healing; and
- The prime importance of access to resources by the powerless and the recognition that access is the poor's most important resource.

These elements of the natural and human environments are added to the figure to emphasise that each and every situation is unique and that attempts to generalise across the globe, continent or a nation state are doomed to failure. Cultures are astoundingly diverse. Social relations are a product of historical patterns that may share some characteristics from place to place but must be unique to any specific location. Similarly, nature represents a set of diverse ecosystems that have evolved and been impacted in many different ways. On this context is overlaid the most important institutional elements of rural society. It is these institutional elements that need regeneration for the achievement of sustainable rural societies. These institutional elements are represented by rectangles and the numbers in the rectangles represent the rural regeneration aspects outlined here.

Sustainable agriculture implies new ways of approaching rural development. It is not so much a criticism of past approaches as a recognition of the shortcomings of narrowly focused technocratic solutions. For convenience of discussion, it is suggested that rural regeneration toward sustainable agricultural and rural development has at least 12 aspects. Further work on the policy implications of this approach to sustainable agriculture in any particular situation will surely change the aspects somewhat and lead to new priorities. The 12 aspects are the following:

1. self-help mobilisation and the creation of many loci of action in rural areas;
2. improved governance and support to catalytic community organisations;
3. constant affirmation of political and human rights, which involves struggle and conflict;
4. constant vigilance and government intervention to correct market imperfections;
5. political mobilisation of the disempowered to target public services more precisely;
6. provision of access to land to reduce poverty and promote equity;
7. making common property resource management a focus of policy dialogue and not merely an academic sideline;
8. recognition of water management and allocation and, especially, irrigation management as key to sustainable

use of water resources;

9. targeting financial services in less-favoured agricultural areas;
10. forming cooperatives, which is essential to reinvigorating smallholder agriculture and creating off-farm employment;
11. State support for appropriate R&D and extension services aimed at less-favoured agricultural lands, smallholders, women, and sustainable agricultural practices; and
12. employment guarantee schemes to reduce vulnerability.

First Aspect

Encouraging and supporting the formation of local people's organisations that will study, analyse, and mobilise local resources. The people's organisations must share interests but not be predicated on the assumption of a homogeneous "community" of shared interests. They are bound to clash with local elites over access to and use of local resources. They must therefore pay careful attention to dispute resolution that recognises asymmetries of power and strives for equity and justice in outcomes.

Water-users groups, forest-users' groups, production and service cooperatives, micro-credit borrowing groups, landless water sellers, and equipment and work-sharing groups, among others, are already active in many countries' attempts to mobilise farmers for livelihood improvement. They have encountered many difficulties, perhaps the most serious of which has been their takeover by the elite and powerful who use them to obtain susbsidised inputs, retain control over resources such as irrigation water or timber, maintain coercive social relations, or head off organising by the poor. Fortunately, many groups have managed to remain cohesive, operate efficiently and effectively and build the power of the poor, women, and other socially excluded groups. Sometimes organisations benefit the communities as a whole, especially those that are more homogeneous, less faction ridden, less stratified, under less pressure from outside market or State forces, and have rural classes with common interests.

The catalytic organisations, goal is to create many loci of action throughout rural areas. They will sometimes oppose and sometimes support. State interventions, but they will always seek to mobilise local creative energies expressed as ideas, traditional knowledge, labour, savings, locally available resources, and aesthetic sensibilities. Their efforts are motivated by the belief that it is necessary to wean people from the idea that the State can and will solve problems of poverty, environmental destruction, social dislocation, and social exclusion. Many of these problems can be solved only by strong local action supported by the State. Local organisations and the State cannot work in isolation (Rahman 1993; White 1999; Chambers 1997; Beck 1995; Hazell *et. al.* 2000).

Second Aspect

Encouraging and supporting government decentralisation that is financially and technically meaningful, as well as responsive to public pressure. Catalytic institutions such as people's organisations, user groups, NGOs, and cooperatives flourish in the fertile and sustaining soil of democracy, which respects human and political rights, has high standards of government accountability and transparency, and listens to and responds to the pleas of the powerless. Decentralisation does not mean divesting higher levels of government of responsibilities that are rightfully theirs, but rather devolving responsibilities and powers to the appropriate level for efficiency and effectiveness. Environmental regulations, for example, will remain the responsibility of non-local authorities, but monitoring and sometimes enforcement can be delegated to accountable local authorities. *Reducing Poverty—Findings and Implications* reveals that decentralisation of authorities and resources to the local level, which weakened governance, has increased poverty. Therefore, such decentralisation must be accompanied or, preferably, preceded by establishment of good governance and capacity building.

A key element of this aspect is fostering public participation, which is seen as public accountability as well as recognition of public knowledge and its worth. Agricultural knowledge, for example, has too often been assumed to be the exclusive realm of the outside expert. More and more, however, it is recognised that sustainable agriculture requires a process of mutual learning between the farmer and the expert and that both can contribute to finding new and better ways to attain sustainability.

Third Aspect

Recognising and exercising political and human rights, including the right to have access to the legal system. The State and its citizens must also recognise indigenous systems of land use and tenure and of resource management. Above all, women's rights to land, inheritance, freedom from violence, equal pay for equal work, inclusion in project decision making and benefit sharing, and provision of public goods such as health care and education must be enshrined in the legal code and practice.

On one level, the issue is access to resources and exclusion of women and other groups from rights to such access. Barriers to equal access to land, credit, extension, education, and health care need to be removed. At a more profound level, however, is the recognition that women's exclusion from resource access stems from inherent structural and institutional discrimination. Change at this level requires mobilisation, organisation, collective action, and increased political representation of women or other socially excluded groups. Legal rights enable such positive change to happen.

Fourth Aspect

Making markets more efficient in allocating resources. Doing so requires three principal changes in government regulatory and fiscal politics:

- Eliminate subsidy distortion of prices, as they nearly always harm the environment and discriminate against the less powerful. Price distortions are caused by implicit or explicit subsidies on fertiliser, fuel, electricity (including that used for irrigation pumping), pesticide, and credit (either through subsidised interest rates or through political tolerance of wide-spread default). Carefully targeted subsidy elements—

such as grants to institutional development and group organising of rural financial institutions—can be non-distoring and non-crowding to competition if correctly designed.

- Incorporate in prices additions that reflect the external costs of use of the commodity. For example, electricity and fuel prices should reflect not only the marginal cost of production and delivery but also the externalities imposed on society and the environment by production and transport.
- Encourage competition and discourage market power. Often, extension agents, trades, and chemical companies work hand in hand to promote input-intensive cropping. It is difficult to break that collusion and foster new ways.

Careful analysis of specific situations often offers glaring examples of noncompetitive practices, especially in the marketing of agricultural commodities, where small farmers lack access to information. Formation of cooperative associations is one answer to this problem.

Fifth Aspect

Targeting the needs of environmental sustainability, women, the poor, a and the socially excluded through agricultural extension, agricultural research and development (R&D), primary-school education, adult literacy training, other non-formal education, user-group formation local government strengthening, infrastructure investments, and rural development projects in general. This aspect requires an informed and organised citizenry and a responsive government, especially at the local level.

The Concept of Rural Development

Rural development means improving the living standards of the low income population residing in the rural areas and keeping the process of development self-sustaining. Y.C. James Yen described the ideology of rural development in terms of four goals of rural reconstruction: livelihood, education, health and group activities.

Dr. Ranaan Weitz attributed four characteristics to effective Rural Development Programs. "It is *action-oriented* through the formulation of projects which are adjusted to the conditions prevailing in each particular area. It is co-ordinated in the sense that it co-ordinates policy, investment and manpower programing between the local and the area level on one hand, and the objectives and constraints at the national level, on the other. It is, therefore, a co-ordinated approach from the top down and from bottom up. It is also *comprehensive* in the sense that it takes into account within the rural space all the relevant sectors of the economy and uses the inter-relationship so as to identify and exploit the linkages and the external effects between those sectors, namely agriculture, industry, and services. It should be described as *democratic* in the sense that active local participation is an integral part of this approach." Action, co-ordination, integration and participation are the four pillars of an effective Rural Development Program.

Thus any rural development program should consist of projects to raise agricultural output, create new employment, improve health and education, provide communications, power, improve housing, improve credit delivery systems, train personnel, develop institutions etc. Such a process would call for series of measures-setting of right priorities, mobilization of resources, chalking out a time frame to develop appropriate skills, technology and implementing capacity. But any rural development strategy should reckon the following factors *i.e.*:

(i) Whatever would be the efforts, the persons depending on low productivity agriculture will continue to be there for long time though in relatively smaller numbers.

(ii) As the available resources and technology are limited, any increase in population will further worsen the economic position of rural masses.

(iii) Effective mobilization of labor, land and available capital through appropriate organization is the key to reduce the incidence of poverty.

The first stage is to recognize the importance of integrating a rural development strategy with the overall development strategy for growth and production. As Robert MacNamara noted "It is here that World Development Report comes to its most shocking conclusion: that even if the growth rates projected for developing countries were to be achieved by 1985, which is by no means certain, and even if that growth were to continue for another 15 years, it seems likely that at the end of the century, there would still remain some 600 million individuals trapped in absolute poverty. The only feasible hope of reducing poverty is to assist the poor to become more productive. Each developing society must formulates specific antipoverty objectives at national, regional and local levels, prepare operational programs to attain these objectives over a reasonable time and determine the level of resources required to meet the minimum goals."

Ultimately, any rural development strategy will be judged from the extent of its contribution to reduction of poverty and human misery-characterized by poor nutrition, inadequate shelter, low health standards, poor literacy and limited accessibility to economic infrastructural facilities which numb their potential productivity. In other words, the yardstick is as to how far it has helped to increase the productivity of poor and in providing them with more goods and services.

Productive work opportunities outside the rural sector will not be able to absorb more than a small fraction of the natural increment in the rural population of working age in the coming decades. Most of these people will have to remain in the rural sector, that is to say, in agriculture, rural industries and other services. Intensification of agricultural production could absorb some, but for a majority of the present and potential rural poor, other avenues have to be identified within the rural sector itself. In India, the National Commission on Agriculture estimated that against an expected increase of 111 million people in the total rural labor force by the year 2001, expansion in the various agricultural programs is likely to generate employment for only about 52 million. For more than half the increase in the total rural labor force productive work will have to be found in non-agricultural rural sectors. The solution to this problem apparently lies in two concurrent approaches, one relating to promotion of rural industries and the other to integrating this approach with an overall rural development strategy. Providing more jobs and higher incomes for poorly paid rural workers would be possible only in such activities where (a) the elasticity of substitution between capital and labor is very high (b) wage rates are not fluctuating upwards too rapidly (c) the price elasticity of product demand is high and (d) technical change is rapid so as to increase the efficiency of both capital and labor use.

The traditional crafts, rural industries and the informal sector, with their labor-intensive processes, have better scope for providing work opportunities to large numbers of people, provided they are efficiently organized and supported. As Dennis A. Rondinelli put it, "The key to development clearly must be in the expansion of participation in productive activity, an objective that depends primarily on the ability of governments to accelerate the commercialization of agriculture and to expand employment through promotion of small-scale industries in both rural and urban areas. These two sectors-agriculture and small industry-provide the greatest potential for achieving equitable growth in every Asian Society."

However, there has not been a universally acceptable definition of rural industry. Various terms such as rural-based industry, small-scale rural sector, agro-industry, village industry, cottage industry, decentralized industries, etc. are being used. One study done by Asian Development Bank defined Cottage industries and handicrafts as those employing up to nine persons, small-scale those employing from 10 to 49 persons, medium-scale from 50 to 499 persons and large- scale more than 500 persons. More appropriately, village industry in India connotes an enterprise whose credit needs do not exceed Rs. 25,000. It includes mainly artisans and small industrial activities for manufacturing, processing, preservation and servicing in villages and small towns which mainly use locally available natural resources and human skills. Although rural-based manufacturing activies technically include a wide variety of primary processing industries *i.e.,* agro-processing, agro-inputs industries, rural consumer goods industries, etc. it is from these decentralized village industries than the rural poor earn a living.

Rural industries atrophied in many developing countries, particularly during the colonial period. As Rajni Kothari noted "The chief casualty of the colonial period was a whole range of rural and semi-rural industries and a number of non-agricultural occupations that gave livelihood to large sections of the people and which in fact made for a society that was far less unequal and unjust than is the case now." While it may not be practical to go back to all those occupations, it is certainly possible and necessary to provide a new basis for fulfilling the same economic functions, namely making work available other than farming. Support to self-employed artisans with finer skills and to small-scale rural industries manufacturing goods needed by the local people can provide a strong basis for rural regeneration.

The rural artisans operate on a tiny scale with meager capital, employ simple technology and mostly hereditary family skills, depend on local raw materials and market their outputs in the nearby areas. In India, a survey revealed that 91 percent of small industries had an investment in plant and machinery up to Rs. 0.1 million and that 73 percent of such industries came under the category of village industries. Five main activities *i.e.,* (a) food products, (b) beverages, tobacco and tobacco products, (c) cotton textiles, (d) textile products including clothing, (e) leather and fur products absorbed 69 percent of all those employed in cottage and village industries in India. A world Bank survey covering many countries revealed that within manufacturing most rural employment is accounted for by (a) food processing (b) textiles and clothing (c) wood including saw million, furniture making and general carpentry, (d) metal, including black-smithing, welding, fabrication and the making of tools and equipment.

The problems faced by village industries mainly relate to competition from organized urban industries, limited marketing avenues, non-availability of raw materials and poor credit rating with banks. As these industries are widely dispersed, they cannot organize themselves into affective local organizations to take advantage of scale economies in purchasing raw materials and marketing finished products. Their access to new technology is also very limited. Positive government support can remove many of these constraints. In India, promotion of village industries has been accepted as an important element in the national development policy, and several steps have been initiated to promote them. District Industries Center are expected to provide the needed support to this sector in each district. They investigate the resource potential of the area, supply machinery and equipment, arrange credit from financial bodies, provide help in marketing and undertake research, extension and training. A specialized national body known as Khadi and Village Industries Commission, supported by the Government, provides much needed assistance to these industries. More than all these, in every country the policy makers should express succinctly their basic approach to industrialization and the role they expect to be played by village industries. They should ensure that there is a fundamental compatibility between the goals of overall industrialization and of protection of village industries. They should create conditions to guarantee the essential viability of these industries through appropriate industrial licensing, location, pricing, reservation and credit policies. At the same time overeagerness to support them on ideological considerations should not result in a long-term drain of the economy in the form of subsidies, tax-relief, restrictive licensing etc. How this balance between these two groups of industries is to be achieved, in the key issue.

The Indian Efforts and Lessons

In India, recognition of the need to uplift village societies and other poor from centuries of stagnation has always been there. During early twenties, the noted poet Rabindra Nath Tagore had initiated a rural reconstruction work at Sriniketan in Bengal. There were several other experiments in rural uplift. The Martandam experiment initiated by Spencer Hatch in Kerala, Mahatma Gandhi's programs at Wardha and Sabarmati, the Nilokheri project of Dey, and the Etawah Project started by Albert Mayer were rural development programs initiated by charismatic leaders without much outside support. The Baroda experiment of Maharaja Gaekwad, the Gurgaon project started by Bryne and the Firka scheme support by Government of Madras were programs which, although started by individuals, had the support of the benevolent governments. Since the beginning of economic planning in the early 1950s, the first such thrust began in 1952 with the organization of Community Development Programs. The essence of these programs was that villages who came together to bring about social change would be assisted by government in building up a new life for themselves. Such government participation with increasing awareness and responsibility in the planning and implementation of projects that were material to their well-being, was thought necessary.

Despite substantial government support and good intentions, the impact of these programs on rural life was marginal. Gunnar Mydral had observed "The disappointments thus have deep roots. From the start the philosophy underlying Community Development presupposed that the village was a unit with a basic harmony of interest among its members. This idea, though consistent with the Gandhian concept of village life, was and is unrealistic. Indian villages, even more than other South Asian villages, are torn by conflicts of interest among their economic and social groups. The original attempt to engender a popular movement was so strangled that responsibility for the operation of the program inevitably passed from the village leaders to civil servants. The long-standing clash of interests within the village hierarchy and the failure to draw up and carry through a consistent land reform program — which if it could not have eliminated these cleavages, could at least have narrowed them—are the fundamental factors responsible for the fate of India's Community Development efforts." India experimented with several other rural development programs. Microlevel planning approaches such as the 'growth center concept,' 'minimum needs program', 'Small Farmer Development Agency Program,' 'Drought-prone Areas Program,' 'Command Area Development Program' *etc.*, were tried. Their limited success could be mainly attributed to inadequate participation by the rural poor, lack of functional integration of activities in different sectors of the rural economy and more important, absence of a technological base for improving the productivity of the rural poor.

Despite all these well-meant programs to uplift the rural poor, about 30 percent of India's 800 million people *i.e.,* around 240 million were still living below the poverty line, mostly in village societies. A more comprehensive rural development program, known as the Integrated Rural Development Program (IRDP), synthesizing various strategies found effective under past programs, was launched in 1978–79 initially in 2300 blocks and later extended to all 5011 administrative blocks of the country in October 1980. A typical administrative block in India has about 30,000 families (150,000 people spread over about 100 villages) of whom about 40 percent are poor. The new program recognized the "block" as the base level unit for planning and implementation. Local planning started from the bottom, reckoning the physical and human resources potential available within the region. The importance of linkages between different sectors of the rural economy on the one hand and between rural and other sectors on the other came to be recognized. It also provided an operational yardstick to identify a poor family so that development activities could centre around them, working upward from the poorest. An income of Rs. 62 per capita per month at 1975–76 price level was considered the minimum desirable consumption standard. Families below this minimum, known as the poverty line, are identified as rural poor on the basis of household surveys. Technically feasible and financially remunerative activities are suggested to these poor. Seeking the preference of the poor ensured that they participated fully in the activity. To make the activity financially viable, subsidies according to prescribed scales are provided. This smoothed the flow of bank credit to the rural poor. Banking arrangements were also simultaneously revamped so that large number of small loans ranging from Rs. 1000 to Rs. 6000 could be given by banks to identified beneficiaries over a wide area. The new program also took care of the other infrastructural needs like extension, technical guidance supply of inputs, marketing and development of local skills. Above all, it viewed development as a total process linking investment activities of the rural poor with public investments in other sectors by the State. Jawaharlal Nehru, the then Prime

Minister of India, while initiating the community development movement, had said, "The Community Projects envisage co-ordination of a number of activities. They cannot be separated or viewed as isolated activities. The object is to build the human being and the group and to make him and the group advance in many ways. Therefore, the activities in the Community Project must be closely co-ordinated and worked to this end." The new IRDP program was another endeavor to achieve this co-ordination.

The basic thrust of IRDP has been provision of subsidized credit to families below poverty line to undertake productive investments in self-employment ventures in agriculture, rural industries, livestock and other subsidiary rural activities and services. During the past decade or so of its working, upto an amount of nearly Rs. 143 billion has been spent on IRDP, Rs. 84 billion as bank credit, Rs. 49 billion as Government Subsidy to beneficiaries under the program (subsidy ranged between 25 percent and 50 percent of the investment cost) and balance about Rs. 10 billion as administrative expenses by banks and Governments. Around 35 million rural families (*i.e.,* around 175 million rural people) received assistance under IRDP. During 1990–91 itself Rs. 12 billion was disbursed as credit and Rs. 8 billion as subsidy to 29 million rural families of which 50 percent belonged to scheduled castes and tribes and nearly 1/3 of the beneficiaries were women. Although, poverty threshold is Rs. 6400 per family per annum (1987 prices), to qualify under IRDP, families should be below Rs. 4800 p.a. income level. 30 percent of the programs benefits are earmarked to Scheduled Castes and Tribes, and 30 percent for women. Block level Government staff survey households, prepare a list of qualified beneficiaries and submit it to the traditional 'Gram Sabha' *i.e.,* village assembly for final approval of candidates. Block officers then assist the selected families in choosing viable investments for *e.g.*: small retail shops, purchasing of milch cattle, animal driven carts, etc., and also in submitting loan applications with the nearby bank branches. Expansion of commercial banks to rural areas in India has been phenomenal. While the commercial banks had about 4000 rural and semi-urban branches in June 1969 (when these banks were nationalized) by 1989, the number of such branches had increased to 44000. In addition there were 13000 branches of Rural banks and nearly 90,000 village co-operatives. The average investment per household under IRDP is around Rs. 5500. Although IRDP could reach the intended beneficiaries *i.e.*, poorest of the poor it could help only about 15 percent of the beneficiaries to cross the poverty line.

IRDP as is being implemented has several drawbacks- there are leakages at several levels, assets are misappropriated to take advantage of subsidies loan repayment to banks is not satisfactory, many of the assets acquired have remained unfructous etc. The other criticisms of IRDP are (i) it is mainly driven by the supply of generous capital subsidy rather than geneuine household demand for credit, (ii) banks participate in it only because of government compulsion and consequently do not put their best in the program. Since borrowers are identified by Government, banks have developed little stake in the program, (iii) the lending rate at 10 percent is too low to cover the high lender transaction costs of reaching the rural poor, (iv) IRDP did not provide a line of credit to the needy, rather it is a one shot investment credit, (v) a large share in subsidy is being skimmed off by the program administrators, bankers, suppliers of assets etc.

Despite these shortcomings, IRDP in India indeed is an unique program of its kind to reach the rural poor. Reaching credit in small driblets to 35 million households (for most for the first time) for undertaking manifold small rural enterprizes is not a small achievement by any standard. These small rural entrepreneurs vindicated the 'Economic Principle'—people will take the opportunity of gaining an advantage when it is presented to them, a term coined by British economist John Hicks. And it is here there are lessons for other developing countries.

Supplementing Rural Incomes Through Livestock Projects

Livestock rearing provides an excellent opportunity to increase the incomes of rural poor by utilizing the idle family labor and agricultural by-products. Such family small-herd farm production is highly suited to conditions where both land and capital are scarce and human labor abundant. Livestock rearing can improve the economic lot of the rural poor, provided such programs are properly organized and supported with improved breeding, better feeding and introduction of quality animals and adequate animal health care. Above all what is imperative is a suitable marketing system, which enables rural producers to get a reasonable return for their products. Recognizing its potential to achieve the core of rural development objective *i.e.,* alleviation of rural poverty (by providing work) and provision of better nutrition to the rural poor (through better food), livestock rearing has been accorded high priority in India's Five Year Development Plans. Several programs have been launched in India to remove the major constraints faced by the rural poor in livestock management. Substantial growth of livestock products in India over the years is partly on account of several such Government supported programs. Milk production had increased from 20 million tonnes in 1960–61 to 50 million tonnes by 1989-90. Over the same period annual egg production registered an increase from 2 billion to 20 billion.

One basic policy issue in livestock development in many developing countries is how to arrive at a balanced mix of cross-bred high yielding livestock (being developed) directly dependent on land, and non-descript low yielding livestock (already existing) dependent on crop wastes and by-products. This is because both the human beings and livestock compete for food grown in the limited land area. The survey conducted by Asian Productivity Organization on Livestock Production Systems in Asia found that "the main problems . . . were not so much technological or marketing but a consequence of massive human population growth demanding an increasing share of available food supplies and the resultant increase in competition for animal feed-stuffs from human beings." The high yielding livestock with greater efficiency in feed conversion will need less land but earmarked for high quality animal feed, whereas the low yielding ones with less efficiency in feed conversion would need more land but coarse feed material including by-products. A local cow, yielding about 400 liters of milk in a lactation has an efficiency of conversion of nutrients of feed into nutrients of milk at about 4 to 6 percent, whereas a cross-bred cow yielding 3000 liters has an efficiency of 25 to 30 percent. Feed conversion rates to a substantial extent determines profitability of dairying, especially because 60 to 80 percent of the cost of milk production is accounted by feed cost. So on economic grounds, it is necessary to reduce progressively the low yielding stock and replace it with high yielding stock. But many factors including religious sentiments come into play in this. Although, there is awareness in many developing countries to reduce the unproductive stock, how fast this change should take place is still widely debated. One view is to reduce the poor yielding ones to such a level that can be supported by-products of human feed and other crop waste as an interim measure.

India's cattle wealth is estimated at 178 million. Excluding the young stock (below 3 years) at 48 million, the balance consists of 78 million work animals, 48 million milch animals and 4 million animals used for other purposes. Most of the productive cattle is used for draught purposes. They contribute over 28 million H.P. of energy per day for agricultural operations. Good animals give about 1 H.P. per pair per day of 8 hours. It is estimated that the average power requirement to produce a yield of 2 tonnes per hectare will be 0.75 H.P. per day. As against this, the current availability of power including those provided by man, animals, farm machinery, *etc.* is only 0.30 H.P. per hectare. Thus, non-availability of power is a major constraint in improving farming efficiency in India and also in most other developing countries. As a matter of fact, farmer looks to cow as a basic source of draught power, their 'living tractor,' rather than as a dairy animal. Apart from farming, he needs them for pulling his cart, drawing water from well, operating his oil 'Ghani' etc. However, dairying his caught on quite extensively in India over the past several years.

Most of the 26 indigenous breeds of cattle in India are draught breeds with low milk potential. The indigenous cow when mated to an exotic bull like. Jersey, Holstein *etc.* produce an off-spring with yield potential of about 2400 liters per lactation as against 175 to 400 liters of a local cow. Such cross-breeds acquire the dual characteristics of high milk production of exotic breeds and stress bearing capacity of local breeds. Full exploitation of this phenomenon has been accepted as the most effective and practical way for increasing India's milk yield under the development plans. Through systematic cross breeding the number of cross-bred cows is expected to increase from 3 million in 1979–80 to about 15 million by 1992. However, experts like Charles Hickman do not wholly approve such massive cross-breeding of native stocks with exotic breeds. He noted, "Experience and research thus far have provided two critical results. First, livestock breeds developed in temperate zones do not survive in radically different environment, such as the humid tropics. Secondly, cross-bred off spring from low-producing native sired by high producing non-adapted stock excel in level of performance in harsh environment. The consequences of these two facts are as obvious as they are disastrous to the preservation of native stock. The urgency for achieving higher production levels encourages widespread cross-breeding, uncontrolled loss of native breeds and the accompanying loss of genetic ability to withstand severe environmental stress. The dilemma arises from the fact that cross-breds themselves cannot reproduce the hybrid vigour that they exhibit. The superior performances is lost because it is dependent upon matching of unlike genes from the two parental breeds. The highest benefit from this matching, known as heterosis, is obtained from the greatest genetic distance between parental breeds, in other words, in the first cross. Any attempt to mate between first crosses results in reduced hybrid vigour and extreme genetic variability.

As regards ensuring backward and forward linkages for rural milk producers, Kaira District Co-operative Milk Producers Union (known as (AMUL) in Gujarat State in India, under the leadership of Dr. Kurier, provided a model suited to Indian conditions. Perhaps with some variations, this model would be well suited to many of the developing countries. In the words of Dr. Kurien "The 'Operation Flood' implies not flooding the cities with milk, but a stop to the taking of cattle from the rural areas to the cities, so that a flood of milk will be generated in the rural areas and flow from there into the cities. Put milk in the city; then cattle will not go to the city. And this is the basis of 'Operations Flood'.... A firm foundation has been laid for the modernization of dairy industry and this is more important than any figures which we cite on the subject." This experiment has shown that the crux of the issue lies in forging a sustained and effective link between product markets and the rural producers through appropriate organizational models.

Experience in many countries has shown that there is no single rural development strategy applicable in all socio-economic and cultural environments, although unfortunately policy makers have often emphasized one strategy or one objective above all others. Thus some have concentrated on land distribution, some others on rural settlement, on green revolution or on creation of family units. In Rural Development planning, it is necessary to consider various objectives and available means at the same time and prioritise them. In many instances, however, the priorities of urban-based national planners have not coincided with those of the rural population.

Three convictions are vital to any large-scale anti-poverty program in the Third World.

(i) Poverty itself is the problem not the individuals who are poor. They represent immense human capital.

(ii) The cause of poverty is not lack of money capital but under-utilization of material and especially human resources.

(iii) Poverty is not removed by simply increasing production for goods and services but only by ensuring that those who need these goods and services have means to acquire incomes to purchase them.

Thus, an holistic approach to rural development means a two-way street. If the poor are to prosper there must be increased production of essential goods. If there is to be increased production there must be commensurate increase in the effective demand of the poor.

CHAPTER 5

Alternatives in Development: A Conceptual Framework

We have presented the traditional definitions of sustainable development as they emerged from the Earth Summit and were operationalised by individuals and organisations, in view of the non-traditional approach taken in this paper to analyse the problem, we need to elaborate on the concept of sustainable development. To most economists, nature is a category of discrete market goods not worthy of accountants' depreciation. Whatever concerns arose from the recognition that marginal returns to input intensification were diminishing, they were readily dispelled as Prometheus' example inspired faith in technology's ability to unshackle human beings from the chains of nature. Industrialisation was the way and nature was to obey.

The assumption of fixed technical coefficient production functions (with engineers' wizardry able to maintain them over time) was complemented by the equally convenient neglect of externalities or effects occurring outside the theoretically closed market system. The messy details of soil erosion and flooding caused by forest clearing, water pollution caused by chemical applications in agriculture, and loss of species caused by combination of development activities could for a long time be excluded from social scientists' purviews. Belatedly discovered, these externalities often over-whelm both market-mediated effects and the best efforts of economists to create conceptual market proxies.

The modern model of economic growth blithely measures progress as GNP, refusing to account for non-marketed activities and to recognise the fundamental importance of nature (through depreciating natural capital, at the very least). Those who blindly accept the model, which is so convenient to industrialisation, give absolutely no value to the nurturing work essential to society's functioning—work performed primarily by women—reinforcing the patriarchal view that only men's work has real value. Similarly, reliance of large numbers of the less powerful on the commons and its bounty enabled accountants to neglect them as long as markets did not function there. The same body of theoretical work further declared that the distribution of income and wealth was outside the realm of respectable economic thought and that poverty was, at most, an embarrassment that would be eliminated as the market was allowed to perform its magic.[9]

As Stiglitz has observed: "Many development strategies have focused narrowly on economics. But this focus on economics has led to a confusion of means with ends: higher GDP is not an end in itself but a means to improve living standards and a better society, one with less poverty, better health, and improved education. Furthermore, past strategies have confused cause with effect: to some extent, the changes in society that may be called modernisation are as much a cause of the increases in GDP as a result. Development itself is a transformation of society, a society-wide shift to new ways of thinking..." (Stiglitz 1998: 1).

The idea that neither nature nor societies nor individuals are dispensable underpins sustainable development, representing a leap beyond economics to include the future, the whole system (and not just the marketable portion), power and conflict within and between human societies, and ethics.

Development and Freedom in Asia

The only reason to direct attention to this vast Continent is precisely that it encompasses so much and is going to provide a testing ground for so much that is at stake in this fast changing world of ours. It is a region that, during the coming years, is likely to become vulnerable to all the traumas of the international power game. As Marek Thee has stated so vividly, it is already extending "from West to East, along the borders of the USSR and China, and in sensitive strategic areas lying athwart the great power divide, which includes the United States and Western interests... With the main world energy resources located in Asia; with the strategic lifelines of all the great powers running across the continent and along the rims of Asia; with the USR and China seeing each other eye to eye across their lengthy common border; with so many nations in Asia in the wake of anticolonial revolutions now only in the early stage of modern nation-building and confronted with numerous unsolved social, ethical, religious and national problems; with such manifold issues susceptible to great power manipulation and interventions: the center of gravity of world conflict is decidedly moving toward Asia."

In the Asian region, development strategies have long been the product of international forces and especially of western domination—or reactions thereto.

This is true of Japan, perhaps the most advanced of the industrial nations of the world, deeply influenced by the West and now showing itself capable of competing with the West on its own terms (though it is also demonstrating the major weak points of such a model of industrialization and modernization).

It is true of the People's Republic of China, which for a good 30 years refused to accept the dominant development strategy preached by the westerners but now finds itself in the middle of such a radical about face that it is in danger of losing its unique identity and becoming prey to the global struggle for power and for the human mind.

It is true of Vietnam, which became an immense battlefield between imperialism and nationalism, but which has since become a battlefield in another kind of war, namely the one within the world communist movement, which of course reflects the titanic struggle for power between China and the USSR.

It is true of the Middle East, which was once seen as the source of the greatest economic challenge to western hegemony, the OPEC offensive since 1973, and which since then presented an even more fundamental challenge to the West, this time to its entire *Weltanschauung*—the great Iranian Revolution, the full implications of which have yet to be worked out, even though it might now appear to be in the throes of much confusion and a lot of violence and anarchy.

It is true of the whole complex of ASEAN countries, in which global corporate capitalism seems to be finding client states keen on economic development at all costs, thus giving rise to a new genre of development strategy known as 'repressive-bureaucratic developmentalism.' This system, though it exhibits several shades of authoritarianism, includes some of the most cynical repressive regimes found anywhere in the world. South Korea could be included in this category.

It is true of Sri Lanka, which chose a moderate path of welfare-type developmentalism by means of which it managed for a long time to promote a minimal level of welfare for the mass of the people without resorting to authoritarian measures, but which now finds itself deeply in trouble, with respect to both economic solvency and political viability, and its desperately seeking external support to bail itself out of problems of its own creation.

It is true of some extreme manifestations of withdrawal from the world political process—Burma, Kampuchea and, in a way, North Korea.

It is true of Pakistan and Bangladesh, split asunder and ruled, as the result of coups, by military regimes in alliance with technocrats and external forces. These countries manifest deep pathologies of inward-looking nation-building with the greatest cost being paid by the mass of the people both in terms of their freedom and in terms of their development.

Above all, it is true of India, an enigma in many ways, beset by some of the worst manifestations of poverty and inequality on a massive, in fact continental, scale and yet somehow struggling both to retain democratic forms and to make important strides in economic self-reliance. Nonetheless, like China and in a different way Japan, it is likely to experience growing convulsions and major reverses under the impact of both internal and external forces in the struggle for both these objectives.

This then is the vast terrain of our subject matter. I am deliberately omitting such areas as the Asian republics of the USSR, most of which are Islamic; Mongolia and the tiny states and principalisties in the Himalayas—Bhutan, Nepal, Tibet; the vast range of border states on the northeast of India in each of which a protracted guerilla struggle is going on; and above all Afghanistan home of a proud mountain people living under the shadow of intense superpower rivalry. But even without these, the picture of development as concerns both the strategy of economic areas and the character of political and cultural development is so diverse that one is in danger of getting bogged down in descriptive and classificatory exercises which only bewilder and do not leave one any wiser for all the analysis.

Dialectic of Development

And yet this need not be so, for we are addressing the topic of development strategies at a time when not just Asia but the whole world is entering an age of diminishing options and is experiencing a loss of confidence and a decline in the capacity to manage change and provide workable, if imperfect, governing structures. There is emerging a deep sense that we have gone wrong somewhere in our whole way of thinking about development, and that there is need for fundamental reconsideration of the whole development problem. To that extent there is a certain unity of the human condition that transcends the great diversity that I spoke of earlier. The diversity we face in Asia combined with the fact that all these various entities face serious problems illustrates this situation of common destiny, and this problem of declining capacities when it comes to responding to new forces of change. What is more, there are global forces at work, both at the base of societies and in the international arena, which seem to focus more on the basic characteristics of this problem than on regional or comparative analysis. We have to consider the problems of Asia in the context of the social transformation that appears to be so far-reaching and so full of dangers to human survival as well as opportunities for building a creative alternative to the present system. We are still struggling to get an intellectual grip on this context, and, I am afraid, not too successfully. A certain dialectic of world history is unfolding before us, arising from the collapse of the western era, and an as yet unarticulated and ambiguous response to it. I have dealt with this dialectic of world history elsewhere in the context of its global manifestations. Here I would like to focus on just one aspect of it, namely the situation arising out of the erosion of the doctrine of development that held sway for so long and is now in crisis. Most of what I have to say has relevance outsides of Asia as well but nonetheless pertains especially to the Asian region.

Let me list a few obvious factors first. We have lived through a period not just of massive increase in populations but also of highly imbalanced increases in terms of their distribution by nation, region, social and ethnic group and resource endowments. The result has been highly unequal economic technological and socio-political burdens. We have also been witness to very large movements of people across political and cultural frontiers. This has given rise to massive dislocations, unprecedented human suffering and rather serious ethnic and racial tensions. But looming above every-thing else is one major factor which, if we fail to handle it with care and discrimination on the basis of an ethic of human solidarity (restraint and self-control by all), will in all likelihood make the human enterprise unworkable and so conflict-ridden as to become unmanageable. In large parts of Asia, there is taking place a serious scarcity of resources in a world that is getting increasingly competitive and crowded. The sudden disappearance of the presumption of continuous availability of resources in the Asian region has given rise to major pressures and conflicts to gain access to them. At the same time the ethic of consumerism has take hold of all classes and all nations and is leading to the relentless destruction of natural resources—forest lands, river beds, coastal terrain, reserves of soil and water and jungle. This process is seriously reducing productive capacities and making technological progress—which is acquiring a momentum of its own—an enemy of the poor.

All over the world, there is a slowing down of growth rates, a crisis in economic relations between States, emanating from the world capitalist centers and spreading to both the developing world and the socialist world where it is in turn amplified by the inherent weaknesses of these two spheres. It affects most severely the poorer parts of mankind, both regionally and socially, and provides the basis for very considerable violence arising both from the restlessness of the poor and the backlash of an elite intent on preserving its privileges, living standards and lifestyle. No issue is going to be more important than this struggle to preserve living standards on the one hand, and the struggle of the poor and the dispossessed to make it in this world, on the other.

More basic than all this is the psychological factor: a growing sense of insecurity at all levels. At the top, governments everywhere are becoming unstable propositions. The most powerful among States, *viz.,* the superpowers, are reeling from sense of insecurity both *vis-a-vis* each other and *vis-a-vis* the rest of the turbulent world that is beginning to assert itself and will not longer accept a passive role. At the other extreme, at the bottom of society, the poor and the oppressed feel insecure because their plight, mainly their economic plight, is getting worse and because the environment around them is crumbling. There is nothing to hang on to, and the political authorities and symbols they have relied on are failing them, leaving them in the lurch.

Then there is the growing spectre of world militarization. The point about insecurity that I made is not found in just psychological and attitudinal forms. It is found in the behavior of States, in their brutalization, in their increasing reliance on force, both internally and externally. Seriously contributing to this is the world power structure, which, partly because it cannot any longer 'manage' the world according to the old *status quo* and partly because of the inherent logic of this stage of world capitalism, which causes an increasing reliance on the production and sale of armaments, is leading to a global arms race from which no one is free and for the sake of which local sources of conflict are exacerbated and a world market created for arms, particularly those of the most modern type.

In sum, we are moving into a period of the growing vulnerability of States and the increasing deprivation of the needy and the deprived. The traditional institutions of a modern State, as the modern State was conceived in Europe and adopted everywhere else, are unable to cope with this situation. This is creating pressures on the elite to hand over power to technocrats and experts who are likewise unable to deal with a crisis that is fundamentally political. This then produces the need for overriding institutions and creates a role for personality and charisma in politics, the only result of which is long-term instability and uncertainty. Internationally, it is a period of growing pressures from the world power structure, politically and economically, strategically and technologically. There has been a striking decline over the last several years in the autonomy and self-reliance of developing countries, although there is some evidence of an opposite tendency, especially in Latin America, though that evidence is still far from conclusive. There is a growing temptation to seek remedies for domestic problems through international co-optation of one kind or another. India provides a striking example of this but it is true of other countries, too. 'Interdependence' is being turned into a process of recolonization.

This then is the scenario of the human condition. It is a scenario that would dishearten, depress and disorient most people. However, it is precisely a scenario that must not be accepted, fatalistically, for that would be the main precondition for the fulfillment of our worst fears. It is a scenario that must be taken up as a challenge, as a gauntlet thrown by dishonest and corrupt interests. We have to pick up that gauntlet and respond to it is a creative, constructive and critical spirit. We have in other words to meet the challenge head-on.

Challenge and Response

I, for one, am convinced that there is room for counteraction against the dominant tendencies of our time; for precisely during this period of growing conflict over resources, increasing hegemony of the world capitalist system, and declining autonomy in various societies, we have also seen some major assertions and reassertions of the human spirit in the form of a challenge to western dominance. For instance, I consider the secular assertion of Islamic power as manifested by the OPEC challenge of 1973 and the Iranian revolution as fundamental challenges to western hegemony. The issue is how does one manage the transition from an initial revolutionary upsurge through the rabble reaction to it (like the Jacobin reaction to the French revolution) to the ultimate victory of the cause. The issue is how to join the various civilizational challenges mounted by the powerful thrust of Afro-Asia and Latin America into a major counter force against the growing backlash of a declining civilization, that of the West, and how to involve the middle-sized powers of the world in the same process.

The issue is also how to develop a set of alternatives that take us beyond the managerial limits of both world capitalism and State socialism, how to repair the weaknesses of the socialist option that have already developed, and how to recreate an authentic alternative to the corrosive competitiveness and individualism of the modern world-view. It is a challenge that must be faced, mediated and managed, but it must be done in a manner that responds to the turbulence and transformation at the bottom of our societies.

We have to recognize quite clearly that we are moving into a fundamentally new age, an age of the people and an age of populist leaders. These are two contradictory forces, one highly democratic and egalitarian to the core and the other highly elitist and authoritarian to the core. The new age is thus also deeply deceptive and cunning. It is a strange combination but very real nonetheless. The very process of democratization also creates the conditions for institutional erosion and heightened expectations from individual personalities. The whole problem of 'charisma' is a problem of taking a shortcut to solving political questions by identifying a whole society with a person. Both people and leaders resort to it out of a sense of insecurity.

It is necessary to mediate in this critical situation and to provide alternatives to the people so that their democratic aspirations may find new channels for crystallization and fulfillment. The very forces that at present seem to succumb to criminality and corruption—the large lumpen element in our cities, the youth, the rural middle classes, the educated unemployed—can be mobilized from the bottom for a constructive crystallization process, rather than succumbing to co-operation from the top.

I cannot emphasize this point too much. The story of most of our societies is a story of lost opportunities and missed challenges of a professional elite that has degenerated into an exploiting, domineering and parasitic stratum because it has lost the capacity to feel inspired by any challenge or avocation and is thus unable to steer society in a positive direction. But this situation can still be reversed and I have no doubt it will be. When and by whom are open questions, but history does not foreclose new possibilities. Indeed, it always throws up surprises.

The Issue of Freedom

Let me draw the various threads of this paper together by dealing with what seems tome to be the basic problem of all human development, namely, the problem of freedom in human affairs and of democracy and the institutions that sustain it. It is a problem of fundamental significance to the Asian region, especially to countries of South and Southeast Asia, and of course to Japan. But I have in mind particularly pluralistic and multi-ethnic societies where the management of power demands an institutions framework that supports both diversity and nation-building.

There is as yet no adequate theory of democracy for multicultural societies. The closer democracy gets to the grassroots, the more the operating elite is found unable to handle multiple polarities and heightened demands from below. As this happens the system take recourse to authoritarian shortcuts and, since they do not work, the politics of sheer survival.

A series of questions arise. Is it inevitable that in pluralistic societies membership on the effective political community is restricted to the dominant groups? How is it possible to respond to the demands of the lower classes in a liberal polity that has no access to external colonies? How does the class factor operate in a multi-ethnic society? Then there is the question of poverty and economic development. According to the dominant theory of development based on liberal internationalism, poor societies lacking adequate production of surplus must rely on foreign aid, preferential trade and technology transfers. But, in fact, these resource transfers have only reinforced the structure of internal disparities and inequities. There is, further, the whole issue of ethnicity and class. Cultural and ethnic pluralism is not a serious problem for a liberal democracy so long as membership in the political community is limited to the upper and middle strata and so long as democracy means the politics of accommodation and co-operation. It is only when politics moves into the mass age, when, in short, ethnic differences take on class or quasi class character, that the problem becomes serious. It is against this background that the parallel phenomena of radicalization at the bottom and authoritarianism at the top, with the left and 'radical' parties either losing ground or becoming part of the dominant structure, have to be perceived.

Faced by these myriad cultural expressions of the political process, the political elite resorts to populist and plebiscitary politics, leading to a gradual undermining of institutional intermediates and the federal structure of government and communication. After that, all that remains is charisma and its direct appeal to the masses, so that mass society becomes the purveyor of an authoritarian polity and a captive State structure. Such a resort to populist politics and a commensurate operating system on the part of the top elite (and their local dependents) also escalates tensions in other fields—in minority politics especially but also in such areas as the politics of language and regionalism. In the course of time, all these processes of tension-generation and the decline in the mediating roe of politics sow seeds of disaffection, parochial separatism and ultimately disintegration, which can only be stopped by resorting to even more repression by transforming issues of social management into problems of law and order and 'security.' All this takes place against a background of heightened consciousness and politicization of the lower strata and peripheral communities.

On the other hand, such a system, based as it is on an ideology of justice without institutionalization thereof, generates pressures from the educated and semi-educated class, and from the relatives of various influential people, to expand the State apparatus far beyond the normal bounds of efficiency, leading to a large 'lumpen bureaucracy' that then becomes a drag on the exchequer. Thus arise the parasitism of the urban middle classes.

In institutional terms, the theory of development has given rise to a growing faith in centralized institutions. In different ways, both the liberal doctrine of a free society and the communist doctrine of a classless society have endorsed the role of a centralized bureaucracy for achieving social ends. During the very decades when participation has become the dominant value with people everywhere, it has come to mean even less in actual practice. The capacity of citizens to actively intervene in the social process that the doctrine of participation requires has been severely circumscribed because of the high degree of centralization in most institutions resulting from the growth of the technocratic State. To sum up, the sources of the decline of democracy are to be found in the transformation in the nature of the modern State under the impact of 'developmentalism'. The post-1945 era of State and nation building in diverse historical contexts, based on a common struggle for political autonomy and human dignity encompassing vast regions of the worked, represented a major new era in human history. What is threatening the creative orientation of the State is the developmental creed and its attempt to turn the State into an economic instrument—an agency for exploitation, control and subjugation—nationally internationally. The crisis of the State arises from a totalitarian vision of State power as a result of the homogenising thrust of developmentalism which is undermining its role as a civilizing agent and as an instrument for the promotion of human values. Herein lies the intellectual and political challenge of our times.

There is need to return to some of these basic issues, for they are among the central questions of our time. They were very much part of intellectual reflection, study and discourse a few decades ago. This has since been discounted due to preoccupation with the so-called 'scientific' study of politics at a time when the ground has been slipping from under most societies, the traditional limitations on the exercise of power are disappearing, and cultural and ethnic identities are being rapidly eroded. There are some indications that out of the present struggle between the centralized and increasingly repressive State that has taken shape in large parts of Asia under the impact of modern forces, on the one hand, and various movements of protest and defiance based on local organizations of the poor, ethnic minorities, and the peasants, on the other, there may emerge and alternative formation that will prove more sensitive to indigenous cultures, their great diversity and essentially decentralized character, their tenacity against the homogenizing thrust of modernization, and their in-built restraints on the exercise of power.

This confrontation between centralizing and decentralizing thrusts, which is already going on and is being waged in various regions as well as nationally(and, in respect to the larger forces at work, internationally is at this moment of time generating a massive backlash from powerful interests, both in the economy and the polity, in the countryside and in the metropolitan areas, against the forces of change. But it appears that the issue has been joined and the basic forces at work cannot be kept down for long.

I am convinced that this task is fundamentally ethical and intellectual, arising out of the fact that old models have become useless as necessary new visions and perspectives are beginning to arise. We face the challenge of providing a conceptual and moral perspective that goes beyond modern capitalism and modern socialism and humanizes the State, puts human beings once again at the center, and at the same time calls upon modern man to control his desires and appetites and live in greater harmony with nature and technology, to redirect technology toward building the sustenance for both the biological and cosmic aspects of the human collectivity. On all this there is much to learn from the wisdom that prevails in large arts of Asia. However, these issues relate as much to the problem of freedom and spirituality as to the problem of power and the organization of the State. While the crisis that we face is fundamentally a crisis of human freedom, it is also a crisis of the State. In saying this I am no more than restating the basic predicament of man: how to achieve freedom while being a member of a civil society, a State. There can be no freedom until the State itself, and with it the economy and the technology under whose impact it is being pulverized, becomes a condition of freedom instead of becoming an impediment to it.

Alternatives in Development: A Conceptual Framework

In July 1955 Bertrand Russell and Albert Einstein issued a 'Manifesto' which, besides urging renunciation of war as a means of settling human disputes, also said that "There lies before us, if we choose, continual progress in happiness, knowledge and wisdom." The appeal, addressed mainly to the scientists of the world, ended thus:

> We appeal, as human beings, to human beings: remember your humanity, and forget the rest. If you can do so, the way lies open to a new Paradise; if you cannot, there lies before you the risk of universal death.

Thirty-three years later, the promise of continual progress and the way to a new Paradise does not seem so clear. Indeed, it seems more and more remote and, short of some basic rethinking on the very premises on which the modern industrial civilization has been based, it seems more impossible of realization than ever. This is not just because a number of wars have been waged since 1955, nor even because the stockpiling of deadly armaments has gone on unabated and has greatly proliferated. This is no doubt a very important reason why human progress has been held up or distorted and diverted into wrong channels. But I submit that there is another and perhaps more basic reason.

Diagnosis

This lies in modern man's approach to science and technology. The very technology that has produced more and more deadly armaments has also produced a more and more wasteful civilization in the very centres where modern science and technology have flourished and has, in consequence of this, given rise to a world structure that has become increasingly inequitous and conflict-ridden, in the process rendering millions of human beings—including in the industrial centers—obsolescent and redundant.

The centers where modern science and technology have ushered in wasteful ways of human consumption are not limited to the rich, highly industrialized, 'developed' North; they are also to be found in the poorer, less industrialized, 'underdeveloped' South. Domination of the nations of the South by those of the North is accompanied by domination of large masses of the people by westernized elites which are more closely tied to the metropolitan centers of the world than to their own peoples.

The problem of persisting 'underdevelopment' and increasing gaps between the rich and the poor nations—and, as a reflection thereof, between the rich and the poor in the poorer nations—have been sought to be explained by reference to a number of misleading diagnoses—the increase in population size, lack of motivation among the people of backward lands, decline in 'aid' from the rich nations, transfer of resources from development to defence in the poor nations, regional, linguistic and ethnic divisions in the latter, and so forth. None of these, however, seem to us basic or even important. They are either (like population growth) symptoms of more basic causes or (like the alleged lack of motivation among the poor) wholly misleading an wrong, arising from the prejudices of scientists and social scientists and the search for alibis by people overcome by guilt but not willing to accept responsibility for basic injustices in the world.

The result is that even the political an intellectual elites of the countries of the Third World remain divided, both within each of them and between them severally. These countries have failed to exert themselves at regional and world levels, and have also failed to pursue policies within their own countries that are called for by their socio-economic, demographic and cultural conditions which happen to be quite different from the conditions that obtained in the developed nations during their respective phase of development. Instead, they (or most of them) are found to indulge in a rhetoric of confrontation, both at global and at domestic levels, and to seek alibis for their failures to restructure a world in which they happen to be in a majority. Thanks largely to the inimical consequences of modern science and technology, the dominant economic model that has resulted from it and has been accepted almost universally, and the politico-philosophical underpinnings of this model by a 'theory of progress' that had stemmed from the presupposition of infinite progression of resources that could become universally and equitably available, the world is being ruled by elites that are incapable of handling the problems confronting it.

But the basic shortcoming underlying all this is intellectual: if the world is 'structured' in a certain way it is because the thinking that has dominated the world for the last hundred years—and more—has been faulty. These have been the years that have been dominated by the idea of a uniform end product to be achieved by all societies—a state of urban, industrial affluence, managed by experts at the top running secular affairs through a 'rational' bureaucracy, and backed by a capital intensive technology. Even today—despite decades of misery and exploitation engendered by this model—the notion of catching up with those who are seen to be more 'developed' and along the same course continues with uncommon persistence. To no small extent this persistence — which is based more on institutionalized interests of a few powerful people than on conscious deliberation by the large majority— accounts for the general scenario of inequity within societies and a state of myopic dependence between them.

Towards a Concept of Alternatives

It is the slow realization of this large context of growing

misery and destitution in the world that provides the background and rationale for the concept of *alternatives*. Most ideas take time in fructifying as general concepts capable of attracting the minds of men. There has to be a certain threshold of collective awareness, normally of a deep sense of discontent with the prevailing state of affairs, before such fructification takes place. In the past few years this threshold has been reached for the concept of alternatives and the various associated thought processes and normative perspectives that go with it. And as with earlier conceptual breakthroughs, the idea of alternatives, implying 'alternatives to what is' signifies a major dissatisfaction with both the existing state of *affairs* and the existing state of *analytics*—in short, with the existing paradigms of both science and politics. A feeling of fundamental dissonance between not only what is and what ought to be but also between what is and what can be (if only human agencies intervened decisively) underlies the recent interest in seeking out alternative ways of attending to human problems. It implies two considerations: that the world is becoming too uniforms, too standardized, too dominated by a single conception of life and its meaning, with little scope for other available cultural and historical propensities and potentialities; and that such domination of a single conception has led to political and cultural domination by a single region of the world over all the others.

The problem posed by the concept of alternatives is at once philosophical in respect of the validity of diverse worldviews and theoretical paradigms, and practical in respect of the struggle for survival and development of literally billions of human beings. It questions both the claim to universality of a model of life by virtue of its sheer dominance and the notion of determinacy of the historical or evolutionary process for all time to come. Instead, it affirms the validity of human intervention in the historical process, and of this intervention taking different forms based on different perspectives on both the ends of life and the problems that life poses when faced by different conditions.

Every few hundred years (in recent times, every few decades) man is faced by a changed reality when earlier models and institutional structures—as well as conceptual paradigms and their underlying metaphysics—which were evolved to meet a different kind of reality are found not to work any longer. The need is to seek for alternatives to meet new situations.

Methodological Issues

This implies two crucial considerations. First, if the search for alternatives is not to be an end in itself (fulfilling some aesthetic desire for change) but related to real needs, it is necessary that the utility and worth of various alternatives be measured be measured by reference to some criteria of values which provide a unifying scheme of human experience and which can judge between alternative perspectives, models and policies; and with the help of which it is possible to pronounce judgment on which alternative is better suited to which needs. Second, if this is the methodology of pursuing the choice of alternatives, then surely while at any point of time and space there can be only one alternative, it may still be possible to have different alternatives for different configurations of space at a single point of time or at different points of time and history in the same place. The two consi-derations—of choice and coherence—must be pursued together. To the extent that human experience is to be guided by some unity of meaning and purpose, this would entail that, depending upon agreement on value criteria, one alternative is to be preferred to many others, at any rate in the overall model of human arrangements. And yet there should be scope for diversities in the details of these arrangements.

Thus, for example, to the extent that the capitalist mode of production and the social system based on it were found to be unsatisfactory, the socialist alternative that was proposed in the last century and realized in this century represented a unified concept. Similarly, as the Third World emerged as a coherent human experience for which neither capitalism nor State socialism were found satisfactory, a third alternative was called for and is currently being evolved through intense deliberation and debate—as a common alternative to both the first and the second worlds. Meanwhile, with the growing realization of the homogenizing tendency of the modern State and the elite that controls it, there has emerged the necessity of insisting on further differentiations within all these three worlds. Taken together, these represent a series of alternatives within the search for one major theoretical alternative to existing arrangements.

Pitfalls

It is necessary to stress this if one is not to be lost in two familiar pitfalls in recent thinking. One is the view that we must somehow find an alternative to the 'western model', expressed as a reaction to the excesses of the western model, at times borne out of animus towards it, often from within western academic and intellectual circles, and then echoed elsewhere. While such a reaction in understandable and constitutes an important step in the growth of consciousness and knowledge, it also tends to distort the response by making it largely negative and without any real direction towards a genuine alternative.

The second pitfall is much larger than the first and has an even greater intellectual pedigree. This is the view based on cultural relativism, namely, that each and every society must evolve its own alternative and that the alternatives before man in society are infinite. I believe that every major new human experience calls for a new theoretical response, different from all earlier ones: a new theoretical paradigm is not just a mental construct but a response to a new empirical reality. But while this is so—and assertions of universality for one particular model of life must be resisted on grounds of their being both arrogant and obscurantist—it is also the case that there is some unity underlying diversi-ties. This is so in two respects, especially in the modern age.

First, the different societies one talks of are interrelated and the causes underlying the problems they face are at least in part to be found in these inter-relationships. Second, there is a unity in the flow of history which gives it some determinacy, no doubt with a lot of scope for intervention for history is no more than a sum total of human interventions, but not without limits. To ask for a different alternative for each micro situation without reference to the basic unity provided by both the interrelations in which different units stand and the determinacies of the historical process would be to ask for infinite fragmentation (which will not stop at national frontiers and will be sought by regions, ethnic groups, and communities within each nation as well). Any search for alternatives that does not seek to foster a new and better unity for all is liable to lead to disintegration and chaos. I think it is necessary to reject chaos as a preferred alternative for civil society.

The Global Context

That brings me to my last theoretical point. The current search for alternatives is not, or ought no to be, simply because the techno-economic model that dominates current thinking in the other two worlds is inadequate for the Third World. It needs to be said that the model is also inadequate for the other two worlds. And it needs to be said that a crucial component of the model is provided by a certain structure of international relations and a set of global distributions and control mechanisms. It is true that the model that dominates the world today is far more inimical to the countries and human beings of the Third World (barring the upper classes everywhere) than to those in the other two worlds. But it is still a world model and has to be attacked as such. The importance of an alternative approach to technology, for instance, may be more immediate for the overpopulated and capital-scarce countries of the Third World but it has relevance for the overabundant and heavily polluted cities of the other two worlds as well, though clearly not in the same manner, for after all one is dealing with quite different situations. The same is true of alternatives in energy, education, public health, urbanization, communication and so forth.

The notion of alternatives as a new intellectual endeavor, involving both theory and action necessitates that it presents not a tangential effort but one that is integral to the strivings of the human species as a whole—indeed to creation as a whole. We ought to value scope for diversity within such striving and respect the autonomy and dignity of diverse entities and to that extent stress the pluralist notion of *alternatives*. But it is at the same time necessary to realize that at any one point of major historical change one is seeking out a new *alternative* which gives unity to the plurality and enables comprehension of each as part of an overall scheme of things. Failure to bear the latter in mind would be both a historical and lead to an accent on reformism for its own sake without a sense of wider purpose that provides unity and meaning to individual efforts.

The concept of alternatives, then, is not to be limited just to development policies; it should entail visions about society and polity, and it should do this in the context of the evolution of the human community as a whole. When available models are found wanting and a new alternative is called forth, this applies not just to social and economic arrangements within a given society, but to the ordering of the world as a whole. Alternatives is a conception not just in the theory of development. It entails a model of (and a perspective for) world order and the transformations entailed for such a world order. It is an exercise in values and their realization at various levels of reality, always taking account of cultural diversities but also of the unities that inform these diversities. It is to just a different kind of model for China or India or Tanzania (or Brazil or Chile) that one is seeking out though no doubt these and other models provide a very large scope for learning and criticism and action. One is also concerned about the making of a different kind of world conceived as a set of inter-relationships. Without seeking to alter these inter-relationships the effort to alter individual societies is not likely to get very far. China is a case in point.

The philosophical perspective that should guide us in such a setting should steer clear of both imperialist claims to universality and the normless striving for relativity: it should affirm both the principle of *autonomy* of each entity (human as well as social) to seek out its own path to self-realization and the principle of *integration* of all such entities in a common framework of inter-relationships based on agreed values. The worlds as it is at present constituted violates both autonomy and integration as principles informing human arrangements. It is a world based, instead, on a framework of dominance that works through endless fragmentation and tensions, one that relies heavily on instruments of violence and institutions of inequity. It is only by seeking a new structure of the world, and as a basis thereof, a new form of technology and a new ethic of individual and group behavior that are in consonance with the changed conditions of our times that we shall be able to perceive the true intertwining of happiness, knowledge and wisdom and to restrain man from overstretching his rationality and undermining his religiosity.

Perspective on Alternative Development Strategies

Having laid out a general theory of 'alternatives in development,' I shall now try to spell out a broad framework of development strategies for our time, especially for a country like India, though large parts of the framework have relevance beyond India. Briefly, three major aspects of development strategy and the need for an optimal relationship between them, may be proposed. These are:

Lifestyles. While retaining a good deal of diversity of a cultural and individual kind, there is need to have a consensus on such matters as desirable and undesirable consumption standards, use and distribution of resources for the gratification of needs, and norms for minima and maxima in incomes and wealth.

Organization of space. There is a need to stop thinking of "rural' and "urban' as separate sets of entities and to think of them as a continuing structure of city, town and countryside, of agricultural and industry, of hinterland and metropolis. Countries like India have a unique opportunity to develop a social continuum in which, while the romantic utopian dream of village self-sufficiency may be left behind (there should be no regret about this for such a system had many negative features), we may also be able to avoid the scenario of huge metropoles draining the resources of the countryside in a parasitic manner. The scenario best suited to us—and to civilized life—is one in which the country is studded by a few thousand localities (regions), each clustering around a medium size town, sharing in its amenities and its economy in a relatively egalitarian manner, in which all strata of society gain from the benefits of entering the modern age but avoid the ills of post-modern consumer societies that are prisoners of highly concentrated production complexes.

Production system and technology. Such a structuring of space will need to be supported by a corresponding continuum of productive orientations and technology relevant to each of them. The strategy that we shall have to evolve will need to be integral to the development of the country as a whole—where both production and administration are decentralized to medium-sized towns and their rural hinterlands, where city growth rates are arrested from becoming grotesque, where employment opportunities in agriculture (which have some natural limits) are supplemented by employment in small and widely diffused industries, where educational institutions are located close to jobs and restructured away from the present emphasis on university degrees, where health facilities are not limited to the privileged, and where the economy derives its strength from the purchasing power of the great numbers of the people and not from the expansion of middle-class consumer industries and their 'export orientation.' Implied in such a restructuring of rural-urban and agricultural-industrial relations is a new techno-economic model for our society which will enable us to reach the goals set out by us in the Directive Principles of the Constitution and often elaborated since. Rural development must be conceived as part and parcel of this model as a whole a model in which we talk less of rural development in our usual segmental fashion and more of development of individuals and communities—of all of them, irrespective of distinctions of locale or class. It is only in this overall context that 'rural development' will make sense.

Future Scenario

It is from an optimal inter-relationship of the above three parameters that our design for the future emerges. It has to be a comprehensive design, of which economic development becomes an integral and a crucial part. I give below the essential components of such a design.

The prime concern of economic policy for a just social order ought to be to generate employment that is able to absorb at least the new additions to the adult population, and where there is a substantial backlog of unemployment and underemployment, to absorb that as well. The major source of injustice today is to be found not so much in a condition of general scarcity as in the fact of the diminishing marginal utility of men and women, in the fact that millions of people find themselves idle and useless, often in their very prime.

Social Continuum

The crux of such a combination of policies designed to raise employment and alleviate mass poverty is to put agricultural and rural development at the core of public policy. But there is a counterpart to this approach in the area of urban development and industrial policy as well. Apart from heavy industries, which require large capital inputs and centralized organization, industrial development should be employment-oriented as much as possible, should produce goods that are needed by broad strata of the population rather than by a small middle class, and should be widely dispersed over the country so that the employment that it generates benefits all areas rather than a few cities or regions as is the case today. Regional disparities constitute a crucial—and visible—dimension of social injustice. Most of the favored regions are those with large urban centers.

Socially, this means that the present duality of city and countryside must give place to a continuum in which agriculture regenerates the villages; small-scale and medium industries are located in the towns; and large-scale industries that necessitate heavy inputs of capital and high technical efficiency are located in the cites. As such a fusion between industry and agriculture takes place, further intermediate links in this continuum—rural social structures in towns, urban amenities in villages—will develop, thus combining the best traditions of both rural and urban life and producing a composite and integrated culture.

My preferred world should be not one made of millions of self-contained villages but, rather, one of thousands, of small nucleating towns towards which the rural landscape gravities, thus doing, away with both the present duality of metropolitan and rural cultures, limiting the large size and concentrated location to just the industries that cannot do without them, while at the same time enlarging the size and horizon of rural communities, and providing them with the necessary infrastructure of welfare and communication facilities. Such a spatial structure—supported by a decentralized structure of community decision-making, as argued below—would provide the necessary framework for the techno-economic alternative to the present dualist model of city *versus* countryside.

Policy on Education

It is not simply by altering the economic basis of rural-urban relationships that a more just social order will be created. We also need to alter the cultural underpinnings of the present patterns of dominance and disparity. An important source of the sharp duality of lifestyles and living standards found in most poor countries is the educational system, the aim of which continues to be to produce colonial type gentlemen, disoriented from the large society and constituting a class apart.

In most ex-colonial countries, formal education was initially meant to produce an elite, mainly to fill the ranks of the bureaucracy, the law-and-order establishment, and the technical positions in public administration and private enterprise. This orientations still persists in spite of the achievement of independence and in spite of the political elite's commitment to democratic and socialistic ideals. Education, far more than property or income, is the basis of privilege in our society.

Meanwhile, a majority of the population continues to be illiterate and unskilled, while the ranks of the highly educated in the urban areas keep swelling. Studies in this area suggest that whereas expansion of literacy and primary education produces very rich and rapid dividends, after a point higher education turns out to be counterproductive. Acquisition of a minimum educational level greatly raises a person's skills and his capacity to enter the employment market; it also raises his sense of potential achievement and his ability to relate to the outside world, his sense of political efficacy, and his general self-confidence and sense of dignity. In contrast, an undiscriminating expansion of higher education beyond the absorptive capacity of the economy produces and alienated class that is unable to relate meaningfully to the rest of society,[1] that rapidly inhabits various levels of the bureaucracy, making it increasingly inefficient and insensitive to the needs of the people and, with growing unemployment in its ranks, loses self-respect and becomes aggressive.

This polarization between a large mass of illiterate and totally unskilled and hence unemployed people on the one hand, and a class of people who are overeducated and hence also unemployed on the other, is a natural result of the hiatus between the elite and the people—and between the parasitic cities and a depressed countryside—discussed earlier. We must alter this condition by a major allocation of resources to mass-literacy, by giving special attention to the economically weak and socially handicapped strata, whose major avenue of mobility seems to be education,[2] and by a re-orientation of the job market so that employment within a wide spectrum of non-technical jobs is available to those without college degrees, thus deflating the importance of higher education and the disparities that result from insistence on degrees.

It is necessary to emphasize strongly the importance of widespread literacy in generating massive social and economic transformation. Poverty is, more than anything else, a cultural condition and if poverty breeds poverty and perpetuates itself, it is because it is located in a particular cultural milieu — a milieu of ignorance, isolation, segregation and an extremely low self-image of the poorer classes, who suffer exploitation without protest and indeed consider exploitation to be the natural state of affairs. This situation cannot be changed except by a basic cultural attack. And the primary precondition for this is literacy and minimum education. This point cannot be over-emphasized and needs to be expressed continuously and loudly.

Finally, higher education itself needs to be reoriented, by restricting university education to its logical role—to provide basic grounding in the main sources of theoretical knowledge. Some commentators appear to dismiss higher education (and institutionalized education generally) as largely unnecessary. I do not share this view. There is urgent need for a very large number of doctors, engineers, geologists, architects, designers, managers, even economists and sociologists. What is at fault is not their availability but their placement, their location. Most of them are unwilling to go where the real jobs are, the institutions where they learn are unwilling to train them for employment in local conditions, and the leadership is unwilling to tell them candidly about their duties and their responsibilities. There is need to look upon education as a political process, upon the attainment of a degree or diploma as a social good that must be capable of being socially used, and upon the relationship between educational output and available work as part of a conscious plan of development. Higher education, instead of becoming an instrument of class privilege and exploitation and a source of disparities, must be made an integrator of human resources ad human needs.

There is also need to undertake a major review of the whole institutional approach that has accompanied the modern view of education: classroom-based, bookish, graded and located in large campuses in large cities. This approach needs to be replaced by a close relationship between education and work—including intellectual work, where education is sought for scientific and literary pursuits—and by bridging the gap that divides the location of one from the location of the other. City-based education must be largely for city people. For others, schools and other institutions a must go where the people are, not the other way around. Unless these various aspects of the educational scene are approached with some perspective on the changing social reality, it is difficult to see how the deep cultural barriers that divide different classes and accentuate economic disparities can be overcome. Education can be made to bridge these gaps or to accentuate them. The need is to move from the latter orientation to the former.

There is need to give special attention to the education of women. In our country, as in most parts of the Third World, women are less educated than men and within the depressed social strata and ethnic minorities the gap is even more pronounced.

Meanwhile, the daughters of the rich are flocking to the universities and some of them are leading women's liberation movements (imitating their counterparts in affluent countries), which in our country means the liberation of the privileged. These gaps in education among women and between them and men are an important source of the persisting duality of cultures, economic levels and consumption standards, the latter more often than not being a direct function of the perennial shopping to which the educated women are so addicted. These differences also account for the wide divergences in the way the children of the rich and the poor are brought up, thus perpetuating sharp disparities for generations to come.

Lack of education of women is an important cause of the exploitation of women, which is a marked characteristic of our society (though in a way that is quite different from that in western countries). The main basis of this exploitation is economic and it is found at its worst in the lower classes and among the scheduled castes—but most of all for women. As a matter of social policy there is need to pay special attention to raising the educational levels of women and mothers from the poor, under-privileged and conservative[4] strata of society in order to achieve a major spin-off process of social reconstruction.

The Ethic of Consumption

Even more fundamental than the gaps in the literary culture are the gaps in the material culture that divide the urbanized upper and middle classes from the people. Perhaps the most important and glaring contrast of today is caused by the extraordinary consumption levels and material possessions of the richer and high-status groups, following almost *in toto* the standards set by the high-consumption societies. The lust for things and for more and more things has become so myopic that it has given rise to all kinds of unethical practices, chief among these being a great deal of corruption among public officials and a thriving black-money economy that is sustained by the availability of a large array of consumer goods.

Apart from the vulgarity of such ostentatious living in a society characterized by massive poverty and malnutrition and apart from the creeping corruption to which it gives rise, such standards of consumption also undermine the whole fabric of economic policy. If a massive program of employment and social welfare is to be generated, a high rate of savings and capital accumulation will be necessary. This implies a high rate of savings among those with large incomes as well as restraint on salary and wage increases among the employed classes, so that resources can be transferred to employing the unemployed (in a poor country to be employed is itself a privilege) and raising income levels of the poorly employed and the underemployed.[5]

All of this calls for an *ethic of consumption* that discourages ostentatious living, cuts down the production and consumption of non-essential items and shifts production priorities towards fulfilling, the needs of the poor. It is, of course, necessary to encourage saving among the peasantry, the lower-middle classes and even the laboring classes as is often advocated. But this will this be an impossible task unless the pace-setters of society themselves adopt a consumption ethic that encourages austerity and reduces the gap in material culture between the different classes. Gandhi put his finger on the most crucial dimension of moving towards a just social order when he called for a *limitation of wants* and warned his countrymen against falling prey to an industrial machine that not only reduces a majority of men to labouring slaves but also dictates what and how they should eat, wear, dress, and house. Today his insights are even more relevant than when he lived. If there is to be an end to exploitation and inequity in our society, the present norm of a high-consumption ethic must give place to one that both meets the minimum needs of all men and limits the needless expansion of wants that have no relationship to the basic requirements of body and mind.

The Nature of Production

Built into such an ethic of consumption is also an ethic of production that is critical to the achievement of justice in society.

The current notions of social justice derive from concept of economic equality that is essentially distributive. It is not surprising, therefore, that both theoretical understanding and empirical evidence have underlined the need for first expanding the cake and then distributing it. Part of the problem is that both production and distribution are thought of in terms in which the mass of the people are reduced to a position of subjects and onlookers. An economic ethic that seeks to meet the consumption needs of all while limiting the flow of inessential commodities involves a simultaneous increase in the income of the poor and the output of goods that they will need to buy with those incomes. This means that instead of conceiving production and consumption as two separate activities, one aims at an economic system that (to echo Gandhi) not only produces for the mass of the people but one in which the mass of the people are also the producers.

As with all visions, perhaps this, too, is an ideal. All that one can hope to initiate is a movement towards such as state. In practical terms this calls for a location policy that, while permitting large-scale organization where it is unavoidable, will encourage a small-scale, labor-intensive, decentralized pattern of industrial development. Similarly, the market economist's retrogressive concept of 'effective demand' (that only the needs that are backed by the existing distribution of purchasing power are worth producing for) will have to give place to a concept of *need-effectiveness*, so that the real needs of the people as a whole determine what goes into the package of production. A combination of such a production system and the consumption ethic outlined above will lead to a climate in which progress towards dispersal and decentralization of economic power becomes possible.

Social Minima

Major casualties of the present structure of consumption and production are the large numbers of people in poor countries who suffer from acute malnutrition and the resulting physical and mental deficiencies. Their numbers are likely to increase in the next few decades. While demographers and bureaucrats are busy propagating birth-control measures to ward off an 'explosion' sometime in the next century, inadequate attention is being paid to the problem of enabling those who are already born and who will be born in the next two decades or so to live a normal life and put in sustained work for their livelihood.

The picture of the culture of poverty that emerges from various studies is highly depressing: it is a picture of large families exhibiting physical and psychic abnormality, incapacity for sustained work even for a few hours, a pronounced inferiority complex, a tendency to deal with patterns of exploitation and coercion by directing them inward and against their own dependents, and a vicious cycle of parents inducting children into these characteristics of deprivation and degradation, turning them into the same kind of adults when they grow up, and thus almost *ad infinitum*. We must give top priority to a program providing basic health care (with more accent on preventive health services) and an adequate supply of protein and other nutrients to the poor and especially to their children, drawing especially on the accumulated wisdom of both traditional society but also on relevant segments of new researches in the bio-medical sciences.

Here it is essential to stress a special advantage that Third World countries like ours have in charting a distinctive course of development in which the human cost that has accompanied economic growth in other societies can be avoided. Given our advantage in the low cost of trained manpower and the considerable plurality of knowledge systems, it is possible to spread the basic essentials of education and health over the whole country, to all classes of people and in a short time through concentrated and devoted effort. This will lay a surer basis for all-round and continuous development than all the investments made in high technology, urbanization, mass media development and the other appendages of 'modernity.' Health and education are the essential pre-requisites of social and economic mobilization for sustained development, for the so-called 'take-off.' Once such a basis is laid, nothing can prevent a society from moving forward. What is more, it will be a process of development that will produce far fewer disparities and less inequity than is the case when the sole emphasis is on economic growth in aggregate terms without regard to the cultural framework in which it takes place.

Minima and Maxima

The above analysis provides the elements of an alternative model. The objective of development, should be to achieve minimum conditions of material welfare for all the people, the *minima* to be defined according to local conditions and norms, but all of them providing at the least a package of minimum items of human necessity such as food. clothing. shelter and nutritional needs to children and mothers in particular, and socially approved minima of health, education, drinking water and public transportation for all. The extent to which these minima should be translated into personal or family incomes or combined with social welfare programs will depend on local conditions and the nature of the future political system. But it should not be difficult for any system to work out a policy on essential minima for all as a basic component of development planning.

A policy of minima entails a policy of *maxima*. Indeed, without the latter the former is, in practice, impossible to realize in reasonable time. Also, beyond a certain point, incomes ought not to be allowed to grow nor human wants allowed to be artificially stimulated by the aggressive salesmanship of modern industry or the demonstration effects from the rich capitalist countries. There are two reasons for this limitation, one which is relative and the other absolute. No one has a right to amass more and more income and riches whine large sections of population live below subsistence standards. Also, it is morally undesirable to go beyond a certain level of fulfillment of human needs. For an unlimited gratification of wants leads to individual decay and social disharmony, an unnecessary destruction of natural resources, a fouling of the human environment, and thus a bartering away of the health and happiness of future generations for the present pleasure and lust of a few. Hence my emphasis on 'limitation of wants' as a necessary principle of my preferred world.

There should be a reasonable scale connecting the minima and maxima, that is to say, an admissible ratio between the two, thus limiting disparities and enabling society to implement the principles of natural justice. Entailed in the norm of such a scale is the further norm of *transfer* of surplus incomes and wealth above the maximum to those who have not yet reached the minimum.

Participation

Implicit in my preferred model for social and economic justice are also a number of other issues. The norms of minima and maxima are not mere economic formulations; they are part of a certain conception of a good and desirable life. Not only should an individual be entitled to a minimum standard of living; he should also be able to participate actively (though he ought not to be forced to do so) in the way things are produced and decisions are made. It is not just a minimum wage that one thinks of here in some kind of contractual relationship, alienated from the work process and the total scheme of ownership, production and distribution of the means of livelihood. Rather, one thinks of an apparatus that men and women themselves control and find meaningful and from which they derive a sense of personal power and significance. Furthermore, to the extent that economic activity is managed and mediated by political and administrative agencies, the whole problem of effective participation in decision-making, at the desirable level and in optimum units, becomes real. Without such participation the economic aims may indeed be difficult to achieve.

There is also the need to prevent the economic process, and what is now sometimes tellingly called the 'industrial-bureaucratic complex' of modern society, from taking on a will of its own and destroying every other value in its inexorable march. In other words, as the values of a participatory democracy and of non-violence in man's relations to man and to the environment are joined with the values of individual autonomy and social justice, it may well be that we should ask ourselves equally basic questions about the kind of institutional superstructure that we want to build. Three major aspects of this issue are (a) the rural-urban structure of the economy, (b) the territorial structure of the State, and (c) the participatory structure of the policy. As we consider these aspects, it will become clear that the current model of modernization is not conducive to our goals; that the norm of a necessary shift from a predominantly rural to a predominantly urban structure based on large-scale industrialization may not be the best thing that human intelligence has devised; and that urban metropolitan life, far from being a 'civilizing' instrument, may turn into a structure of manipulation, exploitation and destruction of the very properties of man's natural environment that are essential to human survival.

Similarly, we may also question the norms of centralized government, large-sized States and big bureaucracies as necessary instruments of national integration and political accountability; and as we question these, we may begin to answer with greater clarity the problems raised about local autonomy, about decentralization of functions, powers, resources and talents, and about the optimum size for genuine participation of the people. Perhaps there is something to be gained in the very short run from large-scale enterprises, modern communication media and centrally planned initiatives, although the real issue here is less of scale than of control. But it is also necessary not to close all options for the generations to come concerning the quality of life they would like to have. As the prospects of the future are vitally affected by what is done in the present—it is no longer possible to think in terms of just a few months or even a few years ahead—it is a matter of considerable responsibility that these various consequences of the present are borne in mind.

It is necessary to consider here a widespread belief that rapid development cannot be carried out in a participatory framework, that only a determined and authoritarian elite can bring it about, that this indeed is the lesson of contemporary history. My answer to such a position is that it mistakes appearance for reality, that the issue is not one of choice between liberal democracy dominated by machine politics and State socialism in which a small bureaucratic elite seeks to perpetuate itself, but that both these systems are authoritarian as far as the majority of the people are concerned (there is far greater similarity between the two than appears at first sight), and that the real issue relates to the classic predicament of political life, namely, the relationship between those in power and those out of power, between the government and the people. Seen in this light it is not surprising that the demand for authoritarianism has normally come from members of the privileged classes (the businessmen, the bureaucrats, the technocrats), often reinforced by the analyses and prescriptions of foreigners.

My model of a participatory system is not conceived in terms of simple political reforms. Rather, it is expressed in a number of sectors: concerning economic organization and its governance, the nature of education, location of work and enterprise, choice of technology, size of units (economic, political, demographic, communications) and the nature of work. Participation is not some process of involving everyone and reducing all to a common denominator. Rather, it consists in evolving institutional structures from which diverse individuals get a sense of dignity and self-respect, as beings that are able to determine their own destinies. (Poverty and inequality are themselves reflections not just of prevailing relations of production but rather of structures and values the deny dignity to the human being.)

Nor is my thinking on participation conceived in terms of establishing idyllic and isolated small communities. My conception (outlined above) of a social and spatial continuum goes against such a utopia. I am also convinced that, given the numbers of human beings we have to deal with, such a utopia is no longer feasible. My concern, rather, is that structures at various levels and of various sizes imbibe the value of participation as integral to my model of a just society and my conception of the autonomy and dignity of all human beings. It is only through such an integrated view of the various components of such a model that an alternative political perspective can emerge and that policy issues can be discussed in a meaningful manner. It would be folly, however, to look upon such a perspective as in any way smooth sailing on some neat course. Nothing is more difficult to realize than change in the social framework of politics—except for the worse.

Every more on such a course needs to be fought for, by organizing for it and building sustained pressures from below in the form of social and intellectual movements. And it is, of course, clear that these will need to be conceived and carried out is not one but many spheres, at not one but many levels. But I am firmly convinced that it is only on the basis of a clear acceptance of a decentralized and highly participatory democratic structure that social justice can be realized. These, then, are the issues that arise when specific problems of economic strategy, political structure, educational policy and the reconstruction of the human space are considered from the integrated perspective provided by a set of values and the criteria that follow from it. Involved in such an approach is what may be called a design for living in which reason, compassion and a regard for the equal worth of all men and women are joined in the cultivation of a truly civilized life.

CHAPTER 6

Sustainable Urbanisation

Provisional data from the Census of 2001 reveal that over 285 million persons, or nearly 28 per cent of India's total population of over a billion (up 21% from 846 million in 1991), live in urban areas, against approximately 26 per cent in the previous census. This rise of two percentage points is lower than most projections made during the 1990s, which suggested urbanisation levels of 30 per cent or more by 2001. But the resulting growth (68 million-up 31% from 1991) in urban population is more than the total populations of major countries such as the U.K. or France. And India's total urban population is the second largest in the world after China's and higher than that of all countries put together, barring China, Russia and the U.S.A.

The overall increase in urbanisation over the decade has not been very dramatic, but its distribution is noteworthy. Nearly 38 per cent of urban India lives in cities of million-plus population—close to 15 per cent in three urban agglomerations (UAs) of over 10 million each, about 9 per cent in five UAs in the range of 3-6 million, and nearly 15 per cent in 27 UAs or cities of 1-3 million. The remaining 62 per cent lives in some 3,600 small and medium towns (5,000-100,000 population) and cities of less than a million. A major part of the growth is directed to about 30 cities in the million-plus category, which added an average of 33 per cent to their populations in a decade.

The Urban-Rural Growth Differential continues to be high.

This has serious implications for the kind of urbanisation happening in India. An important concomitant of development, urbanisation has to be viewed in its regional context. The city serves as an important service and exchange centre for its hinterland. It draws upon the resources and assets—material, human and environmental—of the hinterland. Urbanisation can be sustainable only if it has a symbiotic relationship with developmental processes in the hinterland.

Over the decade since Rio, India has taken a number of noteworthy initiatives to address problems and issues of sustainable urbanisation.

Initiatives at the International Level

India's status as signatory to a number of environment-related agreements has encouraged better environmental performance in some areas, notably in management of hazardous wastes, emissions of pollutants and Green House Gases by motor vehicles, in polluting industrial processes and in CFCs, all of which have significant bearing on the urban environment.

Initiatives at the National Level

A legislative milestone in governance is the Constitution 74th Amendment Act (1992), which devolves significant functions and powers to Urban Local Bodies, especially in respect of protection of environment and 'promotion of ecological aspects'. This amendment has created possibilities of building institutional mechanisms to involve citizens more closely in local governance, and has also led to some innovative urban finance mechanisms being attempted.

The National Housing and Habitat Policy, 1998, significantly lays down the role of all the stakeholders in achieving the goal of providing shelter to all.

Another important legislative initiative with far-reaching implications, particularly in the area of habitat and shelter, was the repeal in 1999 of the Urban Land (Ceiling and Regulation) Act of 1976.

In the area of policy, "despite the Report of the National Commission on Urbanisation (NCU), 1988... the country is yet to evolve a National Urban Policy... The Planning Commission ... constituted a National Task Force on Urban Perspectives and Policy in 1995. Three Technical Groups were constituted on the subjects of Urban Perspectives and Policy, Urban Infrastructure and Urban Planning... After the reports of the Technical Groups are available the Task Force will finalise its recommendations. These will provide inputs for the National Urban Policy" [Government of India, Ministry of Urban Affairs and Employment, 2002].

As a result of the NCU report, the Eighth Five-Year Plan (1992-97) "for the first time explicitly recognised the role and importance of the urban sector for the national economy. While the growth rate of employment in the urban areas averaged around 3.8 per cent per annum, it dropped to about 1.6 per cent in the rural areas. Therefore, the urban areas have to be enabled to absorb larger increments to the labour force. The Plan identified key issues in the emerging urban scenario:

The widening gap between demand and supply of infrastructural services badly hitting the poor, whose access to drinking water, sanitation, education and basic health services is shrinking.

Unabated growth of urban population aggravating the accumulated backlog of housing shortages, resulting in the proliferation of slums and squatter settlements and decay of city environment.

High incidence of marginal employment and urban poverty as reflected in the National Sample Survey 43rd round... 41.8 million urban people live below the poverty line [*ibid*].

Other initiatives with significant implications for the urban environment consisted of the notification of rules such as the Hazardous Wastes (Management and Handling) Rules, 1989; the Biomedical Waste (Management and Handling) Rules, 1998; the Motor Vehicles Act, 1998 which requires that vehicles obtain regular 'Pollution Under Control, certification to monitor levels of suspended particulate matter and noxious gas emissions; and the Recycled Plastics Manufacture and Usage Rules, 1999. The last named in fact cover even the use of virgin plastics, especially in respect of bags made of sheets less than 20 microns thick. The Batteries (Management and Handling) Rules, 2000, applying to lead batteries, make it compulsory for manufacturers, assemblers, recyclers, importers, retailers and customers to ensure that used batteries are recycled in an environmentally sound way and by authorised dealers, and that new batteries are sold only after confirming that the old batteries which they replace have been given for proper recycling. A committee constituted by the Supreme Court to look into Solid Waste Management in Class I cities (pop.> 100,000) submitted its detailed recommendations in 1999.

An important development at the national level is the growing awareness and expression of concern in various quarters—citizens, NGOs, Government—about the environmental and sustainability issues connected with urbanisation. The judiciary, driven by public interest litigation or by *suo motu cognizance* of the situation, has delivered a number of judgements supportive of urban environmental concerns.

Initiatives at the Local Level

The various notifications issued by the Government, cited above, are being progressively implemented in several urban areas. Besides this, a few cities have published annual reports on the state of their environment. Partnerships between Urban Local Bodies, NGOs, stakeholder groups and, in some cases corporate entities, in critical aspects of environment such as solid waste management, reduction of industrial pollution, water harvesting, urban greening and slum improvement have emerged in some places. Initiatives at varying stages of fruition are on to corporatise urban services in order to make them functionally and financially more efficient and accountable. Some, such as slum-networking and corporatisation of water supply and sanitation, seek to integrate cross-sectoral demands and needs, for example between the industrial and the domestic sectors. There have also been efforts by corporate providers of some urban services (notably electric supply) to promote reduction of waste and introduction of efficient practices by shifting focus from Supply Side to Demand Side Management.

The Local Agenda 21 mechanism, emanating from Rio, does not appear to have worked as well in Indian urban centres as it is reported to have worked in some other parts of the world. But wherever stakeholder groups with focused agendas have acted, the outcomes have often been promising, in keeping with the spirit of Local Agenda 21 objectives.

Among the various post-Rio urban initiatives at the global level, the Sustainable Cities Programme (UNCHS-UNEP) is being implemented with varying degrees of intensity and effectiveness in five major cities, with official as well as spontaneous actions in the areas of environmental sustainability through legal, infrastructural and environmental management actions; social equity through affirmative policies and rights movements; economic growth with redistribution through poverty alleviation, housing and shelter programmes; and political empowerment through decentralisation of urban governance and NGO-led capacity-building activities. Some cities have received the UNCHS Best Practice Awards for particular projects. However, all these achievements have been isolated events, not part of a countrywide process of mobilisation to address urban environmental concerns.

New Issues to be Addressed

In the decade since Rio, a number of new factors bearing on sustainable urbanisation have emerged, which must be added to the official perception evident in the Government statement quoted above.

- Liberalisation of the economy has accelerated the pace of industrialisation, but in some of the most developed (and most rapidly urbanising) parts of the country, polluting chemical industries play a significant part in this development.
- The increase in economic activities and livelihood opportunities accompanying this industrial growth, without matching access to infrastructural resources for the urban

poor, is an important cause of growth in urban informal sector housing lacking in basic services.

- Because of unregulated urban development, natural and man-made disasters, though not inherently a new phenomenon, are causing unprecedented scales of damage to both private and public urban property.
- The number of motorised vehicles has increased, with growth of personal transport far exceeding that of public transport, leading to higher levels of air pollution.
- Increased consumption has led to generation of more waste and pollution.
- The use of water and energy by urban areas has dramatically increased, leading to shortages and an urgent need for better sharing of these precious resources, both between the different economic classes and sectors within urban areas and between urban and rural areas.
- Many livelihoods are perceived to be under threat from the forces of Liberalisation, Privatisation and Globalisation in general, and from global business in particular.

For urban as well as rural India, these manifestations of urbanisation are placing tremendous stress on the environment, giving cause for grave concern.

Urbanisation today is inextricably linked with development, which one writer explains as "(the) fundamental structural and social changes that, once accomplished, cannot be undone. (Its) classic indices include: birth rates, levels of education, consumption patterns, life expectancy, household size, and the status of women" [Polese, 1997].

The major impetus to urbanisation in modern times has been a shift in livelihoods from primary to secondary and tertiary sector-based occupations. It places economic, social, infrastructural and environmental pressures on both urban and rural areas, leading to serious concerns about its sustainability.

The foregoing discussion leads to the conclusion that while many desirable initiatives have already been taken to set India on the path to sustainable urbanization, much more has to be done in order to fulfill the objectives of these initiatives. India's record at the policy and legislative levels has been good. The obstacles to realising the underlying intentions lie mainly in the areas of governance, planning, management and education. Some of the key interventions needed to overcome these obstacles are discussed below:

Learnings and Perspectives

Integrating Urban and Rural Issues within Urban Policy and Planning

The resources which support cities—food, energy, water, raw materials for economic activities, human resources—flow largely from outside urban limits, often at the cost of the developmental and environmental capital of the areas contributing them. Urbanisation can be sustained only if overall regional development is sustainable and equitable. For this, an integrative approach is necessary between urban and regional development planning in terms of land-use, resource allocation, equitable and mutually complementary resource flows between the city and its hinterland, and institutional and infrastructural mechanisms to enable these to happen.

- Urban growth must not be incrementally agglomerative, consuming forest and agricultural land, water bodies and other environmental assets. It should be directed in a planned and locale-specific manner, to existing contiguous settlements, which can receive it, leaving intervening open accommodate growth must be enhanced by improving transport and other infrastructure to and in them.
- Land use planning and regulations must be made comprehensive to support the goals of sustainable urbanisation. Special attention must be paid to the issue of land recycling to create assets compatible with contemporary needs of the urban environment.

- Cities produce large amounts of waste, which pollutes and degrades the environment both within and outside their limits. Planning and management mechanisms (including waste minimisation) must be evolved and implemented to correct those aspects of urbanisation which promote such negative cross-boundary impacts.

Making Cities and Urban Systems More Energy-Efficient

Cities consume high levels of energy for water supply, transport, waste management, commerce, industry and many other functions. Much of this consumption is inefficient and wasteful, leading to deprivation or scarcity in sectors which could use the same energy in more productive ways. Policy interventions and management mechanisms which minimise such waste of energy are necessary.

- Building heights should be regulated to reduce the energy costs of lifting water and vertical movement of people and material.

- Measures should be adopted to encourage recovery and reuse of wasted energy in commercial and industrial processes.

- New energy saving technologies should be aggressively promoted in all sectors including the domestic and commercial, with imaginatively conceived demand side management, pricing and subsidy mechanisms to make them attractive and viable.

Use of private transport should be regulated for optimal capacity utilisation.

Promoting R&D in and Use of Alternative Energy Sources

The commercial energy presently used in the urban sector is produced mainly from non-renewable resources, or by methods potentially harmful to the environment or both. The efforts made so far to produce energy from non-conventional, renewable sources—

mainly based on technologies developed by countries of the North in their own environmental and economic contexts—have moved in fits and starts at the policy, research and implementation levels. Often such energy is either commercially unviable compared to that produced by traditional technologies, or (as in the case of solar cooking) it requires radical changes in established cultural practices.

- Locally appropriate R&D to develop non-conventional energy sources should be encouraged and promoted, especially in the area of solar energy, which is abundantly available in most parts of India, as well as wind energy wherever practicable.

- Imaginative costing and recovery mechanisms should be evolved to make energy from non-conventional sources commercially competitive with conventional energy.

- In the urban context in particular, R&D in human waste-based biogas generation to supplement other commercial fuels must be undertaken, supported by a programme of awareness building, skill development and education. This is one case where the supply of raw material is bound to keep pace with population growth.

- R&D work should also be targeted at deriving organic manure from municipal and agricultural waste in order to reduce the quantum of such waste requiring disposal.

Investing in and Development of Relevant Economic, Social and Environmental Infrastructure

People must be placed at the center of planning concerns. The quality and efficiency of infrastructure play a major role in determining the quality of urban environment, and consequently the quality of life of citizens. Sustainable urbanization is not possible without appropriate physical, economic, social and environmental infrastructure. Such infrastructure includes water and sanitation, public health and education facilities, recreational spaces, open spaces and transport.

- Scarcity of potable water is an emerging crisis area. Approaches to addressing it, such as new and better methods of reduction of waste, managing demand, harvesting rainwater, recharging aquifers, and recovery of water from sewage, sullage and industrial effluents should be seriously explored.

- The existence of a number of coastal urban settlements also calls for exploration of viable desalination technologies to augment water supply.

- Inherently interdependent infrastructural services, such as water supply and sanitation, must be integrated to derive maximum equity, performance efficiency and investment returns. Integrated planning of urban water supply and sanitation networks is an important first step towards addressing water scarcity.

- The provision of adequate water and sanitary facilities for the urban poor must be a high priority item on the agenda for urbanisation.

- Slum Networking Programmes in some Indian cities such as Indore and Vadodara have demonstrated that a sewerage network servicing the most deprived pockets of the city can in effect service the entire city economically. (Slums are usually spread across the city in low-lying areas which naturally attract, under gravity, flow from the entire city; laying sewers mainly along natural gradients minimises both their depth below ground level and the need for pumping stations, while extending the area serviced to include non-slum pockets built on higher ground). The gains of and learnings from such initiatives must be consolidated, improved upon and applied in other cities.

- The emphasis in the role of public health services should progressively shift from curative to preventive and positive health care. A significant proportion of morbidity in society is environment-related. It is more appropriately addressed through emphasis on education and awareness of the served population and empowering it to participate in managing preventive health care related to environmental sanitation and hygiene.

- The focus of urban transport must shift from private to public modes, and the shift made viable with effective incentives and disincentives (including investment in public transport reinforced by cross-subsidisation from private transport, modification of land-use and building density regulations, Floor Space Index, vehicular access restriction and other regulations). According to some estimates, the urban poor spend as much as 25 per cent of their income on essential transport. It is necessary for urban policy and planning to provide them access to affordable transport.
- Ways and means to reverse the trend of sacrificing pedestrian thoroughfares to facilitate vehicular traffic should be explored. Traffic arteries and parked vehicles must not dominate over the urban fabric at the cost of pedestrian and civic spaces.
- Use of bicycles must be encouraged where possible, with infrastructure (such as dedicated bicycle tracks) to facilitate it and incentives to encourage it.
- Travel reduction strategies must be explored and encouraged through the urban planning process. Intermediary public transport (*e.g.*, taxis and autorickshaws) must be regulated to make it complementary to and not a substitute for public transport.
- While progressively stringent emission standards for new motor vehicles entering the market will fulfill part of objective of reducing pollution, this achievement must be reinforced and sustained by evolving and enforcing similarly progressive standards for the maintenance of vehicles in use, and the creation of appropriate monitoring, training

and certification mechanisms towards this end.

- For large urban agglomerations, the feasibility of providing appropriate mass-transit systems must be explored and translated into ground reality. In places where the rudiments of such systems already exist (Mumbai, Chennai, Kolkata) they must be extended and updated using state-of-the–art technology). The town planning and management interventions necessary to make a success of mass-transit systems must also be actively pursued.

- New and emerging information and communication technologies are leading to a gradual decrease in the premium on location in urban areas, making the distinction between 'place of work' and 'place of residence' less critical to urban dynamics and form. They have the potential to effect changes in land use and use and traffic patterns. Transport and land use planning must harness this potential to influence the course of sustainable urbanisation.

Focus on Shelter

In the urban informal sector, slums are places of both residence and work. They contribute significantly to the creation of wealth in the urban economy. The urban poor have capably demonstrated their ability to invest in and improve on shelter given even notional security of land tenure. It must be recognised that slums are not a problem but a solution to a problem, evolved by people using their own ingenuity and resources. Official policy must encourage this process, intervening only to the extent of making it orderly, integrating it with overall urban development, and focusing on the provision, with people's participation, of infrastructural services—which lies beyond the capacity of individuals and small groups—in the areas of investment technical inputs and management. Urban housing must be viewed not as a product but as a process with appropriate enabling mechanisms of legislation, management, technical support and finance, together with a legitimate recognition of the propensity of people to invest in their own shelter.

- Shelter at minimum acceptable standards of habitability, guided by economically realistic building and planning codes (especially for the urban poor) is crucial to urban infrastructure. Those living in self-created substandard shelter should be given help and guidance in progressively improving it according to their capacity for investment in a convenient time frame.

- Building and planning codes for the lowest income groups should be reviewed and revised taking cognisance of the fact that for many people in this group the same shelter serves as living space and work space.

- At least a notional security of land tenure must be granted to inhabitants of unorganised sector housing, in order to encourage them to invest in the improvement of their own shelter and to facilitate the provision of infrastructure by local bodies.

- Innovative housing finance mechanisms for the urban poor should be evolved, including affordable loans at concessional interest rates and realistic collaterals.

- To help the urban poor invest in housing stock, assistance should be made available in terms of building material banks, technical guidance in construction and planning for integration into citywide networks such as water-supply and sewerage.

Ensuring Security of Livelihoods

All development affects livelihoods. It creates new opportunities while posing a threat to some traditional occupations. In order to be sustainable, development must offer, to those whose jobs and occupations are at risk, opportunities which they can recognise and convert to their own advantage. For the urban poor in low-skill, marginal occupations, livelihood has several critical dimensions. Rapid economic changes in response to changing market currents may place not just individual livelihoods but entire livelihood categories under threat. Such vulnerable groups in urban areas must be provided with appropriate security nets, opportunities for developing new skills, appropriate entrepreneurial skills and social welfare programmes for basic survival.

- Sustainable development, especially in the urban based sectors, demands urgent and strong policy measures to safeguard the livelihoods placed at risk by the forces of liberalisation, privatisation and globalisation.

- Programmes of skill and versatility development, backed by support for promoting small-scale entrepreneurship, management and marketing must be developed for those whose occupations and livelihoods are at risk.

- Basic education for function literacy, livelihood skills and responsible citizenship is a precondition for sustainable development. Such education must be appropriate to the social, economic and environmental context, must be of the highest quality possible within that context, and must be available to every child and youth as a fundamental right. Facilities for each child to acquire such education without being discriminated against on the basis of economic class, geographical location or cultural identity, are a must.

Emphasising Environmental Concerns in the Agenda for Urbanisation

An unpolluted, healthy and aesthetically satisfying environment, natural as well as built, conducive to overall well-being, is a fundamental right of every citizen. In urban areas health, in its broadest sense of physical, mental and spiritual well-being, is to a great extent dependent on the access of the citizen to environmental assets which support such well-being.

- Clean air and water, and places for recreation and relaxation in the public domain (such as waterfronts, parks, lakes, wooded areas, hills etc.) are necessary components of a sustainable urban environment, and must be provided for in the planning for that environment, both in terms of conserving existing assets and developing new ones.

- Tree plantation in urban open spaces (common and waste lands, lands subject to inundation, lands on the margins of roads and railway tracks etc.) should be encouraged, to serve (a) the biomass fuel needs of the poor who, for want of affordable alternatives, use toxic forms of fuel such as rubber tyres and plastics; (b) as green cover; (c) as a deterrent to environmentally incompatible encroachment; (d) as livelihood opportunity for the poor (in partnership with various stakeholders in the urban environment); and (e) as a protective measure against the destruction of forests to meet urban fuel-wood demands.
- Clear policies, and planning and implementation mechanisms, should be laid down for the protection and conservation of urban water bodies.
- Monuments, precincts and civic artifacts forming the cultural and historical heritage of urban areas, which are important as aesthetic features of the built environment and as symbols and rallying points of civic pride, must be conserved and protected from encroachment and vandalism, awareness about them promoted among citizens and visitors, and ways and means explored to involve citizens as well as urban local bodies in this process.

Bringing Gender Issues to the Mainstream of Urban Policy and Governance

Women at all levels in society tend to be discriminated against. Urban women in particular, while continuing to perform their traditional domestic roles (thereby conforming to a gender stereotype), are also increasingly involved in earning livelihoods; in many poor households they are often the principal or the sole breadwinners. A major thrust at the policy level is necessary to ensure equity and justice to women in the urban environment. The Constitution 74th Amendment has made a beginning by ensuring representation for women. But much remains to be done in the areas of access to social and economic services, social as well as domestic violence and crimes against them, and attitudinal prejudices in the establishment.

A policy of positive discrimination in favour of women, especially women from deprived social, economic and educational backgrounds, should be adopted in order to empower them to become functionally equal members of society with men.

Child-care support for working mothers should be provided to enable them to function efficiently as productive members of the workforce.

The equality of women with men should be recognised in matters such as opportunities in education and employment, and access to institutional finance for entrepreneurial ventures.

Laws aimed at prevention of discrimination against women must be reinforced with social awareness and education programmes to promote gender sensitivity.

Evolving Appropriate Partnerships for Local Governance

The educational, occupational, cultural and economic heterogeneity of the urban population is a major asset in making urbanisation sustainable; but in times of crisis the same heterogeneity can lead to conflict and social insecurity, with adverse consequences for law and order and human rights. It is imperative to evolve participatory mechanisms of urban governance, involving citizen groups and local authorities, which will provide effective means of conflict resolution.

The Constitution 74th Amendment has opened up opportunities for the devolution of governance to the lowest political strata of society. These have been successfully and positively used in some cases. More should be done to make devolution effective across a broader spectrum of citizens. There is a potential role for partnerships involving citizen groups, social workers, NGOs academics and professionals, and the lower levels of the legislative, judicial and executive wings.

Despite some sincere, motivated and upright individuals in its ranks, the bureaucracy as a whole is perceived as being opaque and obstructionist rather than transparent and facilitative. This mindset inherited from the past is not in keeping with present-day developmental aspirations and ideals. The bureaucracy must be sensitised to simplify and streamline its procedures so as to minimise mandatory citizen-bureaucrat interfaces to the barest essential.

It is imperative to decentralise and devolve environmental management to the lowest levels of governance and to capacity-build local government and citizen groups to participate in and take charge of such management as partners. The establishment of ward committees, with appropriate awareness, education and skill development inputs, needs to be encouraged and strengthened towards this end.

On one hand, there is a surfeit of laws, many of them outmoded and irrelevant. On the other hand, effective enforcement is lacking in respect of those laws which are relevant to contemporary concerns and conducive to good governance. While this is often blamed on lack of political will or undue political interference, most lapses in enforcement are purely due to bureaucratic indifference and unconcern, or to corruption which is in the first place bred by the irrelevance or the irrationality of the laws themselves. All systemic barriers to governance should be reviewed and eliminated, and the influences and powers at various levels which allow perversion of governance drastically curtailed.

The emphasis in urban governance must shift from excessive regulation to an enhanced use of essentially economic instruments in the form of levies, tariffs, tradable environmental performance mechanisms and a range of other incentives and disincentives.

The role of awareness generation and education must extend across a wide spectrum of the legislative, judicial and executive wings. It has been found that in many instances well-meant judicial directives pertaining to environment have run into stumbling blocks because they were not backed with adequate information about the administrative, technical and financial preconditions for implementing them. Similarly the bureaucracy, which is usually well-informed about the nature (if not always the structural causes) of various issues, must learn to anticipate problems and have alternative options ready to solve the problems. It is a waste of both judicial and executive time for each contentious issue to be brought to court before even serious thinking for action on it can begin. The role of Urban Local Bodies in this context must include the creation of environmental monitoring mechanisms involving citizen groups, academics, professionals and media persons.

Making Cities Increasingly Self-financing and Evolving

Urbanisation heavily dependent on the deflection of resources from the hinterland cannot be sustainable in the long run. The two major finance mechanisms currently available at the local government level to Indian cities are property tax and octroi. The former is not buoyant enough to meet increasing investment and administrative demands. The latter, while buoyant, is not viewed favourably because it impedes the smooth flow of goods and commodities across the country [Rakesh Mohan, 1996]. Octroi is gradually being phased out in the country. A viable and buoyant substitute, under autonomous control of the Urban Local Body is yet to emerge. A vigorous effort is necessary to explore innovative methods of generating revenue for local bodies.

Private participation in the provision and maintenance of many services traditionally perceived as local government responsibilities can free some financial resources for diverting to sectors which must be addressed by local government. Privatisation should open up two kinds of options: (1) converting services such as urban waste management (especially composting of organic wastes) into profit making ventures and (2) livelihoods for the urban poor functioning in an organised manner to provide essential services for urban environmental management. However, "liberating local bodies from government regulatory and legislative controls may oblige (them) to come under the direct or indirect control of financial institutions, resulting in dilution of their social commitments (Kundu, 2001). It is necessary to ensure that privatisation does not end up favouring those who can afford to pay for services at the cost of those who cannot, accentuating the divide between the haves and the have-nots. To the extent that such services are equally necessary for all segments of the urban population, the local bodies must not abdicate their responsibility of ensuring equitability in the provision of urban services. Cities are places of opportunity, for learning, earning and living fulfilling lives. In order to make them financially sustainable, local government bodies must seize upon the potentialities to exercise every possible option to raise finances by fair and equitable means. Those who derive the maximum profits from cities must be willing to pay for the privilege of living in them and using them.

CHAPTER 7

Towards Sustainable Development

To enhance development of these, legislation was created to promote clearing of land for agriculture and to permit mineral exploration and promote mining (Bolton, 1981: Lines, 1981: Lines, 1991 and Dover, 1992). Agriculture and pastoralism were the most extensive form of development and this has continually expanded up until the 1980's when a moratorium was declared by the goverment banning further clearing of native vegetation for agricultural production. The affect of rapid expansion especially in the agricultural and pastoral areas in the current and continuing extent of land and water resource quality decline (Department of Conservation and Environment, 1987 and Select Committee on Land Conservation, 1990a, 1990b and 1991a).

The Commonwealth of Australia (1989) list reasons for land and water resource degradation and attribute these to ignorance of the environmental constraints such as soil stability, soil water balance, nutrient balance and pest control. That is, many management techniques were in appropriate. Bawden and Sriskandarajah (1993) describe the evolution of land development in Australia as relating directly to changes in community perspective's. They discuss the shifts as being from pioneering to production, productivity and more recently to persistence perspective's and suggest these shifts in community perspective entail significant changes in their thoughts about the land and their relationships with it.

A brief description of Bawden and Sriskandarajah's (1993) concepts of development phases and the reasons for the shift between each follows:

1. *Pioneering.* This phase is characterized by "rugged" individual eking an existence from new lands. This was a period of subjectivism where individuals learnt from their own subjective experience. It was also a period of reductionist outlooks, for example, "... a tree to be cleared was a tree to be cleared; no more, no less." The land was cleared purely for increasing the area of crops and pasture, without necessarily improving increases in production per unit area.

2. *Production.* This phase began in the 1880's when government agencies were established to improve production. It indicated a profound community paradigm shift from subjectivism to objectivism. This resulted in four fold improvements in production. It also established a technocratic perspective but excluded, like the pioneering phase, consideration of constraints to environmental and natural resource quality and consequences in short and long term. This also excluded the possibility that there could be negative impacts on the socio-economic or cultural environments with which development interacted.

3. *Productivity* . By the 1960's the community perspective began to change more from "...one based not on the amount of physical production that could be realized, but on the efficiency with which it was produced." That is, this phase returned to objectivism but rather than in a reductionist mode it was now a noises perspective. Improving efficiency in these perspective's also lead to extension of economics but also the initiation of the role of ecology.

   However, even though in the 1970's it was fashionable to speak of ecologically sound development, it was not until the 1990's that the problems incurred from past practices were quantified. Quantification of problems such as salinity led to a realization that some current development practices were beyond the safe minimum standards and ecologically sustainable development constraints.

4. *Persistence.* This phase is described as being holistic but with increasing community perspective's focussing on subjectivism. That is, recognizing that current systems of development, such as farming "... are not likely to persist into the future as they fall victim to the very environmental damage they themselves have triggered in the first place."

As described in these phases, community attitudes and development of land uses such as agriculture has been varied. In particular, the first three phases, management objectives did not include cognisance of consequent resource quality.

The Soil and Land Conservation Council (1991) and the Select Committee on Land Conservation (1991b) have identified 15 different types of land and water degradation. However, the Commonwealth of Australia (1989), the Soil and Land Conservation Council (1991) and the Select Committee on Land Conservation (1991b) together recognize that although degradation can be attributed to inappropriate management by farmers, miners, foresters and other land use managers, legislation also contributed by promoting economic growth without due regard for the sustainable development constraints for each of the natural resources supporting land use production.

Evolution of Resource Development

Imperatives of Western Australian Governments for rapid expansion of economic development described by Bolton (1981), Lines (1991) and Dovers (1992) initially reflected "a development at all costs" approach. Thus approach still prevails in some legislation such as the Land Act (1983) however, the Environmental Protection Act 1986 provides that development growth is within environmental constraints be permitted.

Barker (1987) outlines four main phases of land use development related legislation in Australia and Briggs (1993) shows that this is also applicable to Western Australia. Barker's four main phases follow:

1. Virtually uncontrolled physical development of resources.
2. Imposition of legislative control over exploitation to ensure its orderly economic development with some basic conservation requirements consistent with the sustainable yield concept.
3. Imposition of specific law in response to political demand during a period of raised environmental awareness designed to alleviate disruption to resource quality.
4. Integration of various resource specific laws (both those that control resources in economic terms and those that protect environmental quality) in recognition of the complex ecological relationship between all resources and their usage.

Briggs (1993) demonstrated that phase one approaches is still applicable in some Acts and that most legislation can be designated in phases two and some in three. Entry into phase four has not yet occurred in regard to Acts but some government agencies have policies which reflect this approach. That is, some government agencies have in part adopted the Ecologically Sustainable Development (ESD) concept described by the World Commission on Environment and Development (1987) and stated by the Commonwealth of Australia (1991).

One of the reasons for this partial adoption of the ESD concept is that government agencies have separate resource management missions and objectives which do not reflect an integrated or co-ordinated approach to natural resource management. A second reasons is because of traditional institutional cultures, innovations have not been readily adopted (Jacobs. 1993). Jacobs (1993) states that even though ESD concept and principles may be adopted, negotiations may result in either weak or strong commitments towards economic development progressing within environmental and natural resource quality constraints.

Evolution of legislation, in regard to government agency natural resource development responsibilities, has also resulted in each agency having its separate administrative areas of which only few are common (Select Committee on Land Conservation, 1991b).

Natural Resource Management Areas

Each government natural resource management agency has in its development during the evolutionary phases of legislation become responsible for specific resources. They also have their own administrative areas which mainly comprise hierarchies of divisions, regions and smaller management units. In Western Australia (WA), there are three essentially different administrative frameworks designating these management units:

* socio-economic areas (*e.g.*. regional resource development, the agricultural and range and regions)
* socio-political areas (*e.g.*, local government authority areas, electoral areas)
* biophysical areas (*e.g.*, water catchments, waterways).

Administrative areas, structures and frameworks have traditionally been created and develcped with a clear distinction between land based resources (*e.g.*, soils, rivers and vegetation) and marine resources. Administration areas do not reflect the full natural resource quality responsibilities. For instance, there is no explicit or implicit legislation referring to the impact of land and water degradation on the outwash zones from rivers and ground water discharge and deposition of wind blown particulates from the land areas into marine environments. This demonstrates a shortcoming of the existing natural resource administrative structure. However, recent developments of coastal zone management refer to near shore marine quality affected by ground water and river discharges.

In 1992, representatives of 178 nations gathered at the Earth Summit in Rio de Janeiro to discuss the future of the world. Economic sustainability, social advancement and equity and environmental stewardship were on the summit's agenda to advance sustainable development. Today, as Asia-Pacific countries cross the threshold of the third millennium, the formidable task of achieving sustainable development has become most critical and urgent.

Even before the historic summit, the Brundtland Commission, which was created by the United Nations (UN) General Assembly in 1983, coined and defined sustainable development as "development that meets the needs of the present without compromising the ability of future generations to meet their own needs". Specifically, sustainable development is a "process of change in which the exploitation of resources, the direction of investments, and the orientation of technological development and institutional change are made consistent with future as well as present needs" (The World Commission on Environment and Development 1987: 8-9). Principle 1 of the Rio Declaration on Environment and Development states that "human beings are at the center of concerns for sustainable development" and "entitled to a healthy and productive life in harmony with nature." Principle 5 affirms that "all states and all people shall cooperate in the essential task of eradicating poverty as an indispensable requirement for sustainable development in order to decrease the disparities in standards of living and better meet the needs of the majority of the people of the world" Sustainable development is about pro-poor and environmentally sound economic growth, social development, and good governance. In this sense, adopting a strategy to reduce poverty should also promote sustainable development.

Sustainable development requires a healthy and productive life of human beings in harmony with nature. In other words, it satisfies economic, environmental, and social requirements as part of international efforts to eradicate poverty. Sustainable development is about providing economic, social, and environmental benefits to the people through a given project or programme

Eight Years After Rio

Environmental degradation, poverty reduction, and sustainable development remain major concerns for countries in Asia and the

Pacific. Decision makers at the highest levels must assess the progress of sustainable development and discuss common challenges posed by critical social and environmental conditions. In order to face these challenges, it is necessary to realise that environment, poverty, and sustainable development are interrelated.

This chapter focuses on Asia and the Pacific at the dawn of a new millennium. It makes evident that although the region has had many successes, achieving broad-based sustainable development is not, unfortunately, one of them. It takes an unconventional approach to some of the root causes of the problem and offers a somewhat unorthodox prescription, which admittedly, will require further in-depth analysis on a case-by-case basis. It highlights three key determinants of sustainable development:

- consumption of goods and services;
- production through conversion of resources to desired goods and to pollution; and
- distribution of consumption, pollution, and the environmental degradation resulting from resource mining.

Consumption beyond reasonable limits set by nature and technological knowledge; production characterized by gross inefficiencies in the use of energy, water, and materials; and starkly inequitable distribution of resources and consumption—all perpetuate poverty and prevent sustainable development.

The challenge can be met if the problem is carefully described, the causes analysed with sophistication, and prescriptions made for curing the disease while nurturing the patient. Production can yield far more with far less expenditure of resources and far less pollution through dramatic efficiency improvements using holistic design concepts and already-existing technology. The eradication of poverty and the just distribution of resources can assure all their basic needs and reinvigorated sustainable social contracts while reorienting consumption and the pressures on environmental resources toward a more balanced state.

Consumption, production, and distribution can be transformed through policy attention given to three facets of society:

- political economy of markets and their imperfections and of access to land, capital, and information;
- quality of governance and its impact on who bears the costs and who reaps the benefits of political decisions; and
- civil society and how social values are communicated and transformed into public policy through processes of public participation.

Asia and the Pacific

Any generalization about Asia and the Pacific can be challenged. Therefore, the diversity of the region's ecological situations, cultures, emphasised. Yet, it is possible to characterise Asia and the Pacific in a way that can set the stage for the discussion to follow. Design and implementation of strategies, polices, programmes, and projects, however, require the careful description and analysis of specific situations. They can be done effectively only with strong and continuous involvement of local people intimately informed about local conditions.

Asia is a continent of rapid change and great dynamism. Not all of the change is for the better, but Asia's very dynamism creates the possibility for altering the trajectory of change in more positive directions. A willingness to try new ways and to effect seemingly impossible changes in social relations was an Asian hallmark of the last century.

We have seen Asia's remarkable economic and social transformation. Many Asians have become richer, healthier, better fed, and more educated in the last 25 years. In 1965-1990, Asia's gross domestic product (GDP) grew by an annual average of 3.8 percent. Regional economic interdependence and integration within Asia was also accelerated by intra-regional investment and trade, the exchange rate appreciation of East Asian currencies, the upward pressure on wages in Japan and newly industrialising economies, and, finally, the technological advancement and capital surpluses of East Asian economies.

In general, Asia and the Pacific are rich in labour and poor in resources, which has great implications for their choice of technology and comparative advantage in world trade. Yet countries often give priority to labour productivity and little attention to resource productivity.

Over half the world's population—about 3.2 billion out of 6 billion people—lives in developing countries in Asia and the Pacific. About 36 percent of the population lives in urban areas. Asia-Pacific developing countries account for 8 percent of world gross national product (GNP)--$2.4 trillion out of $28.9 trillion—but for 24 percent of world commercial energy use.

Nine out of the world's 17 megacities, each with a population over 10 million, are in Asia. Eleven more cities are predicted to attain megacity status by 2025, by which time Asia's urban population is expected to be 2.5 billion or half the world's urban population.

Large numbers of Asians lack access to basic needs. Variations across countries are great: for example, 95 percent of the rural population in Afghanistan lacks access to safe drinking water, 70 percent in Cambodia, 68 percent in Papua New Guinea, 57 percent in Viet Nam, 56 percent in Lao People's Democratic Republic (Lao PDR), 40 percent in Burma, 39 percent in Solomon Islands, and 29 percent in Nepal.

Child malnutrition is a good indicator of poverty and the absence of the provision of basic needs. In 1990, there were more under weight preschool children in South Asia (60 percent) than in any other region. Asia and the Pacific (outside South Asia) also had a high rate of 25 percent, with the region as a whole accounting for 77 percent of malnourished preschool children in the world.

Compounding poverty are high levels of environmental stress. For example, water with-drawals in Central Asia were about 85 percent of available water resources, and in South Asia, about 48 percent, indicating high water stress. Water resources per capita in South Asia have declined by as much as 70 percent since 1950 (ADB 2000). These indicators of water stress reflect not only population growth, but, more significantly, also gross inefficiencies in water use in irrigation, manufacturing, and urban water supply.

Gross inefficiencies also characterise energy use throughout Asia and the Pacific.[1] Energy waste and rapidly growing energy use have caused severe air and water pollution in many urban areas. Energy demand in East Asia was doubling every 12 years before the financial crisis of 1997, and electricity demand was growing two to three times faster than GDP. Energy efficiencies are only 15 percent those in Japan. Use of solid fuels such as coal, tree biomass, and agricultural residues in households in inefficient, costly in terms of the time of women and children, and a serious household and community health hazard. Dirty household fuels burned in inefficient stoves, dirty industrial emissions (70 percent of urban air pollution in Indonesian cities, for example, is industrial in origin), and dirty, inefficient vehicles have sent average levels of particulates shooting up to five times higher than those in Organisation for Economic Co-operation and Development (OECD) countries and to twice the world average. Toxic production and pollution is also rising rapidly. In 1976-1984, the toxic intensity of GDP increased 5.4 times in Indonesia, 3.05 times in Malaysia, 2.48 times in Thailand, and 2.5 times in the Republic of Korea (henceforth referred to as Korea)

Asia is the most polluted and environmentally degraded part of the world. The range of its environmental problems is huge.

Air Pollution. Air pollution in Asian cities is among the worst in the world. The levels of ambient particulates—smoke particles and dust—are generally twice the world average. Lead emissions from vehicles are well above safe levels. The ambient level of sulfur dioxide, which causes acid rain, is 50 percent higher in Asia than in either Africa or Latin America. As two of Asia's giant economies—the People's Republic of China (PRC) and India—rely heavily on coal, Asia's share of greenhouse gas emissions, which is responsible for global climatic changes, is increasing. The extent of air pollution, however, varies within the region. Efforts to improve air quality should focus on particulates in South Asia and the PRC, lead in Southeast Asia, and sulfur dioxide in East Asia and Eastern PRC.

Water Pollution and Water Scarcity. Asia's rivers are far more polluted than the rest of the world's. They typically have four times the world average of suspended solids. The region's biological oxygen demand is 1.4 times the world average. Asian rivers contain three times as much fecal coliform than the world average and 20 times more lead than those in OECD countries, mainly from industrial effluents. The levels of suspended solids have almost quadrupled since the late 1970s, and, while biological oxygen demand in inland waters was reduced in the early 1980s. The increase in biological oxygen demand will exacerbate the current decline in water resources caused by lowering of water tables, deforestation of watersheds, and wasteful water use.

Solid and Hazardous Waste. On average, municipal authorities in Asia spend 50-70 percent of their revenues on municipal waste management. Yet, collection services remain low, with only 50-70 percent of residents receiving any service. A bigger concern is the growing quantities of hazardous toxic wastes that hospitals and certain industrial and commercial establishments generate. Of these hazardous wastes, about 60-65 percent is put in dumpsites or landfills, 5-10 percent dumped in the ocean, and the rest incinerated or chemically treated. In most cases, proper safeguards are absent or largely ineffective.

Deforestation. Asia's forest cover is shrinking by 1 percent a year. With 13 percent of the world's forestland and half its population, Asia has just one third the world average of forest per person, and only one tenth that of Latin America. A great deal of deforestation has already occurred in South Asia, resulting in increased desertification, soil erosion, flooding, and biodiversity loss. Deforestation is particularly acute in South-East Asia.

Land Degradation. In 1992, Asia had only 0.3 ha of agricultural land per person, compared to 1.6 ha in the rest of the developing world and 1.4 ha in OECD countries. Asia's soil is also of poorer quality; less than 4 percent can be used to grow a variety of crops. Soil erosion is equally severe in South-East Asia, South Asia, the PRC, and India. Around 130 million ha of Asian cropland (mainly in the PRC, India, and Pakistan) are salinised and waterlogged because of poor irrigation practices. Desertification is also an increasing problem, with as much as 63 million ha of rain-fed land and 16 million ha of irrigated land already lost to desertification. Denuded forests are being rapidly colonised by imperata grass, which is difficult to eliminate and prevents anything else from growing.

Biodiversity Loss. Asia is home to about 40 percent of the world's species of flora and fauna. Encroachment on wildlife habitats for agriculture and infrastructure, deforestation, land degradation, and water pollution have taken their toll on these biological resources and reduced their diversity. Except for Bhutan and Malaysia, Asian countries have lost 70-90 percent of their original wildlife habitats. Only 7 percent of Asia's total land area is protected, and none of the region's developing countries is particularly effective at managing protected areas. Asia's coastal and marine fisheries, mangroves, and coral reefs are among the most diverse in the world. Two thirds of the world's coral reefs are in Asia. However, more than half of Asia's wetlands has been lost, and more than half of the mangroves in the Indo-Malayan realm cleared.

Nearly every environmental indicator shows an alarming trend in Asia and the Pacific. Take, for example, acid rain caused by sulphur dioxide emissions. As estimated 34 million tons of sulphur dioxide were emitted in Asia in 1990, over 40 percent more than in North America. Acid deposition levels are particularly high in downwind areas due to the use of high-sulfur coal in Southeast PRC, Northeast India, Korea, and Thailand. Impacts on crop yields and forestry growth have already been documented in the PRC, India, Korea, and else-where in Asia.

In summary, the dynamic Asia-Pacific economies have lifted many out of poverty and improved many quantitative indicators of well-being. Improvement has been unevenly distributed, however, and the environmental repercussions of rapid economic growth have been severely deleterious.

Economies and Ideas in Ferment

The consensus demanding free markets, export-oriented production, and severely constricted State functions has foundered on the shoals of economic, social, and environmental crises. Fresh winds are blowing, often from the East and South. Sustainable development is embraced by multitudinous parties of diverse political persuasions, all searching for better ways to improve the human lot without destroying nature and society in the process.

Convergent forces have discredited facile solutions. A rash of hundred-year natural disasters, financial crises in Central and East Asia, deepening polarisation between rich and poor, seemingly intractable poverty, new and continuing environmental and health crises (forest fires, coral reef bleaching, ocean fisheries collapse, urban air pollution, groundwater depletion, new diseases such as HIV/AIDS, hormone mimicry, spreading persistent organic and heavy metal pollutants), and widespread civil strife and violence—all have combined to discredit laissez-faire policies. There is a resurgence of interest in better methods, the role of power in government and market behaviour, and the non-economic sides of individual and social actions. The juggernaut of globalisation and homogenisation is facing opposing forces that focus attention on why the majority has benefited so little and bears so much of the cost of progress. This is not an argument against globalisation, which is a reality and probably here to stay. This is a cautionary point made to analyse factors that could ensure and enhance the benefits of globalisation to the poor.

East Asian experience and viewpoints are critical to the demise of the facile solutions of the 1980s and early 1990s. The "miracle" economies, the financial crisis, deepening environmental problems, pressures for democratisation, and increasing inequalities all converge to distill lessons for the future. East Asia has shown the importance of the State to economic growth. Governments played a major role, especially during the foundation-building stages of growth, by doing the following:

- assuring broad-based access of farmers to financial services technology, crop inputs, and marketing facilities;
- formulating industrial policy and establishing State-owned enterprises;
- intervening successfully in trade;
- regulating financial markets, although perhaps insufficiently;
- heavily emphasising education and technology; and
- supporting a broad-based sharing of development through investments in infrastructure, especially primary health and education (including women's education).

East Asia has shown how important it is to provide access to land, credit, technology, and inputs to as many farmers as possible in high-potential and irrigated areas. In East Asia, health care and primary education are accessible to the poor, and women's education is especially emphasised.

The success of high-input food-cropping systems was a key factor in the East Asian "miracle." Agricultural growth emphasized broad-based access to land and other inputs. Irrigation, new rice varieties, and high input levels dramatically increased production, farmer incomes, and rural employment, while lowering food prices, increasing rural demand for urban products, generating foreign exchange and tax revenues, and mobilising savings. Rural non-farm employment surged.

Progress, however, reached its limit. What worked so successfully in East Asia and parts of South Asia under the rubric of the "green revolution" stalled, unable to penetrate new areas or to continue to increase production where it was initially so successful. Several factors are responsible for the stagnation:

* Advances in technology have slowed.
* Serious environmental problems have become widespread,

including water-logging and salinisation; groundwater quality and quantity depletion; soil erosion; degradation of soil structure and fertility; pesticide resistance; and chemical damage to fisheries, ecosystems, and human health and safety.

* The technology package uses much less labour.[1]

* The best areas have already converted to the new technology; other areas have no ready-made technology packages.

* The partial removal of subsidies for fertilizers, pesticides, credit, fuel, and, in some cases, irrigation water has made adoption of a new green revolution technology less profitable.

* Lower food prices in developing countries and wider spreads between export prices and consumer prices in industrialised countries (that is, greater food cartel markups) have diminished farmer profits.[3]

* Privatisation of agricultural services such as research and development (R&D) and extension has diminished access to new technologies, further burdening farmers with quality control demands and timing requirements of monopsonist buyers. Inequality of access to modern inputs (including extension) and to markets and the takeover of farmer cooperatives by the larger farmers have led to marginalisation of vast numbers of small farmers.

Those who were quick to adopt the new technology—whether individual farmers or regions within countries—generally did well. They profited from land agglomeration, high prices for high-value crops before market demand was saturated, and investments in rural non-farm enterprises. They also invested in private high-quality education and health care. As governments have withdrawn from providing services, however, those left out of economic growth have fallen even farther behind.

Much of Asia and the Pacific suffer from worsening distribution of income and wealth, caused mainly by the following;

- public sector retrenchment in public goods areas such as health, education, and infrastructure;
- rising investment/GDP ratios;
- rising levels of foreign investment;
- difficulty in directing investments into labour-intensive sectors and enterprises;
- privatisation;
- agglomeration of agricultural land;
- adoption by landowners of labour-saving investments (such as trees over rice) to avoid conflict with farm labourers or tenant farmers; and
- shedding of social welfare functions by State-owned enterprises.

Still, many significant improvements in quality of life have benefited large numbers of people. With a few exceptions (Afghanistan, Mongolia, and the Central Asian republics), on the average, life expectancy has become longer, illiteracy has decreased while primary education has advanced, and child mortality rates have steadily fallen. However, disparities among nations, within nations, and across social groups have widened.

Equally distressing, few developing countries have social safety nets, as the financial crisis showed so starkly. Those in Mongolia and the Central Asia republics have been shredded and those in the PRC and Viet Nam are under constant threat. Natural disasters, civil strife, and increasingly variable weather patterns combine with wildly erratic capital flows to produce a volatile mixture of risk and uncertainty. Coping mechanisms invariably favour the more powerful.

The financial crisis has also highlighted the serious nature of poverty. Although East Asian countries for the most part have made impressive strides in reducing poverty, the fragility of their achievement became all too clear in the late 1990s. Poverty has also worsened in the transition economies—although the PRC (earlier) and Viet Nam (more recently) have greatly reduced poverty—and seems a depressingly stubborn feature of much of South Asia. More people are poor now than in 1990.

With millennium fever has come globalisation hype. While little is truly new in "globalisation,"[2] at least one feature does qualify as novel: the dramatic increase in the flow of short-term, speculative capital. Capital movements now exceed trade flows by 60 times and, without regulation, will grow even faster.[3] Given the extreme difficulty of ensuring well-functioning capital markets and discouraging the speculative nature of the bulk of the capital flows, it is obvious that the capital shock of 1997 may be repeated in the open economies.[4] As Joseph Stiglitz, former chief economist of the World Bank, points out: "the seeds of calamity had… been planted in the early '90s [when] East Asian countries had liberalised their financial and capital markets—not because they needed to attract more funds (savings rates were already 30 percent or more) but because of international pressure". As professor Robert Gilpin notes when discussing the Asian financial crisis: "Unfortunately, the international community, which had pushed for openness, failed to push for regulation of the financial sector, and the governments were too inexperienced to appreciate the dangers of an unregulated financial market" (Gilpin 2000). It is striking how blind the experts were to the dangers inherent in this process.

A highly competitive global economy has dampened developing countries' political resolve to strengthen environmental protection. In the absence of any global environmental framework, nations have been reluctant to risk driving away investors with tough environmental regulations. They have also accepted the unsustainable production and consumption processes and practices spread by globalisation. Pollution is, in fact, becoming globalised.

Globalisation undermines social contracts and promotes social fragmentation as owners of capital and their managers avoid labour conflict by opting to relocate their operations. Community spirit is actually enhanced by the presence and resolution of conflict. Consistent patterns of conflict avoidance through capital flight might actually weaken social cohesion both by "exacerbating conflict over fundamental beliefs regarding social organisation and by weakening the forces that would normally militate for the resolution of these conflicts through national debate and deliberation". It this way, partial global integration may be hastening national disintegration and the proliferation of disgruntled spin-off States. In a recent article, *Newsweek* editor Michael Elliott advocates globalisation but cautions: "For millions, globalisation is a process that transforms what is familiar in ways that can be deeply unsettling. And even for those who think they live the global life, nagging questions of loyalty and identity come unbidden to the mind like sea monsters surfacing form the vast deep. Pico Iyer in his book 'The Global Soul' expresses globalisation as 'our dreams, of disconnection, of displacement, of being lost within a labyrinth of impersonal places'"

It is now recognised that unregulated privatisation in the transition economies was a serious mistake. After 10 years of capitalism, Eastern Europe and the former Soviet Union have failed to return to 1989 levels of GDP. There have been dramatic down-turns in social indicators, with life expectancy having fallen in 18 out of 25 countries. Poverty incidence has risen from 4 to 45 percent. The expansion of the market economy (and the destruction of social welfare institutions) can lead to great inequities and can contribute to poor governance and high levels of corruption.

It took the collapse of State capitalism in the former Soviet Union to force general recognition of the severe limitations of the competitive-capitalism model. Imperfect competition (monopoly and oligopoly); incomplete markets for goods, labour, capital, and land; incomplete and costly information; and increasing returns especially to R&D and experience—all undermine whatever legitimacy theoretical models of the competitive-capitalist system may have had.[5]

This implies that mere change of ownership is far less important than subjecting firms to real competition. Innovation, efficiency, and rational incentive structures derive from the competitive process, not from the formality of changing a firm's ownership from the public to the private sector. The mere assigning of property rights does not ensure efficiency. Privatisation has meant the loss of government rents and a consequent serious fiscal problem. As Stiglitz observes; "Efficient corporate governance—the main argument for swift privatisation—is highly unlikely, whatever privatisation model is used, and there is no plausible answer to the intriguing question of who would monitor the monitors" (Stiglitz 1999). It is becoming clear that it is wrong to separate efficiency and equity concerns. Government can and often has done, better than the private sector in providing services. There are many examples in the region of both government and market failures, and a sophisticated and open-minded attitude is needed to assess the best approach in any situation.

Certain roles of the State must also be questioned. For example, one of the reasons for poor performance of many countries' poverty programmes is an over reliance on the State as the principal antipoverty agent. The conventional wisdom is that poverty is an economic problem to be solved through policy prescriptions, a result of insufficient State-financed and directed R&D and extension or a product of the lack of public infrastructure or State-provided welfare. The "poverty sector" is seen as having little capital, no resources, and no solutions—all of which must come from outside. However, more and more people now realise that poverty will be intractable unless numerous sites of action are identified and numerous agents of change mobilised, that the "poverty sector" does not exist in isolation, and that poverty is often created by the dynamics of shifting social relations.

Market and Policy Failures

Market and policy failures have been identified by many experts as the major underlying causes of environmental degradation. Market failures occur when freely functioning markets produce prices that do not reflect the true social cost or benefits of an action. Policy failures include both failure to intervene when necessary and beneficial, and failure to refrain when intervention is unnecessary or detrimental. Some examples of policy and market failures are as follows:

Coexistence of overuse, waste, and inefficiency with growing resource scarcity. In most irrigation systems in Asian countries, water is uncontrollably used by some farmers, resulting in water-logging and soil salinisation while leaving other farmers within the neighbouring irrigation system with short water supply. The latter immediately suffer from production loss while the former can expect to experience the same net effect in the future.

Putting increasingly scarce resources into inferior, low-return, and unsustainable uses when superior, high return, and sustainable uses exist. In some Asian countries, valuable forests have been slashed and burned to grow crops of lower economic value.

Exploitation for extractive purposes of a resource which otherwise could be renewably managed. The rate of deforestation in some Asian countries is several times the rate of reforestation, which suggests that tropical forests are "mined" rather than managed for sustainable use.

Putting a resource into a single use when its multiple use would generate a larger net benefit. Tropical forests are mostly exploited for timber production alone even though multiple usage such as for non-timber goods, water and soil conservation, enhancement of biological diversity, and a host of other environmental services would generate a higher return.

Depriving local communities of their customary rights of access to resources even though they may be the most effective resource managers. Forest dwellers possess the specialised knowledge of the ecosystem needed for sustainable management. But instead of giving them the responsibility for managing the resources and vesting them with sufficient authority, protection, and security of tenure to do so, they are ignored. Rights of management are often awarded to distant logging companies, which exploit the resources.

Not recycling resources and byproducts even though it could generate both economic and environmental benefits. Inadequate recycling means more exploitation of natural resources, more pollution, and loss of salvageable economic value. Even when recycling is more costly than primary production, the environmental benefits such as less waste disposal and less degradation of the environment can be of great value.

Irreversible loss of unique sites, eco-systems, and species in the quest for marginal economic benefit. The uniqueness and the contribution of threatened environments and species to diversity are of immense value that their irreversible loss cannot be justified except in cases of famine or when large indisputable economic benefits are expected. However, wanton neglect continues, which includes coral mining, driftnet fishinga and deforestation in many Asian countries.

Simple notions have had to give way to more complex understandings. The household or the community can no longer be conceptualised as homogeneous units. Cooperation, power, and conflict are ubiquitous. Power, command over resources, knowledge, decision-making, and personal autonomy are ever present. They have instrumental importance for the design of successful policies and intervention strategies, and have implications for human rights and equity.

It is now recognised that development is not a purely technical problem. It is not sufficient to get prices right, adjust trade and investment policies, and improve the macroeconomic environment. Deprivation can be lessened, even without raising incomes, by increasing assets, basic services, and legal rights, and by including people in the development process and decision making. Political rights, power and conflict, social exclusion, land reform, corporate and government corruption, environmental accountability, the role of social institutions, cultural integrity, local knowledge, and ethics and values are now all on the agenda. A potpourri, no doubt, but a creative, chaotic one that is especially conducive to thinking about sustainable development.

The above paragraphs are not meant to sound gloomy, but rather to set the stage for a rethinking of sustainable development and for a reassessment of directions. The immediate and ugly face of unsustainable development—air and water pollution, deterioration of forest and fisheries, destruction of communities and cultures, corruption of power, and the ostensibly ineluctable nature of Asian poverty—can overshadow the dynamism and spirit aflame in Asia today. We have many reasons to be hopeful: people demand democratic government; NGOs are linked across the region; countless communities are engaged in self-help; communities have begun to manage their own natural resources; women and cultural minorities demand recognition of their human rights, and changes in social norms; and more and more people now realize the possibilities inherent in holistic thinking applied to industry and agriculture.

Although we have presented the traditional definitions of sustainable development as they emerged from the Earth Summit and were operationalised by individuals and organisations, in view of the non-traditional approach taken in this paper to analyse the problem, we need to elaborate on the concept of sustainable development.

To most economists, nature is a category of discrete market goods not worthy of accountants' depreciation. Whatever concerns arose from the recognition that marginal returns to input intensification were diminishing, they were readily dispelled as Prometheus' example inspired faith in technology's ability to unshackle human beings from the chains of nature. Industrialisation was the way and nature was to obey.

The assumption of fixed technical coefficient production functions (with engineers' wizardry able to maintain them over time) was complemented by the equally convenient neglect of externalities or effects occurring outside the theoretically closed market system. The messy details of soil erosion and flooding caused by forest clearing, water pollution caused by chemical applications in agriculture, and loss of species caused by combination of development activities could for a long time be excluded from social scientists' purviews. Belatedly discovered, these externalities often over-whelm both market-mediated effects and the best efforts of economists to create conceptual market proxies.

The modern model of economic growth blithely measures progress as GNP, refusing to account for non-marketed activities and to recognise the fundamental importance of nature (through depreciating natural capital, at the very least). Those who blindly accept the model, which is so convenient to industrialisation, give absolutely no value to the nurturing work essential to society's functioning—work performed primarily by women—reinforcing the patriarchal view that only men's work has real value. Similarly, reliance of large numbers of the less powerful on the commons and its bounty enabled accountants to neglect them as long as markets did not function there. The same body of theoretical work further declared that the distribution of income and wealth was outside the realm of respectable economic thought and that poverty was, at most, an embarrassment that would be eliminated as the market was allowed to perform its magic.[6]

As Stiglitz has observed: "Many development strategies have focused narrowly on economics. But this focus on economics has led to a confusion of means with ends: higher GDP is not an end in itself but a means to improve living standards and a better society, one with less poverty, better health, and improved education. Furthermore, past strategies have confused cause with effect: to some extent, the changes in society that may be called modernisation are as much a cause of the increases in GDP as a result.

Twelve or thirteen years later, with the much greater deepening of the environmental consciousness and its maturing into a total vision of the human *problematique*, combining in its sweep both the ecological and the developmental paradigms and correcting the apolitical perspectives of both conservative conservationists believing in stability for its own sake and growth-economists believing in growth for its own sake on the assumption that it would automatically lead to the welfare of all, the "Tragedy of the Commons" argument appears inadequate and one that in fact begs the question. For the issue is not any longer that unmanaged commons lead to disaster—which is rather self-evident—but that of restraining individualistic rationality of capitalist societies by in fact managing them in the large interests of both human survival and human welfare.

Hardi's arguments themselves lead to this conclusion. Both his abstract logic and his illustrations point to moving out of either privatism or what he calls 'communism' (a "system in which the commons is *not* managed") into some variety of 'socialism' and social management. If unmanaged commons lead to tragedy, surely the answer is to manage the commons. But as this obvious solution to Hardin's restatement of the age-old predicament of man-in-society (stated best in Hobbes's *Leviathan* and after him by many a philosopher interested in civil society)[4] does not suit his intellectual polemic and must less his politics, he dismisses the whole issue in one sentence: "The comparative merits of privatism and socialism need not concern us here."

Somewhat later in his argument, while discussing the growing danger of the polluting effects of rapid industrialization on the atmosphere, he in fact does say that "since privatism is hardly an option for the air and waters of the world, socialistic or semi-socialistic regulation is called for." But once again he withdraws into his own distaste for commons as such. "Within national boundaries we known something about the requirements of good management even though we are often unwilling to meet these requirements, but how we are to secure the international co-operation of many sovereign States is still a mystery." In point of fact, there is no mystery about it except that the capitalist nations are consistently opposing gang proposals for global management, whether at the Law of the Sea negotiations or in the North-South dialogue or in the prolonged negotiations on controlling wasteful uses of energy, not to speak of their opposition to any international agreements on controlling private traffic in armaments and other hazardous technologies. Hardin not only fails to examine proposals for controlling the menace of unmanaged commons, he sees in them all a design for robbing the rich nations of their wealth.

The 'rational herdsman' of Hardin is a wholly capitalistic creature, his 'utilities' taken out of elementary textbooks of capitalist economics, his argument about the relentless logic of such herdsmenleading to ruin wholly based on the calculus of pleasure and pain of the English Utilitarians.

Obsessed by his logic of the tragedy of the commons, Hardin refuses to face the common tragedy that faces all of mankind if we refuse to evolve common solutions to common problems based on massive inequities co-existing with wasteful lifestyles, both lading to an impending ecological disaster (of which overpopulation is an important component but which is itself caused by a world of such massive inequity and economic insecurity for large numbers of the poor and the dispossessed).

In his wholesale rejection of all practices and proposals for global commons—all of which he presumes, without empirically examining them, to be as unmanaged as his prototype pastureland, Hardin overlooks the good that they have down. He is insensitive to the starvation deaths that have been avoided through the supply of food from international sources. Perhaps, as appears from his discussion of food aid to Bangladesh, he is at bottom against mush prevention of starvation deaths as this would lead the survivors to reproduce themselves, thus adding to the burden on the 'carrying capacity' of the earth which, according to hardin's basic thesis, sust be accorded greater sanctity than the sanctity of life of such Bangladeshis and similar others. He seems equally insensitive to the fact that the proposal of global food reserves is meant to reduce the political arm-twisting that usually accompanies direct fool aid by rich nations, especially the United States. Hardin's theoretical blindness is, however, more basic.

REFERENCES

1. In irrigated and high-potential areas of India, the employment elasticity has fallen from about 0.7 in the 1970s to 0.1-0.3 today. A 1 percent increase in agricultural output therefore generates a much smaller increase in employment than it did in the early days of the green revolution (Hazell *et.al.*, 2000: 60).

2. Since the 1970s, commodity prices have fallen in international markets while consumer prices in industrial countries have risen.

Spreads have dramatically increased to the advantage of international trading companies (Killick *et.al.,* 1999).

3. Labour is less mobile than in times past. Trade and investment as a proportion of GDP is about the same as it was a century ago. Official development assistance (ODA) flows are severely restricted, and agriculture has so far seen limited effects of trade liberalisation. While there are new institutions such as multinational corporations, the World Trade Organisation (WTO) regional blocs, and the like, they are only superficially different from the imperialisam of the 19th century. Foreign direct investment in 1997 was seven times its level in the 1970s. but 58 percent went to OECD countries and the rest was heavily concentrated in a few developing countries such as the PRC. As the UNDP (1999: 31) notes: "The top fifth of the world's people in the richest countries enjoy 82 percent of the expanding export trade and 68 percent of foreign direct investment..."

4. As Peter Gowan notes in his discussion of the financial crisis: "Of course, not all the East Asian economies were dragged directly into the crisis. Those which had refused to bow to American pressure to dismantle their capital account controls escaped the onslaught because the hedge funds could not hit them. The factor that turned a state's failure of macro-economic adjustment into a catastrophe was the degree to which the Asian development model had been breached by liberalism of the capital account.

5. This and the following two paragraphs lean heavily on an interview with Joseph Stiglitz by Martin Schrenk in *Transition Newsletter* (May/June 1996) regarding Stiglitz's 1995 book *Whither Socialism*?

6. The classic basic economics textbook in the United States is P. A. Samuelson's *Economics*. The 14th edition (1992) proclaims that economists should "try very hard to keep positive science [economics] clearly separated from normative judgements" and "as free as is humanly possible from the taint of wishful thinking and ethical concern.

CHAPTER 8

Sustainable Development in a Globalising World

Globalization hereby comes first as a process that is set in a global context, without problematizing that context. It occurs as an 'out there' process, but what does that context envelop and who does it concern? Global from whose perspective and according to which process? Only in a neo-liberal and then in an anti-liberal range of thought does globalization get its meaning. This means that globalization acquires a very specific meaning, with an emphasis on macro-political and macro-economical interconnectedness. Within gender and development literature a comparable development seems to be taking place. Literature that refers to topics such as the influence of structural adjustment programs, internationalization of the job market, and the position of women within the global economy largely reflects a pessimistic vision (Sen, 1997; Wichterich, 1998). They are approaches in which changing macro-economical relations and their alleged negative effect on local circumstances are central. The image that is put forward by these analyses is that women are victims of neo-liberal processes.

Some speak even about the economistics turn among academics specializing in gender and development and find this turn to be a historical and ignoring potential socio-political dimensions of restructuring (Marchand, 1996:580). Even those who criticize this development as such seem only to want to reproduce the occurrence of globalization as a neo-liberal logic. Within this literature the economic worldwide restructuring in the form of one global capitalism in turn has an often-assumed influence on international governments and on households and families (Connelly *et al.* 1995; Spike Peterson, 1996:5). We will come back to the supposed character of this influence later.

In 1972, the then Prime Minister of India, Mrs. Indira Gandhi emphasised, at the UN Conference on Human Environment at Stockholm, that the removal of poverty is an integral part of the goal of an environmental strategy for the world. The concepts of interrelatedness, of a shared planet, of global citizenship, and of 'spaceship earth' cannot be restricted to environmental issues alone. They apply equally to the shared and inter-linked responsibilities of environmental protection and human development.

History has led to vast inequalities, leaving almost three-fourths of the world's people living in less-developed countries and one fifth below the poverty line. The long-term impact of past industrialisation, exploitation and environmental damage cannot be wished away. It is only right that development in this new century be even more conscious of its long-term impact. The problems are complex and the choices difficult. Our common future can only be achieved with a better understanding of our common concerns and shared responsibilities.

Poverty Eradication and Sustainable Livelihoods

Poverty and a degraded environment are closely inter-related, especially where people depend for their livelihoods primarily on the natural resource base of their immediate environment. Restoring natural systems and improving natural resource management practices at the grassroots level are central to a strategy to eliminate poverty.

The survival needs of the poor force them to continue to degrade an already degraded environment. Removal of poverty is therefore a prerequisite for the protection of the environment.

Poverty magnifies the problem of hunger and malnutrition. The problem is further compounded by the inequitable access of the poor to the food that is available. It is therefore necessary to strengthen the public distribution system to overcome this inequity.

Diversion of common and marginal lands to economically useful purposes' deprives the poor of a resource base which has traditionally met many of their sustenance needs.

Market forces also lead to the elimination of crops that have traditionally been integral to the diet of the poor, thereby threatening food security and nutritional status.

While conventional economic development leads to the elimination of several traditional occupations, the process of sustainable development, guided by the need to protect and conserve the environment, leads to the creation of new jobs and of opportunities for the reorientation of traditional skills to new occupations.

Women, while continuing to perform their traditional domestic roles' are increasingly involved in earning livelihoods. In many poor households they are often the principal or the sole breadwinners. A major thrust at the policy level is necessary to ensure equity and justice for them.

Literacy and a basic education are essential for enabling the poor access the benefits offered by development initiatives and market opportunities. Basic education is therefore a precondition for sustainable development.

At sizeable proportion (about 60 per cent according to some estimates) of the population is not integrated into the market economy. Ensuring the security of their livelihoods is an imperative for sustainable development.

Changing Unsustainable Patterns of Consumption and Production

Within increasing purchasing power, wasteful consumption linked to market driven consumerism is stressing the resource base of developing countries further. It is important to counter this through education and public awareness.

In several areas, desirable limits and standards for consumption need to be established and applied through appropriate mechanisms including education, incentives and legislation.

Several traditional practices that are sustainable and environment friendly continue to be a regular part of the lives of people in developing countries. These need to be encouraged rather than replaced by more 'modern' but unsustainable practices and technologies.

Development decisions regarding technology and infrastructure are a major determinant of consumption patterns. It is therefore important to evaluate and make development decisions which structurally lead to a more sustainable society.

Technologies exist through which substantial reduction in consumption of resources is possible. Efforts to identity, evaluate, introduce and use these technologies must be made.

Subsidies often lead to wasteful and unsustainable consumption by distorting the value of a resource. All pricing mechanisms must be evaluated from a sustainable development point of view.

Protecting and Managing the Natural Resource Base of Economic and Social Development

The integration of agriculture with land and water management, and with ecosystem conservation is essential for both environmental sustainability and agricultural production.

An environmental perspective must guide the evaluation of all development projects, recognising the role of natural resources in local livelihoods. This recognition must be informed by a comprehensive understanding of the perceptions and opinions of local people about their stakes in the resource base.

To ensure the sustainability of the natural resource base, the recognition of all stakeholders in it and their roles in its protection and management is essential.

There is need to establish well-defined and enforceable rights (including customary rights) and security of tenure, and to ensure equal access to land, water and other natural and biological resources. It should be ensured that this applies, in particular, to indigenous communities, women and other disadvantaged groups living in poverty.

Water governance arrangements should protect ecosystems and preserve or restore the ecological integrity of all natural water bodies and their catchments. This will maintain the wide range of ecological services that healthy ecosystems provide and the livelihoods that depend upon them.

Biomass is, and will continue for a long time to be, a major source of fuel and energy, especially for the rural poor. Recognising this fact, appropriate mechanisms must be evolved to make such consumption of biomass sustainable, through both resource management and the promotion of efficient and minimally polluting technologies, and technologies which will progressively reduce the pressures on biomass, which cause environmental degradation.

The traditional approaches to natural resource management such as sacred groves and ponds, water harvesting and management systems, etc., should be revived by creating institutional mechanisms which recapture the ecological wisdom and the spirit of community management inherent in those systems.

Sustainable Development in a Globalising World

Globalisation as it is taking place today is increasing the divide between the rich and the poor. It has to be steered so that it serves not only commercial interests but also the social needs of development.

Global business thrives on and therefore encourages and imposes, high levels of homogeneity in consumer preferences. On the other hand, for development to be locally appropriate and sustainable, it must be guided by local considerations which lie in cultural diversity and traditions. Therefore, recognition at the policy level, of the significance of diversity, and the need to preserve it, is an important precondition for sustainable development.

In an increasingly globalising economy, developing countries, for want of the appropriate skills, are often at a disadvantage in negotiating and operating multilateral trade agreements. Regional cooperation for capacity building is therefore necessary to ensure their effective participation in all stages of multilateral trade.

Globalisation is driven by a vast, globally spread, human resource engine involving millions of livelihoods. Their security is sometimes threatened by local events causing global distortions (*e.g.*, the impact of the WTC attack on jobs in India or, in a wider context, sanctions against countries not conforming to international' prescriptions in human rights or environment related matters). Mechanisms to safeguard trade and livelihoods, especially in developing countries, must be evolved and negotiated to make globalisation an effective vehicle of sustainable development.

War and armed conflict are a major threat to sustainable development. It is imperative to evolve effective mechanisms for mediation in such situations and to resolve contentious issues without compromising the larger developmental goals of the conflicting parties.

Health and Sustainable Development

Human health in its broadest sense of physical, mental and spiritual well-being is to a great extent dependent on the access of the citizen to a healthy environment. For a healthy, productive and fulfilling life every individual should have the physical and economic access to a balanced diet, safe drinking water, clean air, sanitation, environmental hygiene, primary health care and education.

Access to safe drinking water and a healthy environment should be a fundamental right of every citizen.

Citizens of developing countries continue to be vulnerable to a double burden of diseases. Traditional diseases such as malaria and cholera, caused by unsafe drinking water and lack of environmental hygiene, have not yet been controlled. In addition, people are now falling prey to modern diseases such as cancer and AIDS, and stress-related disorders.

Many of the widespread ailments among the poor in developing countries are occupation-related, and are contracted in the course of work done to fulfil the consumption demands of the affluent, both within the country and outside.

The strong relationship between health and the state of the environment in developing countries is becoming increasingly evident. This calls for greater emphasis on preventive and social medicine, and on research in both occupational health and epidemiology.

Because of the close link, there needs to be greater integration between the ministries of Health and Environment, and effective coordination and cooperation between them.

Basic health and educational facilities in developing countries need to be strengthened. The role of public health services must give preventive health care equal emphasis as curative health care. People should be empowered through education and awareness to participate in managing preventive health care related to environmental sanitation and hygiene.

Most developing countries are repositories of a rich tradition of natural resource-based health care. This is under threat, on the one hand from modern mainstream medicine, and on the other from the degradation of the natural resource base. Traditional medicine in combination with modern medicine must be promoted while ensuring conservation of the resource base and effective protection of IPRs of traditional knowledge.

Developing countries should also strive to strengthen the capacity of their health care systems to deliver basic health services and to reduce environment-related health risks by sharing of health awareness and medical expertise globally.

Means of Implementation

Finance

Overseas Development Assistance (ODA) is declining. The commitments made by industrialised countries at the Earth Summit in Rio a decade ago remain largely unmet. This is a cause for concern which has been voiced by several developing countries. Industrialised countries must honour their ODA commitments.

The new instruments and mechanisms, *e.g.*, the Clean Development Mechanism, that are trying to replace ODA need to be examined closely for their implications for the developing countries.

In view of the declining trend in ODA, developing countries must explore how they can finance their sustainable development efforts, such as by introducing a system of ecological taxation.

Private investment cannot replace development aid as it will not reach sectors relevant for the poor. Such investments and other mechanisms can at best be additional to, not replacements for, development assistance.

Conditions attached to financial assistance need to be rigorously scrutinised and the assistance accepted only if the conditionalities are acceptable. Financial support for sustainable development programmes must not be negatively influenced by political considerations external to the objectives of the assistance.

Trade

Trade regimes, specifically WTO, are sometimes in conflict with sustainable development priorities. Imperatives of trade, and the concerns related to environment, equity and social justice however need to be dealt with independently.

Environmental and social clauses which are implicitly or explicitly part of international agreements must not be used selectively to erect trade barriers against developing countries.

Developing countries will suffer a major trade disadvantage if the efforts to put in place globally acceptable Process and Production Methods (PPMs) are successful. Instead existing disparities between the trade regimes and multilateral environmental agreements, such as those between Trade Related Intellectual Property Rights (TRIPS) regime and the Convention on Biological Diversity (CBD), should be thoroughly addressed. Mechanisms to resolve such conflicts between multilateral agreements should be set up.

Technology

Developing countries need not follow the conventional path to development with regard to technologies but must use to their advantage the cutting-edge technology options now available to 'leapfrog', and put the tools of modern technology to use.

Mechanisms must be put in place to make available to developing countries the latest technologies at reasonable cost.

Technology transfer must be informed by an understanding of its implications in the social, economic and environmental contexts of the receiving societies.

Technologies must be usable by and beneficial to local people. Where possible, existing local technologies must be upgraded and adapted to make them more efficient and useful. Such local adaptations shoudlalso lead to the upgradation of local technical skills.

Local innovatiosn and capacity building for developing and managing locally relevant and appropriate technologies must be encouraged and supported.

Integrating highly-sophisticated modern technology with traditional practices sometimes produces the most culturally-suited and acceptable solutions, which also makes them more viable. This trend should be encouraged.

Science and Education

The paramount importance of education in effecting social change is recognised. Mainstream education must now be realigned to promote awareness, attitudes, concerns and skills that will lead to sustainable development.

Basic education which promotes functional literacy, livelihood skills, understanding of the immediate environment and values of responsible citizenship is a precondition for sustainable development.

Such education must be available to every child as a fundamental right, without discrimination on the basis of economic class, geographical location or cultural identity.

Adequate resources and support for education for sustainable development are essential. An understanding must be promoted among key decision makers of the potential of education to promote sustainability, reduce poverty, train people for sustainable livelihoods and catalyse necessary public support for sustainable development initiatives.

The empowerment of women and girls must be supported by actions to improve their access to basic and higher education, training and capacity building. The emphasis should be on gender mainstreaming.

Greater capacity needs to be built in science and technology through improved collaboration among research institutions, the private sector, NGOs and government. Collaborations and partnerships between and among scientists, government and all stakeholders, on scientific research and development and its widespread application need to be improved.

Population

With India's population crossing a billion in the year 2000, the National Population Policy announced in that year has special significance. Its change in focus from merely setting target population figures to achieving population control through greater attention to socio-economic issues such as child health and survival, illiteracy, empowerment of women, and increased participation by men in planned parenthood, gives it greater breadth and depth, thereby holding forth better promise of achieving its long-term objective of a stable population by mid-century.

The official realisation, that population is not merely about numbers but about the health and quality of life of people in general and women in particular, must be reinforced and sustained by an informed debate to bring key population issues into ever sharpening perspective at various levels of policy making from the national and state legislatures to local government institutions.

There is need for a better and more widespread understanding that the number of children desired by any couple depends on a large and complexly interrelated number of socio-economic and cultural factors, and that any policy action seeking to control population must seriously take all these variables into account.

An important part of empowering women in matters pertaining to population is to explicitly recognise and respect their rights over their bodies and their reproductive behaviour. This recognition must permeate society in general, and religious, judicial and law-enforcement institutions in particular, through continual campaigning and dialogue.

There pursuit of population control must not be allowed to compromise human rights and basic democratic principles. Such compromises are often implicit in the disincentives aimed at controlling family size; in comments on the fertility of particular social groupings; and in the occasional demands to control in-migration to metropolitan areas. It is essential to place these matters in a balanced and rational perspective through informed public discourse supported by the wide dissemination of authentic data.

Strengthening Governance for Sustainable Development at the Local, National and International Levels

Local

Effective management of resources requires participation by all stakeholders. At the local level, strengthening democratic institutions generally leads to better and more sustained management of natural resources.

To enhance effectiveness of people's participation in local governance, committees comprising both elected and executive members of local bodies and representatives of community groups, must be formed. Appropriate capacity building would enable them to undertake local development activities according to community priorities, monitor project implementation and manage community assets. Where the conditions for such community empowerment have already been created as in India through the 73rd and 74th amendments of its Constitution, effective implementation of the provisions should be ensured.

All members of society are the stakeholders of sustainable development. Women make up half of this group. Affirmative action to ensure representation and power to women in local governance, and appropriate capacity building, are necessary to make them effective and equal partners in the development process.

Social groups which have been traditionally discriminated against much be represented in local governance and empowered to ensure that they become effective and mainstream partners in development.

Children are a valuable asset of every society. It is the responsibility not only of the parents but of the community that children realise their potential fully, growing up in a healthy, enriching and fulfilling environment. Ensuring the provision of such an environment is a major challenge of governance at the local level.

The occupational, cultural and economic heterogeneity of population is on the whole a major asset in making development sustainable; but there are times of crisis when the same heterogeneity can become the basis of conflict and social insecurity. It is imperative to evolve participatory mechanisms of governance involving citizen groups and local authorities which will provide effective means of conflict resolution.

National

Sustainable development is achieved through optimising gains from several variables, rather than maximising those from a single one. This requires government departments, by convention sectorally organized, to work together, or in some cases as single multi-disciplinary authority. For this joint planning, transparency and coordination in implementation are required.

The richness of skills available in society must be harnessed through partnerships involving institutions in civil society, such as NGOs, CBOs, corporate (including private) bodies, academic and research institutions, trade unions, etc., which must be made an integral part of planning and implementation for sustainable development.

There is on the one hand a surfeit of laws, many of them outmoded and irrelevant. On the other hand, effective enforcement is lacking in respect of laws relevant to contemporary concerns and conducive to governance. This calls for a thorough review of laws, elimination of those which are outmoded, and simplification of the procedures for implementing those which are relevant.

Internal reviews as well as learnings from international experience should be the basis of identifying and filling gaps in existing laws. It must, however, be recognised that laws in themselves do not provide solutions, unless there are mechanisms to effectively enforce them.

There are many traditional systems and practices whose value and validity needs to be recognised and brought into the mainstream of governmental development thinking and policy. Appropriate mechanisms for integrating them need to be created.

Many policies were framed either before sustainable development became a major concern or in a sectoral perspective. These need to be reviewed from the point of view of sustainable development. All future policies must be guided by considerations of sustainable development.

Areas lacking policies should be identified and adequate policies compatible with the imperatives of sustainable development framed, taking into account successful examples, of policies and initiatives in similar areas.

International

There is both a need and a scope for regional and global cooperation in sustainable development. Some of the areas of common concern are marine and riparian issues, transboundary environmental impacts, management of bioresources, technology sharing and sharing of sustainable development experiences.

Efforts must be made, especially by developing countries, to work towards synergising experiences and raising shared regional concerns as a strong united front in international forums. Mechanisms must be put in place to facilitate such international exchange of domestic and global experiences in sustainable development.

There must be mechanisms for monitoring the compliance of countries to their obligations under various environmental agreements. Currently there is a multiplicity of institutions with fragmented responsibilities. A better governance regime is required to ensure cooperation and compliance.

India's Approach to Sustainable Development

The Earth Summit 1992 is widely regarded as being one of the most important events of the century to address issues of global environmental degradation, inequities between nations and possible strategies to protect the future of life on Earth. Agenda 21, which emanated from the Earth Summit, reflects a global consensus and political commitment at the highest level on development and environment cooperation. It provides a framework for governments in their endeavour to seek a balance between population and pathways of development. It strives to formulate plans of action that meet the needs of people while providing for the ecological security of natural systems.

The main policies and programmes contained in Agenda 21 provide a major re-affirmation of a number of traditional values inherent in the Indian culture. It is also in conformity with all those values that are enshrined in the Indian constitution. The notion of 'sustainable development's is not a new one. The history of the country is replete with innumerable initiatives undertaken by people that demonstrate not just concern for environment, but also the awareness of the need to balance it with livelihood resources. This 'tradition' of care, conservation and preservation of environmental resources is also reflected in the spirit of the Constitution of India, which has acted as the guiding inspiration of the nation now for over half a century. The strength of the Indian Constitution lies in the fact that it does not advocate any new or imported principles, instead it builds on the deep-rooted and therefore, resilient, practices of sustainable development that have evolved over time in the country. (See Box 1). Thus, the congruity of Agenda 21's objectives of sustainable development with India's own traditional values provided renewed thrust to several initiatives in the country. It also provided new direction in sectors that have emerged as areas of global concern.

India has over a billion people spread across 3.28 million sq. km. of land and associated water resources, surviving on an astonishing range of biodiversity and other natural resources. Policy makers struggle with the choice of pathways to development in a country that presents a spectrum of lifestyles that ranges from the very rich, comparable with those of the most developed countries, to those that are among the poorest. The complex poverty issues in the country force a large number of persons to remain at low levels of resource consumption. Despite the seemingly desperate race by people of all classes to use all means available to exploit resources, there are still institutions of management that advocate caution. Over hundreds of years the people of India have evolved refined mechanisms of conservation and prudent utilisation of their livelihood resources. Many of these have survived the test of time; others that have not, have given way to newer and more apposite institutional arrangements. The question is how can the available land/water mass (2.5% of the world) sustainable provide for a rapidly increasing population (16% of the world)? The positive answer to the question requires the most unprecedented mobilisation of people's minds, ideas, institutions and resources to come up with a socially just and environmentally sustainable blueprint for survival. More than165 countries that subscribe to Agenda 21, have over the last decade adopted varied and innovative means of interpreting and implementing Agenda 21, suitable to their respective contexts. The Indian context presents a unique mosaic of biological, anthropic, cultural, physiographic and climatic diversity, with a population as diverse as its geography. Approximately one fourth of them live in extreme poverty and amongst them are included the tribal people. One fourth of world's tribal people are habitants of India.

Population and resource dynamics determines the context. The following brief into people of India, its geography and natural resources, selected human and environmental parameters will provide conceptual clarity and present a proper perspective on the magnitude of the task at hand.

People of India

Population: 1.03 billion as estimated in 2001 with an average annual growth rate of 1.95% (between 1991 to 2001). Much of this population resides in rural areas of the country with the average population density of the country at 284 persons per sq km. 23 cities have a population of more than 1 million. Diversity amongst the people of India is immense.

Health: Life expectancy at birth for men stands at 64.9 years whereas for women it is 67.7 years. Infant mortality (as of 1998) was at 72 per 1,000 live births. There are inter regional and inter economic class variations.

Poverty: Declined from 44.48% in 1983 to 35.97% in 1993-94 and further to 26.10% in 1999-2000. The rate of decline in the incidence of poverty was much faster in the decade of the '90's than in the '80's. In absolute terms the number of people living below the poverty line declined from 323 million people in 1993-94 to 260 million in 1999-2000. Poverty profile if India shows that it is concentrated in specific regions and specific segments of population.

Languages: Four major language 'families' of the world are found here with 18 Scheduled languages recognised by the constitution. 4,365 unique communities of people speak an estimated 179 – 188 languages including 112 'mother tongues' in about 544 distinct dialects.

Geography and Natural Resource Endowment

The anthropic diversity as depicted above is equally matched by the diversity of ecosystems, flora and fauna and other resources. (See Box 2)

Geography: The country can be classified into four broad geographical areas including the Himalayas (East & West), Indo-Gangetic Plains, the Thar Desert and the Southern Peninsula flanked by the Western and Eastern Ghats. In addition there are also the island systems of Lakshadweep & Minicoy Islands in the Arabian Sea and the Andaman and Nicobar Islands in the Bay of Bengal. 14 major river systems, besides a number of smaller water bodies, drain through the land-mass of the country.

Forests: Forest area stands at 63.73 million ha (19.39 of geographical area) including 37.74 million ha (11.48%) dense forest, 25.5 million ha (7.76%) open forest and 0.49 million ha (0.15%) mangroves. 16 major groups comprising 221 forest types are found.

Biodiversity: 45,000 plant species (including 6% of the world's flowering plants) have been identified. Of these, a third of the 15,000 flowering plants are endemic to India. Of the 81,000 identified species of animals in the country, 14% of its 1,228 bird species, 32% of its 446 reptiles and 62% of its 204 amphibians are endemic to India. The country also has 330 species of mammals. Two of 18 internationally recognised biodiversity hotspots are the Eastern Himalaya and Western Ghats.

Protected Areas: A network of 586 legally designated protected areas that include 89 national parks and 497 sanctuaries. This covers 4.3% of the country's geographical area. It also includes 13 Biosphere reserves and 27 Project Tiger Reserves.

Cultivated Diversity: 167 species of crops, 320 species of wild crop relatives besides several species of domesticated animals are known to have originated here. Among these are 50,000 varieties of rice, 1,000 mangoes, 5,000 sorghum, and 500 pepeer varieties; 27 breeds of cattle, 22 goats, 40 sheep, 18 poultry and 8 breeds of buffaloes.

Enabling Framework for Sustainable Development

The challenge before India is to conserve the enormous natural wealth that it has and at the same time use it to improve the living standard of its citizens. The growth of democracy as a system of governance supported by an independent election system, emergence of a planned development process, independence of judiciary, an active civil society and media, devolution of power to states and local bodies, transparency and people's participation in development and potential of information technology constitute the basic favourable structure that would enable India to meet this challenge.

Democracy and Governance

The unbroken democratic continuum and fundamental principles of governance, like democracy, equality and rule of law, articulated in the Constitution have taken deep roots in the country. The basic democratic character of the Indian state has become stronger, wider and deeper. A strong and vibrant legislature with an independent judiciary is in place and has acted balance to the executive. Democracy as a system enables people to participate in determining the development priorities, restrains unjust pressure for imprudent resource exploitation and sets rules within which the development has to take place. One of the factors that make Indian democracy functional is the division of power between the executive, legislature and judiciary. The legislature has the power to approve, reject, modify all legislation as well as review the overall performance of the government.

Elections

An independent Election Commission, whose objectivity is safeguarded by the Constitution, supervises election to the legislature, both at the centre and the state. Elections in India are amongst the largest of its kind in the world. In the last fifty years the election process of the country has gained worldwide respect for its independence and objectivity. Approximately 619 million men and women participate in elections for the national legislature. They also vote for their state legislature as well as local bodies.

Planning for Development

Planning in India is based on an iterative process involving interaction between the centre, the state and the local bodies. Multiple stakeholder participate in the planning process. At the national level, India's priorities are reflected in the series of Five Year Plans (The Tenth Five Year Plan, 2002-2007, is currently in operation). Various working groups and task forces are constituted with substantive participation of civil society to prepare plans for various sectors. The Planning Commission takes these reports into consideration while finalising Five-Year Plans for the entire country in consultation with various central ministries and state governments. Commitments to the Five Year Plans as well as the specific resource needs of each state are the basis for Annual Plans that set prioritised short-term development goals. Development plans are implemented through decentralised and broad-based government machinery. A uniform pattern exists of devolution of responsibility between the centre and the states on one hand and the states and local bodies on the other.

Sustainable Development – Enabling Factors

- Democratic continuum
- Devolution of power
- Independent judiciary
- Civilian control over armed forces
- Independent media
- Transparency
- People's participation

Devolution of Power

The Constitution has provided a basis for enduring federal structure by providing the division of power and responsibility between centre and the states. Thus issues requiring national perspective like defence and external affairs are with the Centre while economic and social issues are shared responsibility. Financial flows to the state are guaranteed by leaving certain taxation powers with the state and distribution of Central taxes through a Finance

Commission. The 73rd and 74th amendments to the constitution have sharpened the process of devolution and now local bodies both in the urban and rural areas exercise substantial powers.

Judiciary

The judiciary too is federal in character with Supreme Court at the apex and High Courts in the states, with other courts below the High Courts. The Judiciary is independent and acts as an effective check on executive and legislature. The Judiciary has been exceptionally effective in the area of environment by achieving greater degree of compliance with the laws and upholding the rights of citizens to acceptable quality of water and air.

Armed Forces

Security of the nation from external aggression and internal disturbances is a pre-condition for sustainable development. One of the factors that enables India to move forward on this path is a strong armed force under the control of elected civilian authority.

Media, Transparency and Information Technology

A large number of NGOs complement and support the formal governance structure. There is an active and fiercely independent press and an equally independent electronic media. Information technology has been playing an increasingly powerful role in creating awareness as well as increasing transparency.

Media: Rise in literacy level combined with the efforts at mainstreaming the less privilegedasection of society have strengthened the decentralised governance system in the country. The media (which includes the electronic media) too has played an important role in upholding the basic rights of the people. The media has in recent years also acted as a forum for people to air their grievances as also an instant barometer to gauge public opinion on contentious issues. With the rise in literacy rate, the effectiveness of the media in moulding public opinion has grown. This has been an effectual instrument in strengthening the basic democratic character of the Indian governance.

Transparency: The trend towards greater transparency in the functioning of the government complements the parallel trend of empowering people to participate at all levels in decision making. All important issues are debated and discussed before a decision is taken. Similarly in the case of environmental clearance major projects have to go through the process of public hearing. Use of independent regulatory committees and commissions is yet another administrative innovation to create greater transparency and people's participation. The Indian system of governance thus has shown remarkable resilience in adapting to changing situations and learning from experience of other countries, in the process strengthening the fundamental principles of democracy.

Information Technology: The development of the information technology in recent years has thrown open new opportunities for mass information available on the Internet on performance of the government and important new initiatives and plans of the future. The Internet is also being used for wider consultations; *e.g.*, important document like the Convergence Bill are placed on Internet for comments. Thus the continuous process of change and progressive improvement has led to an increase in openness of the system and a greater degree of responsiveness – an unmistakable sign of basic health of the governance structure.

Sustainable Development: Challenges

* Adverse social indicators
* Poverty and inequity
* Deteriorating quality of resources
* Environmental health risks

Challenges for Sustainable Development

The fact that India is the second most populous country that survives on just 2.4% of world's landmass, creates its own population-resource tension. Combined with the colonial legacy of systems that sub-served the exploitative objectives of the then colonial administration, was made the task of change that much more difficult. Thus, despite the creation of an enabling framework for sustainable development, India continues to face enormous challenges in search of options for development that are environmentally sound and suitable to its specific social conditions.

Social Development

The dynamics of having a large population being sustained on a comparatively low resource base has several disturbing repercussions. Over the last few decades, while India has made significant progress in the areas of poverty eradication, improvement of literacy rates and health standards, etc., there still remains a disparity between India and the rest of the world on various social development indicators.

The Human Development Report (HDR 2001) places India at the 115th position in the world as judged by the Human Development Indicator (HDI). India's HDI was estimated at 52.9. In comparison, the average HDI of all other developing countries was 64.5. On other parameters such as infant mortality, literacy rates, Indicators in Box 3 point to indicate that the challenge before the nation in terms of improving the basic factors that provide a decent quality of life to it's populace is rather onerous.

Poverty and Inequity

Combating poverty and its eventual eradication has been the central theme of all the major policies and programmes of the Government of India since Independence. In the decade of the '90's, the 'focussed intervention' of the Government on various social development sectors bore fruit. At the beginning of the '90's, an estimated 320 million people or 36% of the total population, were below the poverty line. However, by the end of the decade, India succeeded in bringing down the number of people living below the poverty line by 18.75% to 260 million. In absolute numbers, a huge 60 million people were brought above the poverty line in 10 year's time.

Despite the impressive statistics, the nation is aware that the absolute number of people still living below the poverty line is huge. The proportions of poor people in rural and urban areas are 27% and 23.62% respectively.

Deteriorating Quality of Resources

Understandably, a 1 billion strong populace has an immense impact on the total volume and quality of resources. The heterogeneous demands emanating from diverse set of claimants, ranging from subsistence goods to seeking support for opulent lifestyles, put pressure on the forest cover and water resources and it's contribution to environmental pollution is enormous.

Forest Cover: Forests constitute an important component of livelihood resource, especially for the tribal people and those living in the forest fringes (estimated to be around 100 million people). The forests also provide environmental benefits such as watershed protection, prevention of soil and water run-off, groundwater recharge, purification of air and water by acting as a sink for greenhouse gases like carbon dioxide, conservation of genetic resources and bio-diversity, recreational services and aesthetic value.

Access to amenities, etc. though there has been a distinct improvement over the last couple of decades, India's performance relative to the other developing countries in the world has been less than satisfactory.

India's Human Development Indicators

* Infant mortality – 72 per thousand live births
* Literacy rates – 65.2%
* Households with access to safe drinking water – 62.3%
* Households with access to proper sanitation facilities – 49.32%
* Households with electricity connection – 42.37%
* Households with electricity, safe drinking water and proper sanitation facilities – 16.1%
* Households with permanent houses – 41.61%
* Households with semi-permanent houses—30.95%

* Households with temporary shelters – 27.44%

However, in India less than 1/5th of the total land area is under forest cover and has remained so for nearly two decades. While the dense forest cover over the same period has stabilised to around 37 million hectares, approximately 25 million hectares are open forests. Since open forests have a canopy cover of less than 40% it affects the quality of ecosystem services and the quality of life some of the poorest people in the country, who derive their sustenance from that resource.

Water Resources: Of the total estimated 432 cubic Km of replenishable groundwater resources, nearly 92% are estimated to be utilisable. So far however, India has been able to exploit only 32% of the same. The total river water resources have been estimated at around 1953 cubic Km. Despite the estimated quantity of available water, it is predicted that the country's total water resources in the year 2050 will barely be able to match the country's total water requirements. This underscores the urgent need to develop an integrated approach to the development and management of water resources in the country. In addition maintaining a balance between the availability and requirements across basins, regions and between sections of the population adds another dimension to the challenge.

The other important issue is the deteriorating quality of our water resources. The task of continually monitoring the water quality standards of the nation's aquatic resources is the mandate of the Central Pollution Control Board (CPCB) in collaboration with the State Pollution Control Boards. The monitoring results indicate that organic and bacterial contaminations are the predominant sources of pollution in the water resources of the country. The unmitigated release of untreated municipal sewage into the rivers and river systems of the country is reducing the level of dissolved oxygen required to support aquatic life. As a result, the pollution levels in terms of Biological Oxygen Demand (BOD) are increasingly leading to the destruction of aquatic life. Chemical effluents released into the water are also similarly having a detrimental effect on the quality of the aquatic resources of the country.

Environmental Health Risks

Environmental health risks emanate from a combination of complex factors. Poverty, among others, is perhaps the most crucial that puts populations at risk. Other factors include access to safe drinking water and sanitation in rural and urban areas, air quality (especially in urban areas), indoor air pollution (especially in poor rural and urban households), solid waste management and agro-industrial pollution. The health effects measured in terms of Disease Adjusted Life Years (DALY) lost are in Figure 11.1.

Some of the factors affecting environmental health are highlighted below:

Air Pollution: The ambient air quality has deteriorated all over the country, especially in the semi-urban and urban areas. Anthropogenic activities result in air pollution on account of 3 major sources: stationary sources (use of fossil fuels in industries and thermal power plants), mobile sources (vehicles) and in-door sources (burning of biomass). The relative contribution of the 3 sources varies across the country depending upon various factors.

The National Human Development Report 2001 (Planning Commission) mentions that the ambient air quality recorded for 23 major cities in the country revealed that the Suspended Particulate Matter (SPM) levels are critical in many cities in the country. What is more startling is the fact that in smaller and medium towns of the country, the SPM levels are far higher than the larger metropolitan cities. Also, in addition to the common air pollutants like sulphur dioxide and the oxides of nitrogen, several toxic and carcinogenic chemicals are being detected in urban air.

In the rural areas, the burning of unprocessed cooking fuels in homes is a major source of pollution. Rural households rely mostly on bio fuels like cow dung, fuel wood, and crop residues and in some cases low grade coal for meeting their fuel and energy requirements. The indoor pollution on account of pollutants released in close and unventilated places is perhaps more harmful than outdoor air pollution in India's rural areas is primarily responsible for 500,000 deaths annually, mostly of women and children under

5. This accounts for 6 to 9% of the Disease Adjusted Life Years. These estimates make the health impact of indoor exposure larger than the burden from all but two of the other major preventable risk factors—malnutrition (15%) and lack of clean water and sanitation (7%).

An integrated approach focussed on civic amenities, appropriate technology and efficiency of public systems has become an imperative for public policy and administration in most of the urban and rural areas of the country. An additional requirement, especially in the rural and semi-urban areas, is the urgent need to make it possible for the people to quickly move up the energy ladder with a view to address the health impact of indoor pollution on account of the use of unprocessed cooking fuels.

Urban Solid Waste Management: The level of urban wastes being generated in different cities poses a serious threat to the environmental quality and human health. Approximately 36.5 million tonnes of solid waste is generated annually. Many cities generate more solid wastes than they can collect or dispose off effectively. Even when there are adequate resources available by way of public provisions to the municipal authorities, the safe disposal of urban solid wastes often remains a major problem. The problem is made worse by unscientific waste disposal system used. Dumping and uncontrolled land filling are the two options that municipal authorities resort to. These methods of waste disposal are the primary cause for the breeding of bacteria and viruses that cause diseases. Due to inadequate collection, improper disposal and lack of proper storage facilities, solid wastes get into open drains and obstruct the free flow of water, which in turn becomes an ideal breeding ground for diseases.

The municipal solid waste sites often receive industrial and hazardous waste including those from hospitals and laboratories adding to serious consequences for the environment and the health of individuals. The system of disposing non-biodegradable urban solid waste is at a very nascent stage in the country.

As is evident then, there is tremendous scope in the country for improving the technological inputs for urban waste management and institutionalisation of responsible social practices that will facilitate an efficient and environmentally safe method of waste disposal.

A major problem in urban solid waste management relates to sewage disposal. With inadequate and often inappropriate and malfunctioning systems of sewage disposal, the mounting threat to the availability of safe drinking water is quite serious in most urban areas of the country. There is an urgent need for revamping and maintaining sewage systems in most cities and more importantly, increasing its coverage to slums and the shanties that are entrenched around most metro cities of the country.

Noise Pollution: Vehicular traffic is the main source of noise pollution. In most Indian cities, noise levels in residential, commercial and sensitive areas (hospitals, educational institutions and courts) exceed the prescribed standards set by the CPCB. Only in the industrial areas, the noise levels are within acceptable limits, but only during the night! In most residential and sensitive areas around the Indian cities, the noise levels even exceed the limits prescribed for industrial areas. This is a cause for serious concern. The existing legal provisions have largely remained un-enforced and adequate social awarensss is yet to surface.

Strategy for Sustainable Development

- Combating poverty
- Empowering people
- Using core competence in science and technology
- Setting environmental standards

  Conservation of Natural Resources

  Improving Core Sectors of Economy.

Emerging Strategy for Sustainable Development

The democratic governance, a forward-looking constitution, an independent judiciary and a vigilant civil society provide the broad framework that facilitates movement towards the path of sustainable development. However the challenges are daunting. After much experimentation by the government and non-government organisations a more comprehensive strategy has emerged that is rooted in Indian realities and strengths. The main features of the strategy for sustainable development in India area:

Combating Poverty

The importance of sustainability of livelihoods of the poor is a pre-condition for sustainable development. People's enterprise, micro credit, their participation in resource management and focussed intervention in poor areas and investment in poor people have shown positive results in the nineties. The target for the end of Tenth Five Year Plan is to bring down the poverty ratio by 5 percentage points by 2007 and by 5 percentage points by 2007 and by 15 percentage points by 2012. Since income is only one of the dimensions of poverty, a concerted effort to invest in social sectors for improvement in the living conditions of the poor is a critical element of this strategy.

Putting People First

Devolution of power to people through constitutional amendments, in the nineties, is already showing remarkable results in a number of areas. By transferring management powers of 29 sectors of economy to village councils and allowing them to raise resources through taxation, the first major step in empowering people to manage their resources has already been taken. The steps contemplated for the future are, sharing of state and central revenue with village councils and their direct involvement in management of social sector activities and village infrastructure. Moving beyond the elected representatives of village councils, a number of initiatives for management of natural resources seek direct involvement of the whole village, for example, Joint Forest Management, Watershed Development Committees and Participatory Irrigation Management to mention a few. Clearly the emerging strategy is to empower people to manage their resources to establish sustainable livelihoods.

Harnessing Scientific and Technological Prowess

India has the third largest pool of scientific manpower in the world. Efforts since Independence have also ensured a well-established scientific and technological institutional base. Institutions of higher learning continuously replenish the stock of trained personnel of highest calibre. Strategically, this prowess is being used to solve not only the complex issue of clean technologies for power, coal and oil sector but also for clean drinking water, eradication of disease and improved food availability by using biotechnology. A mutually beneficial relationship between large public financed laboratories and the private sector and usage of information technology to bridge the rural urban and poor-rich gaps in access to knowledge are other key elements of this strategy.

Bibliography

Albrow, Martin (1997), *Globalization after Modernization: A New Paradigm for Development Studies?* Paper presented at the workshop Globalization and Development Studies, Nijmegen, 30 October—1 November, 1997.

Alexander, Jeffrey C. (1994), "Modern, Anti, Post and Neo: How Social Theories Have tried to understand the 'New World' of "Our Time,'" *Zeitschrift für Soziologie*, 23 (3).

Anderson, B. (1983), *Imagined Communities: Reflections on the Origin and Spread of Nationalism*, London, Verso.

Appadurai, Arjun, (1999), "Disjuncture and Difference in the Gloal Cultural Economy." In: Featherstone, Mike (ed). *Global Culture: Nationalism, Globalization and Modernity*, London, Sage.

Appadurai, Arjun (1996), *Modernity at Large: Cutural Dimensions of Globalization*, Minneapolis, University of Minnesota Press.

Braidotti, R. (1994). *Nomadic Subjects. Embodiment and Sexual Difference in Contemporary Feminist Thought*, New York Columbia University Press.

Chant, Sylvia (1997), *Women-Headed Households: Diversity and Dynamics in the Developing World*, London, MacMillan.

Chuchryk, P. (1994), "From dictatorship to democracy: the women's movement in Chile." In: J. Jaquette (ed.), *The women's Movement in Latin Americal: participation and Democray*. Boulder, CO: Westeviewer Press.

Connelly, M. Ptricia, Murray Li, Tania, MacDonald, Martha, and Parpart, Jane, L. (1995), "Restructured Worlds/Restructured Debates: Globalization, Development and Fender," *Canadian Journal of Development Studies*, Vol. 16, special issue.

Craske, N. (1999), *Women and Politics in Latin American*. New Brunswick, New Jersey: Rutgers University Press.

Davids, Tine and Driel, Francien van (1999), "Van vrouwenstrijd wereldwijd naar meerstemmigheid en diversiteit." In: Hoebink, Paul Haude, Detlev, and Velden, Fons van der (eds) *Doorlopers en breuklijinen: van globalisering, emancipatie en verzet,* Assen, van Gorkum.

Davids, Tine, and Willemse, Karin (1993), "Inleiding themanummer In het lichaam gegrift; feministische antropologenop opgrens van kennisoverdracht en representatie." *Tijdschrift voor Genderstudies*, Jrg, 2, no. 1, maart.

Davids, Tine (Forthcoming), *From Marias to Machas: Gender, Images and Political Representation in Mexico*, PH.D. Dissertation.

Driel, Francien van (1994). *Poor and Powerful: Female-headed Households and Unmarried Motherhood in Botswana*, Nijmegen Studies 16, Verlag für Entwicklungspolitik Breitenbach GmbH, Saarbrücken.

Driel, Francien van (1997), *Global Economic Developments and Changing Local Family/household Compositions*. Paper presented at the workshop Globalization and Development Studies, Nijmegen, 30 October—1 November, 1997.

Driel, Francien van, and Deuss, Marleen 1997), "Met vrouwen een andere ontwikkeling? Theorieen, strategieen en verschuivingen in debatten." In: Lieten, Krittoffel and Velden, Fons van der, *Grenzen aan de Hulp, Beleid en effecten van ontwikkelingssamenwerking,* Amesterdam, het Spinhuis.

Geschiere, Peter, and Meyer, Birgit (1998), "Globalization and

Identity: Dialectics of Flows and Closures, Introduction, Development and Change," 29 (4).

Ghorashi, Halleh (forthcoming), *The Ways to Survive the Battles to Win: Iranian Women Political Activists in Exile*, Ph.D. Dissertation.

Giri, Ananta Kumar (1995), "The Dialectic BetweenGlobalisation and Localization: Economic Restructuring, Women and Strategies of Cultural Reproduction", *Dialectical Anthropology,* Vol. 20, no. 2, 1995.

Hannerz, U. (1987), The World in Creolization.' *Africa, 57* (4).

Harding, Sandra (1986), *The Science Question in Feminism*, London, Cornell University Press.

Hartsock, Nancy (1997), "Foucault on Power: A Theory for Women?" In: Leijenaar, Monique et al. (eds) *The Gender of Power*, Leiden, VENA.

Jackson, Cecile (1998), "Rescuing Gender from the Poverty Trap." In: Jackson, Cecile, and Parson, Ruth (eds) *Feminist Visions of Development, Gender Analysis and Policy*, London, Routledge.

King, Anthony D. (1991), "Spaces of Culture, Spaces of Knowledge, Introduction," In: King, A.D. (ed.) *Culture, Globalization and the World-System*, London, MacMillan.

Kirkwood, J. (1986), *Ser Pollitica en Chile*, las Feministas *y los Partidos*. Santiago de Chile: FLASCO.

Lareg. Marnia (1988), "Feminism and Difference: The Perils of Writing as a Woman on Women in Algeria." In: *Feminist Issues*, vol. 14, no. 1.

Mencher, Joan P. and Okongwu, Anne (1993), *Where Did All the Men Go? Female Headed/Female Supported Households in Cross-Cultural Perspective*, Boulder, Colorado, Westview Press.

Mohanty, Chandra Taipade (1991), 'Under Western Eyes: Feminist Scholarship and Colonial Discourses." In Mohanty, Chandra Taipade, Russo, Ann, and Torres, Lourdes, *Third World Women and the Politics of Feminism,* Bloomington, Indiana University Press..

Moore, Henrietta (1994), *Is There a Crisis in the Family*? United Nations Research Institute for Social Development (UNRISD), Geneva.

Pearson, Ruth, and Jackson, Cecile (1998), "Interrogating Developmnt: Feminism, Gender and Policy, Introduction", In: Jackson, Cecile, and Pearson, Ruth (eds) *Feminist Visions of Development: Gender Analysis and Development*, London, Routledge.

Peterson, V. Spike (1996), "The Politics of Identification in the Context of Globalization. In: Women's Studies International Forum," vol. 19, nos 1/2, 1996.

Rogers, Beatrice Lorge (1995), 'Alternative Definitions of Female Headship in the Dominican Republic.' *World Development*, vol. 23, no. 12.

Said, E.W. (1978), *Orientalism*, New York,Vintage Books.

Schuurman, Frans (1997), *Emancipatory Spaces in the Global Era*, Paper presented at the workshop Globalisation and Development Studies, Nijmegen, 30 October, 1 November, 1997.

Scott, Joan Wallace (1989), "De constructie van gelijkheid versus verschil. De bruikbaarheid van de poststructuralistische theorie voor het feminime." In: *Tiende jarrboek voor de vrouwengeschiedenis*, Nijmegen, SUN.

Sen, A. (1990), "Gender and Co-operative Conflicts." In: I. Tinker (ed) *Persistent Inequalities: Women and World Development*, New York, Oxford, Oxford University Press.

Sen, Gita (1997), 'Globalization, Justice and Equity: A Gender Perspective.' *Development,* vol. 40, no. 2

Third World Centre (1999), *Research Programme 1998-2003, Globalisation, Governance and Development: Actors and Structures in Processes of Inclusion and Exclusion*, University of Nijmegen, 12 February.

Tonkens, Evelien (1998), "Gender in welke lagen? Kanttekeningen bij de gelaagde genderconcepten van Scott, Harding en Hagemann-White en hun toepassing in empirisch onderzoek." *Tijdschrift voor Genderstudies*, jrg. 1, no. 1.

Tomlinson, John (1996), "Cultural Globalization: Placing and Displacing in the West," *European Journal of Development Research*, 8 (2).

Uyl, Marion den (1995), *Invisible Barrier: Gender, Caste and Kinship in a Southern Indian Village*, Utrecht, international Books.

Venagas Aguilera, L. (1994), Mujeres en la militancia blanquiazul. In: Massolo, A. (ed), *Los Medios y los Modos Paticipation Politica y accion colectiva de las mujeres*, Mexico D.F., El Clegio de Mexcio.

Villarreal, Magdalena (1994), *Wielding and Yielding: Power, Subordination and Gender Identity in the Context of a Mexican Development Project*, Wageningen, Ph.D. dissertation.

Wieringa, Saskia (1994), "Women's Interests and Empowerment: Gender Planning Reconsidered," *Development and Change*, no. 25.